Especially for

....

From

....

Date

....

Mornings
with Tozer

Devotional Journal

Mornings with Tozer

Devotional Journal

BARBOUR
PUBLISHING

© 1991, 2008 by Zur Ltd.

Mornings with Tozer is a revised edition of *Renewed Day by Day, Volume 2,* compiled by Gerald B. Smith.

Print ISBN 978-1-62416-203-9

All scripture quotations are taken from the King James Version of the Bible.

Published by Barbour Publishing, Inc., P.O. Box 719, Uhrichsville, Ohio 44683, www.barbourbooks.com

Our mission is to publish and distribute inspirational products offering exceptional value and biblical encouragement to the masses.

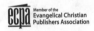 Member of the
Evangelical Christian
Publishers Association

Printed in China.

Preface

Mornings with Tozer is a collection of 366 daily readings from the heart and mind of Dr. A. W. Tozer, the beloved pastor in the mid-twentieth century. The selections have been gleaned from his taped sermons, with additional excerpts from his published books and from his incisive editorials while he was the editor of *The Alliance Witness* magazine (now titled *Alliance Life*). His helpful personal illustrations, testimonies, and spiritual concerns have been scattered throughout these pages, all glorifying the Person of Jesus Christ, our Savior and Lord.

Dr. Tozer would be the first to say to prospective readers: "Don't let the reading of this devotional book replace your own personal study of God's Word." He would want the reader to explore the full context of the scripture reference presented at the beginning of each devotional reading.

A prayer has been added at the conclusion of each day's devotional message. The editors of this volume suggest that the reader uses these prayers as "fire starters." Personalize and expand each prayer. Name specific family members, loved ones, people at the workplace, neighbors, local church leaders, missionaries, unreached people groups, world leaders, etc. Then enter into an extended time of worship.

Dr. Tozer would want the reader to meditate on each devotional thought throughout the course of the day. He would suggest that readers acknowledge specific sins or temptations they are dealing with and confess them to the Lord.

Lastly, as a result of reading these devotional selections, Dr. Tozer would desire that each reader stand firm in his or her faith and do random acts of kindness in the strong name of the Lord.

THE EDITORS

Created for Eternity

Having made peace through the blood of his cross,
by him to reconcile all things unto himself. . .
whether they be things in earth, or things in heaven.
COLOSSIANS 1:20

Men and women without God are helpless and hopeless human beings. We do well to remember that sin is to the human nature what cancer is to the human body!

Who can argue with the fact that sin has ruined us?

Our feverish activity is only one sign of what is wrong with us—sin has plunged us into the depths and so marked us with mortality that we have become brother to the clay—but God never meant it to be so.

Men and women may argue and make excuses, but it does not change the fact that in our human society we are completely surrounded by three marks of the ancient curse: Everything is recent, temporal, and transient! That is why the Holy Spirit whispers faithfully, reminding us of the Christ of God, eternity walking in flesh, God Almighty come to live among us and to save—actually to give us eternity!

This we know: When we turn our faces toward the Eternal One, asking, "God have mercy on me, a sinner," we are finally being what God intended us to be in the first place!

Almighty God and Eternal Father, help me to journey
through the coming year with a new set of eyes.
Enable me to see life from Your lofty, eternal perspective.

In the Beginning

In the beginning was the Word. . .
and the Word was God.
JOHN 1:1

———✦———

*N*one of us can approach a consideration of the eternal nature and Person of Jesus Christ without sensing and confessing our human inadequacy in the face of the divine revelation.

John, in his Gospel, provides a beautiful portrait of the eternal Christ, starting with those stark, incredible words: "In the beginning!" My brethren, that is where we start with the understanding and the revelation of Christianity!

Many others have made a variety of claims, but only our Christ is the Christ of God. Certainly it was not Buddha and not Mohammed; not Joseph Smith, not Mrs. Eddy and not Father Divine! All of these and countless others like them had beginnings—but they all had their endings, too.

What an incredible difference! Our Christian life commences with the eternal Son of God. This is our Lord Jesus Christ: the Word who was with the Father in the beginning; the Word who was God; and the Word who is God! This is the only one who can assure us: "No man cometh unto the Father, but by me" (John 14:6).

Loving heavenly Father,
help me to live each day this year as a humble,
grateful child of the eternal God.

....

....

....

....

....

....

....

....

Man Has Lost God

Thou takest away their breath, they die,
and return to their dust.
PSALM 104:29

The average person in the world today, without faith and without God and without hope, is engaged in a desperate personal search and struggle throughout his lifetime. He does not really know what he is doing here. He does not know where he is going.

The sad commentary is that everything he is doing is being done on borrowed time, borrowed money, and borrowed strength—and he already knows that in the end he will surely die! It boils down to the bewildered confession of many humans that they have lost God somewhere along the way.

Man, made more like God than any other creature, has become less like God than any other creature. Created to reflect the glory of God, he has retreated sullenly into his cave—reflecting only his own sinfulness.

Certainly it is a tragedy above all tragedies in this world that love has gone from man's heart. Beyond that, light has gone from his mind. Having lost God, he blindly stumbled on through this dark world to find only a grave at the end!

Dear Lord, thank You for the hope that I have found in Christ.
And thank You for giving meaning and purpose to my life.
Help me to glorify You today.

Savior and Lord

For by grace are ye saved through faith...
it is the gift of God.
EPHESIANS 2:8

---

*G*od chose His only begotten Son as the channel for His grace and truth, for John witnesses that "grace and truth came by Jesus Christ" (John 1:17).

The Law was given by Moses—but that was all that Moses could do. He could only "command" righteousness. In contrast, only Jesus Christ produces righteousness.

All that Moses could do was to forbid us to sin. In contrast, Jesus Christ came to save us from sin.

Moses could not save anyone—but Jesus Christ is both Savior and Lord.

Grace came through Jesus Christ before Mary wept in the manger stall in Bethlehem. It was the grace of God in Christ that saved the human race from extinction when our first parents sinned in the Garden.

It is plain in history that God forgave Israel time and time again. It was the grace of God in Christ prior to the Incarnation that made God say: "I have risen early in the morning and stretched out my hands to you!"

Dear Lord, I want to be a reflection of Your grace and truth
in the lives of my family and coworkers today.

....
....
....
....
....
....
....
....
....
....

Our Charter Is from God

Upon this rock I will build my church;
and the gates of hell shall not prevail against it.
MATTHEW 16:18

While we are right to thank God in appreciation for all of the great and good men in the history of the Christian church, we actually "follow" none of them. Our charter goes farther back and is from a higher source. They were rightly looked upon as leaders, but they were all servants of God, even as you and I are.

Luther sowed. Wesley watered. Finney reaped—but they were only servants of the living God.

In our local assemblies, we are part of the church founded by the Lord Jesus Christ and perpetuated by the mystery of the new birth. Therefore, our assembly is that of Christian believers gathered unto a Name to worship and adore the Presence. So, in that sense, the strain is gone. The strain and pressure to abide by traditional religious forms all begin to pale in importance as we function in faith as the people of God who glorify His name and honor His presence!

If all of this is true—and everything within me witnesses that it is—we may insist that God is able to do for us all that He did in the days of the apostles. There has been no revocation of our charter!

Dear Lord, thank You for the people in my life who have helped to shape me spiritually.
And thank You that You alone are still the Source of new life.

Yes, God Loves Us

We love him, because he first loved us.
1 JOHN 4:19

---

*I*f we are to have any satisfying and lasting understanding of life, it must be divinely given. It begins with the confession that it is indeed the God who has revealed Himself to us who is the central pillar bearing up the universe. Believing that, we then go on to acknowledge that we have discovered His great eternal purpose for men and women made in His own image.

I heard a brilliant Canadian author being interviewed on the radio concerning world conditions, and he said: "I confess that our biggest mistake is the fond belief that we humans are special pets of Almighty God and that God has a special fondness for us as people."

We have a good answer: Man as he was originally created is God's beloved. Man in that sense is the beloved of the universe. God said, "I have made man in My image and man is to be above all other creatures. Redeemed man is to be even above the angels in the heavens. He is to enter into My presence pardoned and unashamed, to worship Me and to look on My face while the ages roll on!" No wonder we believe that God is the only certain foundation!

Dear Lord, thank You for Your unconditional love for me. I pray that I will not act like a spoiled child but that my life will honor You in all my relationships.

....

....

....

....

....

....

....

....

....

....

Riches of Grace

*God. . .hath in these last days spoken unto us by
his Son. . .by whom also he made the worlds.*
HEBREWS 1:1–2

———

Would it startle you if I dared to say that the living God has never done anything in His universe apart from Jesus Christ?

Christians seem to be woefully unaware of the full meaning and measure of the grace of God. Why should we question God's provision when the Holy Spirit tells us through the apostle John that the Word who became flesh is "full of grace and truth"? Brethren, the stars in their courses, the frogs that croak beside the lake, the angels in heaven above, and men and women on earth below—all came out of the channel we call the eternal Word!

In the book of Revelation, John bears record of the whole universe joining to give praise to the Lamb that was slain. Under the earth and on the earth and above the earth, John heard creatures praising Jesus Christ, all joining in a great chorus: "Worthy is the Lamb that was slain to receive power, and riches, and wisdom, and strength, and honour, and glory, and blessing" (5:12).

Yes, surely the entire universe is beneficiary of God's rich grace in Jesus Christ!

*Lord, I praise Your name. You alone are worthy of all my adoration.
Help me to walk uprightly today as a testimony to Your presence in my life.*

Benefits of Grace

But now in Christ Jesus ye. . .
are made nigh by the blood of Christ.
EPHESIANS 2:13

⁓

*O*nly a believing Christian can testify, "I am a sinner—saved by the grace of God!" But that is not the whole story. All that we have is cut of His grace. Jesus Christ, the eternal Word who became flesh and dwelt among us, is the open channel through whom God moves to provide all the benefits He gives, both to saints and to sinners—yes, even to sinners!

Even though you may still be unconverted and going your own way, you have received much out of the ocean of His fullness. You have received the pulsing life that beats in your bosom.

You have received the brilliant mind and the brain without which you could not function. You have received a memory that strings the events you cherish as a jeweler strings pearls into a necklace.

When we say to an unbelieving man, "Believe on the Lord Jesus Christ," we are actually saying to him: "Believe on the One who sustains you and upholds you and who has given you life. Believe in the One who pities you and spares you and keeps you. Believe on the One out of whom you came!"

Lord, You are such a merciful God! Your offer of salvation is available to all men,
women, and children. You send Your rain on both the just and the unjust.
Lord, open my eyes to those in my sphere of influence who don't know You.

....

....

....

....

....

....

....

....

God's Gracious Act

The Word was made flesh, and dwelt among us.
JOHN 1:14

—❧—

We do well to remember that mankind is only one order of God's beings or creatures. So we wonder: How could the Infinite ever become finite? And: How could the Limitless One deliberately impose limitations upon Himself?

In the book of Hebrews, we learn to our amazement that God took not upon Him the nature of angels, but He took upon Him the seed of Abraham.

We would suppose that God in stepping down would step down just as little as possible. But instead He came down to the lowest order and took upon Himself the nature of Abraham—the seed of Abraham.

I like what John Wesley said concerning this mysterious act of God in stooping down to tabernacle with us: We should be sure to distinguish the act from the method by which the act is performed. Do not reject a fact because we do not know how it was done, Wesley advised.

With the saints of all ages, we do well just to throw up our hands and confess: "Oh Lord, Thou knowest!"

Heavenly Father, thank You so much for leaving the heights of heaven and stooping down to our lowly level. We didn't deserve this amazing visitation from above, but we are so grateful.

Grace Can Be Costly

For it is a good thing that the heart be established with grace. . .
grace be with you all. Amen.
HEBREWS 13:9, 25

Christians all around us are trying every shortcut they can think of to get "something for nothing" in the kingdom of God. Talk to them and they will predictably flare up: "Isn't grace something for nothing?"

That depends upon what kind of grace we are talking about.

Pastor Dietrich Bonhoeffer gave his life as a martyr in Hitler's Germany, but he left a book now known around the world: *The Cost of Discipleship*. He pointed out a sharp distinction between "cheap grace" and "costly grace." Although God's grace has been given freely to humans who do not deserve it, Bonhoeffer believed it rightly could be called "costly grace" because it cost our Lord Jesus Christ even the suffering of death.

Some men and women have actually turned God's grace into lasciviousness. They do not know what the word *grace* means—that God gives us out of His rich and full goodness although we are unworthy of it. When I preach about the grace of God and point out that Jesus commanded us to take up our cross and follow Him, those who do not know the meaning of grace respond: "Oh, Tozer is now preaching legalism."

Father, as I go about the activities of my day today—and for each month of this year—I want to be mindful of Your "costly grace" and desire to grow more deeply in my understanding of it.

United with Christ

We are in him that is true, even in his Son Jesus Christ.
1 JOHN 5:20

---

*T*he Spirit of God has impelled me to preach and write much about the believer's conscious union with Christ—a union that must be felt and experienced. I will never be through talking about the union of the soul with the Savior, the conscious union of the believer's heart with Jesus.

Remember, I am not talking about a "theological union" only. I am speaking also of a conscious union, a union that is felt and experienced.

I have never been ashamed to tell my congregations that I believe in feelings. I surely believe in what Jonathan Edwards termed "religious affections." That is man's perspective.

I am aware also that from God's perspective there are qualities in the Divine Being that can only be known by the heart, never by the intellect!

Long ago John wrote: "Hereby perceive we the love of God, because he laid down his life for us" (1 John 3:16). So it is best for us to confess that as humans we have difficulty in understanding what God has said when He says that He loves us!

Heavenly Father, help me to be conscious of Your presence in
my life today. And I pray that others will see You through me.

Dealing with Sin

For the wages of sin is death; but the gift of God is eternal life.
ROMANS 6:23

---

*M*any evangelical teachers insist so strongly upon free, unconditional grace as to create the impression that sin is not a serious matter and that God cares very little about it! They make it seem that God is only concerned with our escaping the consequences. The gospel, then, in practical application, means little more than a way to escape the fruits of our past!

But the heart that has felt the weight of its own sin and has seen the dread whiteness of the Most High God will never believe that a message of forgiveness without transformation is a message of good news. To remit a man's past without transforming his present is to violate the moral sincerity of his own heart.

To that kind of thing God will be no party! For to offer a sinner the gift of salvation based upon the work of Christ, while at the same time allowing him to retain the idea that the gift carries with it no moral implications, is to do him untold injury where it hurts him most!

Father, thank You for changing me from the inside out.
Empower me by Your Spirit to live in the light of Your forgiveness today.

Love without Measure

Yea, I have loved thee with an everlasting love.
JEREMIAH 31:3

I once wrote something about how God loves us and how dear we are to Him. I was not sure I should put it down on paper—but God knows what I meant.

I wrote: "The only eccentricity that I can discover in the heart of God is the fact that a God such as He is should love sinners such as we are!"

On this earth a mother will love the son who has betrayed her and shamed her and is now on his way to a life in prison. That seems to be a natural thing for a mother. But there is nothing natural about this love of God. It is a divine thing. It is forced out by the inward pressure within the heart of the God of all grace. That is why He waits for us, puts up with us, desires to lead us on—He loves us!

My brethren, this should be our greatest encouragement in view of all that we know about ourselves: God loves us without measure, and He is so keenly interested in our spiritual growth and progress that He stands by in faithfulness to teach and instruct and discipline us as His own dear children!

Dear Lord, this morning I'm struck with the thought of how much You have put up with me—because of Your endless love. Lord, help me take another baby step toward spiritual maturity today.

....
....
....
....
....
....
....
....
....
....

The Wonder of Redemption

For in him dwelleth all the fulness of the Godhead bodily.
COLOSSIANS 2:9

My brethren in the Christian faith, stand with me in defense of this basic doctrine: The living God did not degrade Himself in the Incarnation. When the Word was made flesh, there was no compromise on God's part!

It is plain in the ancient Athanasian Creed that the early church fathers were cautious at this point of doctrine. They would not allow us to believe that God, in the Incarnation, became flesh by a coming down of the Deity into flesh, but rather by the taking of mankind into God. That is the wonder of redemption!

In the past the mythical gods of the nations were not strangers to compromise. But the holy God who is God, our heavenly Father, could never compromise Himself!

He remained ever God, and everything else remained not God. That gulf still existed even after Jesus Christ had become man and dwelt among us. This much, then, we can know about the acts of God—He will never back out of His bargain. This amazing union of man with God is effected unto perpetuity!

Heavenly Father, thank You for making it possible for
mankind to become redeemed. Praise to the most high God!

Our Life Is in Christ

Thanks be unto God, which always causeth us to triumph in Christ.
2 CORINTHIANS 2:14

⸻⸺⸻

Certainly not all of the mystery of the Godhead can be known by man—but just as certainly, all that men can know of God in this life is revealed in Jesus Christ!

When the apostle Paul said with yearning, "That I may know him" (Philippians 3:10), he was not speaking of intellectual knowledge. Paul was speaking of the reality of an experience of knowing God personally and consciously, spirit touching spirit and heart touching heart.

We know that people spend a lot of time talking about a deeper Christian life—but few seem to want to know and love God for Himself.

The precious fact is that God is the deeper life! Jesus Christ Himself is the deeper life, and as I plunge on into the knowledge of the triune God, my heart moves on into the blessedness of His fellowship. This means that there is less of me and more of God—thus my spiritual life deepens and I am strengthened in the knowledge of His will!

Dear Lord, this morning and throughout this day,
may there be more and more of You and less and less of me.

God Sets No Limit

Let no man deceive you with vain words.
EPHESIANS 5:6

❧

Do you know that there are Bible "interpreters" now who believe they can set up rules as to how much we can have of God? However, the Lord Himself has promised that as far as He is concerned, He is willing to keep the candles of my soul brightly burning!

So my heart tells me to ignore the modern scribes whose interpretations, I fear, are forcing the Spirit, the blessed Dove, to fold His wings and be silent. I turn rather to one of Dr. A. B. Simpson's hymns rarely sung now, probably because very few believers have this experience of which he wrote:

> *I take the hand of love divine,*
> *I count each precious promise mine*
> *With this eternal countersign—*
> *I take—He undertakes!*
>
> *I take Thee, blessed Lord,*
> *I give myself to Thee;*
> *And Thou, according to Thy Word*
> *Dost undertake for me!*

Lord, fill me anew with Your precious Spirit.
I pray that others will see You living in me today.

....
....
....
....
....
....
....

Explore God's Word

Thy word have I hid in mine heart.
PSALM 119:11

———❧———

What a strange paradox! The atheistic freethinker rants and raves about the Bible being a "dangerous" book at the very same time that the Word of God is speaking life to my soul!

Strange indeed that some humans have the idea that the Word of God can only be approached with shivering fears. But that is true only of those who love their sin and hate their Savior.

The blessed truth is that if I hate my sin and love my Savior, the Word of God is a wonderful revelation, indeed, and a trustworthy guide.

We need to be aware always that if we do not keep the Word of God on our side, we will be miserable in our souls continually. It is up to us. What do we sincerely will to do with God and His revealed Word?

Years ago, the saintly George Mueller said he had read the Bible hundreds of times, and then he added: "with meditation!"

Let us see to it that we read the Word. More than that, we should actually explore it!

Thank You, Lord, for giving us Your Word. I pray that it will not only illuminate my own heart, but I pray for those translating the Word into other languages so that it will illumine theirs as well.

....
....
....
....
....
....
....
....
....

Faith and Obedience

For whosoever shall call upon the
name of the Lord shall be saved.
ROMANS 10:13

What is our answer to the many confused persons who keep asking: "How can we know that we have come into a saving relationship with Jesus Christ?"

First, we stand together on the basic truth that Christ Jesus came into the world to save sinners. A second fact is that men and women are saved by faith in Christ alone, without works and without our merit.

However, the fact that Christ came to save sinners is not enough—that fact in itself cannot save us. Now in our day, the issues of believing faith and the gift of eternal life are clouded and confused by an "easy acceptance" that has been fatal to millions who may have stopped short in matters of faith and obedience.

Faith is believing and receiving, as in Acts 16:31: "Believe on the Lord Jesus Christ, and thou shalt be saved"; and as in John 1:12: "But as many as received him, to them gave he power to become the sons of God, even to them that believe on his name."

I praise You, Lord, for accomplishing the mission for which You came
to this earth. I pray today for my family members and coworkers who
have not put their faith in You. Bring them to Yourself, Father.

Salvation's Price

But without faith it is impossible to please him.
HEBREWS 11:6

❧

*T*oo many Christian leaders, acting like enthusiastic promoters, are teaching that the essence of faith is this: "Come to Jesus—it will cost you nothing!"

The price has all been paid—"it will cost you nothing!"

Brethren, that is a dangerous half-truth. There is always a price connected with salvation and with discipleship.

God's grace is free, no doubt about that. No one in the wide world can make any human payment toward the plan of salvation or the forgiveness of sins.

I take issue on Bible grounds with the statement that "everyone in the world has faith—all you have to do is turn your faith loose."

That is truly a misconception of what the Bible teaches about men and God and faith. Actually, faith is a rare and wonderful plant that lives and grows only in the penitent soul.

The teaching that everyone has faith is simply a form of humanism in the guise of Christianity. I warn you that any faith that belongs to everybody is not the faith that saves. It is not that faith which is a gift of God to the broken and contrite heart!

Lord, I praise You for extending Your grace so freely to me. I repent of any sins I have committed, both knowingly and unknowingly. Help my faith in You to grow today.

God's Faithful Voice

And take heed to yourselves. . .and cares of this life.
LUKE 21:34

---

*I*n a day when judgments are soon to come upon the earth, we are often warned by doctors that we eat too much—and that we worry too much. More of us suffer from mental illness than suffer from major physical illnesses.

In our self-centered lives, even those who are professing believers are prone to think they will hear the trumpets of woe in time to do something about all this. But at that time, it will be too late!

The voice of God is a quiet voice. The voice of God's love and grace is constant—never strident, never compulsive. God has sent His messengers to every generation. He has spoken urgently and faithfully through His prophets, through the concerns of preachers and evangelists, even through the sweet voices of the gospel singers. Further, God has spoken through witnessing men and women: plain, sincere, loving men and women transformed by a spiritual birth which is from above.

This is the voice of God we hear in this day of grace—the voice of the Savior calling wandering sinners home.

Loving Father, I am humbled that You have called me, a hopeless sinner, to Yourself.
Enable me to reach out today to someone who has been putting You off.

....

....

....

....

....

....

....

....

....

Christ as He Really Is

One like unto the Son of man. . .
out of his mouth went a sharp twoedged sword.
REVELATION 1:13, 16

———————

The Christian message has ceased to be a pronouncement and has become instead a proposition. Scarcely anyone catches the imperious note in the words spoken by Jesus Christ.

The invitational element of the Christian message has been pressed far out of proportion in the total scriptural scene. Christ with His lantern, His apologetic stance, and His weak pleading face has taken the place of the true Son of Man whom John saw—His eyes as a flame of fire, His feet like burnished brass, and His voice as the sound of many waters.

Only the Holy Spirit can reveal our Lord as He really is, and He does not paint in oils. He manifests Christ to the human spirit, not to our physical eyes.

These are strenuous times, and men and women are being recruited to devote themselves to one or another master. But anything short of complete devotion to Christ is inadequate and must end in futility and loss.

Lord, help me to see You as You truly are—
mighty, righteous, just, and holy.

....

....

....

....

....

....

....

....

....

....

Guidance Is by the Spirit

Bringing into captivity every thought to the obedience of Christ.
2 CORINTHIANS 10:5

———— ❧ ————

We can always trust the moving and the leading of the Holy Spirit in our lives and experiences, but we cannot always trust our human leanings and our fleshly and carnal desires. That calls for another word of balance. We know that the emotional life is a proper and noble part of our total personality. But by its very nature, it is of secondary importance, for religion lies in the will, and so does righteousness.

God never intended that such a being as mankind should become the mere plaything of his or her feelings. The only good that God recognizes is the willed good. The only valid holiness is a willed holiness. That is why I am always a little suspicious of the overly bubbly Christian who talks too much about himself or herself—and not enough about Jesus. That is also why I am more than a little concerned about the professing Christian whose experience does not seem to have resulted in a true inner longing to be more like Jesus every day in thought, word—and deed!

*Dear Lord, today I want to be more like You in everything I do—
what I say to my family and colleagues, how I react in
difficult situations, and what I think about in my free time.*

Majesty—and Meekness

I will speak of the glorious honour of thy majesty, and of thy wondrous works.
PSALM 145:5

———

When the prophets try to describe for me the attributes, the graces, the worthiness of the God who appeared to them and dealt with them, I feel that I can kneel down and follow their admonition: "He is thy Lord—worship thou Him!"

They described Him as radiantly beautiful and fair. They said that He was royal and that He was gracious. They described Him as a mysterious being, and yet they noted His meekness.

The meekness was His humanity. The majesty was His deity. You find them everlastingly united in Him. So meek that He nursed at His mother's breast, cried like any baby, and needed all the human care that every child needs.

But He was also God, and in His majesty He stood before Herod and before Pilate. When He returns, coming down from the sky, it will be in His majesty, the majesty of God; yet it will be in the majesty of the Man who is God!

This is our Lord Jesus Christ. Before His foes He stands in majesty. Before His friends, He stands in meekness!

Dear Lord, You are both my King and my Friend. Lead me through this day,
O King, and pick me up when I stumble, dear Friend.

....
....
....
....
....
....
....
....
....
....

Bringing Us to Glory

For it became him. . .bringing many sons unto glory.
HEBREWS 2:10

---

*A*s Christian believers (I am assuming you are a believer), you and I know how we have been changed and regenerated and assured of eternal life by faith in Jesus Christ and His atoning death. On the other hand, where this good news of salvation by faith is not known, religion becomes an actual bondage. If Christianity is known only as a religious institution, it may well become merely a legalistic system of religion, and the hope of eternal life becomes a delusion.

I have said this much about reality and assurance to counter the shock you may feel when I add that God wants to fully prepare you in your daily Christian life so that you will be ready indeed for heaven! Many of us have been in God's household for a long time. Remember that God has been trying to do something special within our beings day after day, year after year.

Why? Because His purpose is to bring many sons—and daughters, too—unto glory!

Dear Jesus, thank You for Your faithfulness in my life—even when I ignore You.
Today I want to be especially attuned to Your holy presence in each of my activities.

Spiritual Readiness

The end of all things is at hand:
be ye therefore sober, and watch unto prayer.
1 PETER 4:7

When the Bible says that God is calling a special people out of the nations to bear the name of His eternal Son, I believe it—and His name is Jesus!

Our pious forefathers believed in spiritual preparation, and they said so. They saw themselves as a bride being prepared to meet the Bridegroom. They regarded this earth as the dressing room to outfit themselves for heaven.

The evangelical church has come through a period when nearly everyone has believed that there is just one prerequisite to readiness: being born again. We have made being born again almost like receiving a pass to a special event—when Jesus returns, we whip out the pass to prove our readiness.

Frankly, I do not think it will be like that. I do not believe that all professed believers are automatically ready to meet the Lord. Our Savior Himself was joined by Peter and John and Paul in warning and pleading that we should live and watch and pray, so to be ready for Jesus' coming.

Dear Lord, help me to "act out" my faith today with seriousness and passion.
Enable me to give spiritual guidance or encouragement to someone who is hurting.

Journey of the Heart

*And they said, Believe on the Lord Jesus Christ,
and thou shalt be saved.*
ACTS 16:31

———— ❧ ————

I object to the charge that "Tozer preaches experience." I preach Christ, the Savior—that is my calling! But I am positive about the validity, the reality, and the value of genuine Christian experience. We can talk to Jesus just as we talk to our other friends.

As a boy, I was not a Christian. I did not have the privilege of growing up in a home where Christ was known and loved. God spoke to me through a street preacher who quoted the words of Jesus, "Come unto me, all ye that labour and are heavy laden, and I will give you rest" (Matthew 11:28).

That invitation let me know that Jesus is still calling "Come now!" I went home and up into the attic. There in earnest prayer I gave my heart and life to Jesus Christ. My feet had taken me home and into the attic. But it was my heart that went to Jesus! Within my heart I consented to go to Jesus. I have been a Christian ever since that moment.

Dear Jesus, I want to thank You for saving me through Your difficult journey to the cross. Give me grace and strength to honor Your sacrifice through my life this week.

....

....

....

....

....

....

....

....

....

....

We Get Around It

If I then, your Lord and Master, have washed your feet;
ye also ought to wash one another's feet.
JOHN 13:14

———

*T*he lordship of Jesus is not quite forgotten among Christians, but it has been relegated to our hymnbook, where all responsibility toward it may be comfortably discharged in a glow of pleasant religious emotion.

The idea that the Man Christ Jesus has absolute and final authority over all its members in every detail of their lives is simply not accepted as true by the rank and file of evangelical Christians.

To avoid the necessity of either obeying or rejecting the plain instructions of our Lord in the New Testament, we take refuge in a liberal interpretation of them. We find ways to avoid the sharp point of obedience, comfort carnality, and make the words of Christ of none effect. And the essence of it all is that "Christ simply could not have meant what He said." Dare we admit that His teachings are accepted even theoretically only after they have been weakened by "interpretation"? Dare we confess that even in our public worship, the influence of the Lord is very small? We sing of Him and preach about Him, but He must not interfere!

Dear Lord, I have to admit that there have been times when I have conveniently ignored the clear instructions of Your Word. Help me to give someone a cup of cold water—in Your name—today.

Ministry of the Church

The house of God, which is the church of the living God,
the pillar and ground of the truth.
1 TIMOTHY 3:15

Not all of the pooled efforts of any church can make a Christian out of a lost man! The Christian life begins with the individual; a soul has a saving encounter with God, and the new life is born.

All else being equal, every individual Christian will find in the communion of a local church the most perfect atmosphere for the fullest development of his spiritual life. There he will also find the best arena for the largest exercise of those gifts and powers with which God may have endowed him.

Unfortunately, the word *church* has taken on meanings which it did not originally have. The meaning of the word for the true Christian was fixed by our Lord and His apostles, and no man and no angel has authority to change it!

The universal Church is the Body of Christ, the Bride of the Lamb, the habitation of God through the Spirit, the pillar and the ground of the Truth.

Without doubt the most important body on earth is the Church of God, which He purchased with His own blood!

Heavenly Father, equip and empower Your Church to
fight the plague of evil rampant in our generation.

....
....
....
....
....
....
....
....

A Believing Remnant

*Even so then at this present time also there
is a remnant according to the election of grace.*
ROMANS 11:5

❧

What is God trying to do with His believing people?—the Bible calls us a remnant according to grace, believers taken out of the great, teeming swarm of so-called religious people in today's world.

I am inclined to join others in wondering if the Lord is postponing His coming because He is trying to get His Bride ready.

For years it has been the popular idea in evangelical Christianity that the whole body of believers in Christ would rise like a flock of frightened birds when the Lord comes. But A. B. Simpson and William MacArthur and others in the past generation said, "Oh no! The Lord will take with Him those who are prepared and ready for His coming!"

I do not presume to give an answer satisfying to everyone in our churches. But I know that many Christians are too smug about this, saying in effect: "I am converted to Christ through grace, so I can live as I please!"

Of some things we cannot be dogmatic; but we know this for sure—God has no halfway house between heaven and hell where He takes us to fumigate us!

Dear Lord, today I pray for my pastor and my local church.
Help us as a congregation not to be surprised on the day of Your return!

....

....

....

....

....

....

....

....

Christ Will Rule

I pray God your whole spirit and soul and body be preserved
blameless unto the coming of our Lord Jesus Christ.
1 THESSALONIANS 5:23

$\mathcal{I}$am not surprised that I still meet people who do not believe that Jesus Christ is going to return to earth. In fact, some of them, armed with their own Bibles and interpretations, are insistent on setting me "straight."

One gentleman has written saying that I have it all wrong, and that Paul did not mean what I had said he meant, as I applied Paul's statement to everyday life.

I took time to write a reply: "When it comes to saying what he meant, Paul's batting average has been pretty good up to now. So, I will string along with what Paul plainly, clearly said."

I did not figure I needed someone to straighten me out—particularly someone who had decided the Bible does not mean what it says.

No one is going to argue me out of my faith in what God has revealed and what God has said. As far as I am concerned, it is a fact that Jesus is coming again! The question I do raise is this: Are we prepared spiritually for His coming? Are we tolerating conditions in our midst that will cause us embarrassment when He does come?

Dear Lord, grant me courage to live today—indeed, every day
of my life—as though You were coming back this afternoon.

....
....
....
....
....
....
....
....
....

A Divine Voice Calls

And the LORD God called unto Adam,
and said unto him, Where art thou?
GENESIS 3:9

———— ❦ ————

There is a divine voice that continues to call. It is the voice of the Creator God, and it is entreating us. Just as the shepherd went everywhere searching for his sheep, just as the woman in the parable went everywhere searching for her coin, so there is a divine search with many variations of the voice that entreats us, calling us back.

If we were not lost, there would be no Father's voice calling us to return, calling us back. So, I say again that we have not been given up.

Think of the Genesis account: Adam fleeing from the face of God, hiding among the trees of the garden. It was then that the sound of God's gentle voice was heard, saying "[Adam,] where are you?"

I would remind you that His seeking voice has never died out. The echo of that voice is sounding throughout the widening years. It has never ceased to echo and reecho from peak to peak, from generation to generation, from race to race, and continent to continent, and off to islands and back to the continent again. Throughout all of man's years, "Adam, where are you?" has been the faithful call.

I pray earnestly, O God, that I may not be found among those with hardened hearts,
no longer able to hear Your voice. Please speak to me today. . .I'm listening.

....
....
....
....
....
....
....
....

Our God: All-Sufficient

In the beginning God created the heaven and the earth.
GENESIS 1:1

———— ❧ ————

*H*ave we modern men and women never given thought or meditation concerning the eternal nature of God? Who are we to imagine that we are "bailing out" the living God when we drop a ten-dollar bill in the Sunday offering plate?

Let us thank God for the reality of His causeless existence. Our God only is all-sufficient, uncreated, unborn, the living and eternal and self-existent God!

I refer often to the great worshipping heart of Frederick William Faber, who in these words celebrated his vision of God's eternal self-existence:

> *Father! the sweetest, dearest Name,*
> *That men or angels know!*
> *Fountain of life, that had no fount*
> *From which itself could flow.*
>
> *Thy vastness is not young or old,*
> *Thy life hath never grown;*
> *No time can measure out Thy days,*
> *No space can make Thy throne!*

Dear Heavenly Father, my daily problems must seem so trivial to You, the eternal God.
Yet You invite Your children to bring their cares and concerns to You. Praise be to God!

....

....

....

....

....

....

....

....

Sharing God's Nature

*Precious promises: that by these ye might
be partakers of the divine nature.*
2 PETER 1:4

⸻

*O*ur heavenly Father disciplines us for our own good, "that we might be partakers of his holiness" (Hebrews 12:10). God's motives are always loving!

I have known people who seemed to be terrified by God's loving desire that we should reflect His own holiness and goodness. As God's faithful children, we should be attracted to holiness, for holiness is Godlikeness—likeness to God!

God encourages every Christian believer to follow after holiness. We know who we are and we know who God is. He does not ask us to be God and He does not ask us to produce the holiness that only He Himself knows. Only God is holy absolutely: all other beings can be holy only in relative degrees.

Actually, it is amazing and wonderful that God should promise us the privilege of sharing in His nature. He remembers we were made of dust. So He tells us what is in His being as He thinks of us: "It is My desire that you grow in grace and in the knowledge of Me. I want you to be more like Jesus, My eternal Son, every day you live!"

*Lord, thank You for allowing us to share in Your divine nature. I want to
become even more like You, but I need Your Spirit's help and encouragement.*

God Reveals Himself

I saw also the LORD. . . . Then said I, Woe is me! for I am undone.
ISAIAH 6:1, 5

———

I often wonder how so many people can live with a continuing hope that they will in some way be able to commune with God through their intellectual capacities. When will they realize that if they could possibly "discover" God with the intellect, they would be equal to God?

Isaiah is a dramatic example of God's revelation of Himself to mankind. Isaiah could have tried for a million years to reach God by means of his intellect. But brainpower is not the means by which we find God!

Brethren, it is true that all of us would still be far from God if He had not graciously and in love revealed Himself to us. In the space of a short second of time, the Lord who loves us can reveal Himself to the willing spirit of a man or woman. It is only then that an Isaiah, or any one of us, can say with humble assurance, "I know Him!"

A committed Christian, then, should have upon him an element that is beyond psychology—beyond all natural laws and into spiritual laws!

Lord, thank You for what we can know about You through the various encounters we read in the Bible. Lord, I want to be prepared in my heart to hear Your voice when You speak.

Jesus Said He Was God

But unto the Son he saith, Thy throne, O God, is for ever and ever.
HEBREWS 1:8

The more we study the words of our Lord Jesus Christ when He lived on earth among us, the more certain we are about who He is.

Some critics have scoffed: "Jesus did not claim to be God. He only said He was the Son of Man."

It is true that Jesus used the term "Son of Man" frequently. But He testified boldly, even among those who were His sworn enemies, that He was God. He said with great forcefulness that He had come from the Father in heaven and that He was equal with the Father.

Bible-believing Christians stand together on this. They may differ about the mode of baptism, church polity, or the return of the Lord. But they agree on the deity of the eternal Son.

Jesus Christ is of one substance with the Father—begotten, not created.
NICENE CREED

In our defense of this truth, we must be very careful and bold—belligerent, if need be! Christ is the brightness of God's glory and the express image of God's Person!

Lord Jesus, the only hope the world has is that You are One with the Father.
You are God Almighty! You are our Messiah! I worship You today.

Both Lord and Christ

God hath made the same Jesus. . .both Lord and Christ.
ACTS 2:36

―――― ∽◦∾ ――――

*N*o Christian believer should ever forget what the Bible says about the Person and the offices of the eternal Son, the Christ of God.

"God hath made the same Jesus, whom ye have crucified, both Lord and Christ" (Acts 2:36). *Jesus* means Savior; *Lord* means Sovereign; *Christ* means Anointed One.

The apostle Peter did not proclaim Jesus only as Savior—he preached to them Jesus as Lord and Christ and Savior, never dividing His Person or His offices.

Remember, also, the declaration of Paul: "If thou shalt confess with thy mouth the Lord Jesus. . .thou shalt be saved" (Romans 10:9).

Three times in the passage to the Roman Christians telling how to be saved, Paul calls Jesus "Lord." He says that faith in the Lord Jesus plus confession of that faith to the world brings salvation to us!

*Sovereign Lord, You are the One I choose to serve. Help me to
meditate on this truth as I journey through some mundane tasks today.*

....
....
....
....
....
....
....
....
....
....
....

Truth Is a Person

Then said Jesus. . . And ye shall know the truth,
and the truth shall make you free.
JOHN 8:31–32

Let me say boldly that it is not the difficulty of discovering truth but the unwillingness to obey it that makes it so rare among men.

Our Lord said, "I am. . .the truth" (John 14:6). And again He said, "The Son of man is come to seek and to save that which was lost" (Luke 19:10). Truth, therefore, is not hard to find for the very reason that it is seeking us!

So we learn that Truth is not a thing for which we must search, but a Person to whom we must hearken! In the New Testament, multitudes came to Jesus for physical help, but only rarely did one seek Him out to learn the Truth. The whole picture in the Gospels is one of a seeking Savior, not one of seeking men.

The Truth was hunting for those who would receive it, and relatively few did, for "many are called, but few are chosen" (Matthew 22:14).

Thank You for this truth, Lord, that You came "to seek and to save that
which was lost." I don't want to keep this truth tucked in my back pocket.
Give me an opportunity to share Your good news with someone today.

Christ Is Not Divided

Jesus answered. . . If a man love me, he will keep my words.
JOHN 14:23

Much of our full gospel literature and much of our preaching tend to perpetuate a misunderstanding of what the Bible says about obedience and Christian discipleship.

I think the following is a fair statement of what I was taught in my early Christian experience and before I began to pray and study and anguish over the whole matter:

"We are saved by accepting Christ as our Savior."

"We are sanctified by accepting Christ as our Lord."

"We may do the first without doing the second."

What a tragedy that in our day we often hear the gospel appeal made in this way:

"Come to Jesus! You do not have to obey anyone. You do not have to give up anything. Just come to Him and believe in Him as Savior!"

The fact that we hear this everywhere does not make it right! To urge men and women to believe in a divided Christ is bad teaching—for no one can receive a half or a third or a quarter of the divine Person of Christ!

Heavenly Father, You are a wonderful Savior and Lord deserving my full
obedience to all of Your teachings. Forgive me, Lord, for the times that I've obeyed
only a portion of Your Word. Show me the areas in my life in which I am weak.

Who Hears the Call of God?

Lord, to whom shall we go? thou hast the words of eternal life.
JOHN 6:68

Who can deny that there are certain persons who, though still unconverted, nevertheless differ from the crowd, marked out of God, stricken with an interior wound, and susceptible to the call of God?

In the prayer of Jesus in John 17:11, He said: "Father, keep through thine own name those whom thou hast given me." Surely no man is ever the same after God has laid His hand upon him. He will have certain marks, perhaps some not easy to detect.

First might be a deep reverence for divine things. A sense of the sacred must be present or there can be no receptivity to God and truth.

Another mark is great moral sensitivity. When God begins to work in a man to bring him to salvation, He makes him acutely sensitive to evil.

Another mark of the Spirit's working is a mighty moral discontent. It does take a work of God in a man to sour him on the world and to turn him against himself; yet until this has happened he is psychologically unable to repent and believe!

*Lord, I pray that Your Spirit will continue to make me
sensitive to the "divine things" at work in this immoral world so that
I may make a difference for Christ among my network of relationships.*

Who Will Come to Jesus?

Whosoever will, let him take the water of life freely.
REVELATION 22:17

———

*G*od's invitation to men is broad but not unqualified. The words "whosoever will may come" throw the door open, indeed, but the church is carrying the gospel invitation far beyond its proper bounds, turning it into something more human and less divine than that found in the sacred scriptures.

What we tend to overlook is that the word *whosoever* never stands by itself. Always its meaning is modified by the word *believe* or *will* or *come*.

According to the teachings of Christ no one will or can come and believe unless there has been done within him a prevenient work of God enabling him to do so.

In the sixth chapter of John, Jesus teaches us that no one can come of himself; he must first be drawn by the Father. "It is the spirit that quickeneth; the flesh profiteth nothing," Jesus said (6:63).

Before any man or woman can be saved, he or she must feel a consuming spiritual hunger. Where a hungry heart is found, we may be sure that God was there first—"Ye have not chosen me, but I have chosen you" (John 15:16).

Heavenly Father, I pray today for evangelists and missionaries around the world who are representing You in teeming cities and remote areas. Through them, I ask that You will draw many people to Yourself who have never heard the gospel message. Amen.

....

....

....

....

....

....

....

....

Christ Came to Save

For God sent not his Son into the world to condemn the world.
JOHN 3:17

———— ❧ ————

*M*illions who have rejected the Christian gospel have generally been too busy and too involved to ask themselves a simple question: "What really is God's intention toward me?"

They could have found the plain and simple answer given by the apostle John: "For God sent not his Son into the world to condemn the world; but that the world through him might be saved" (John 3:17).

This is a gravely significant message from the heart of God Himself! Yet, even in the full light it provides, people are indifferent. Upon our eyes there seems to have fallen a strange dimness; within our ears, a strange dullness. It is a wonder, and a terrible responsibility, that we should have this message in our possession and be so little stirred about it!

I confess that it is very hard for me to accept the fact that it is now very rare for anyone to come into the house of God, silently confessing: "Dear Lord, I am ready and willing to hear what You will speak to me today!"

Dear Lord, how grateful I am that You do not condemn, but by Your
Spirit You do convict. Help me to hear and act upon Your promptings today.

We Are Not Orphans

The steps of a good man are ordered by the LORD.
PSALM 37:23

❦

I once wrote in an editorial that Christian believers are not orphans in this world, making the point that the divine Shepherd goes before us and that we travel an appointed way.

A reader wrote to question my allusion to our traveling an "appointed" way, asking: "I was brought up a Methodist. In your comments, do you mean this to be foreordination? That is what the Presbyterians believe. Just what did you mean?"

I replied that I had not meant to go down that deep into doctrine—that I had not been thinking of foreordination, predestination, or the eternal decrees.

"I was just satisfied that if a consecrated Christian will put himself in the hands of God, even the accidents may be turned into blessings," I told him.

Anyway, I am sure the Methodist brother can go to sleep at night knowing that he does not have to become a Presbyterian to be certain that God is looking after him!

Dear Lord, in these quiet moments this morning, prepare my
mind and heart for the encounters You've arranged for me today.

....
....
....
....
....
....
....
....
....
....
....

Think Like God Thinks

Search me, O God. . .try me, and know my thoughts.
PSALM 139:23

———— ❧ ————

If God knows that your intention is to worship Him with every part of your being, He has promised to cooperate with you. On His side is the love and grace, the promises and the atonement, the constant help and the presence of the Holy Spirit.

On your side there is determination, seeking, yielding, believing. Your heart becomes a chamber, a sanctuary, a shrine in which there may be continuous, unbroken fellowship and communion with God. Your worship rises to God moment by moment!

We have all found that God will not dwell in spiteful and proud and selfish thoughts. He treasures our pure and loving thoughts, our meek and charitable and kindly thoughts. They are the thoughts like His own!

As God dwells in your thoughts, you will be worshipping—and God will be accepting. He will be smelling the incense of your high intentions even when the cares of life are intense and there is activity all around you.

This leaves us no argument. We know what God wants us to be. He wants us to be worshippers.

Lord, I worship You this morning. I look forward to our
fellowship throughout the busy activities of this day.

Our Highest Happiness

If ye know these things, happy are ye if ye do them.
JOHN 13:17

---

*L*et me call it to your attention that the happiness of all moral creatures lies in the giving of obedience to God, the Creator.

The psalmist cries out in Psalm 103:20: "Bless the LORD, ye his angels, that excel in strength, that do his commandments, hearkening unto the voice of his word."

The angels in heaven find their complete freedom and highest happiness in obeying the commandments of God. They do not find it a tyranny—they find it a delight!

Here is something that we should know and realize: heaven is a place of surrender to the whole will of God, and it is heaven because it is such a place.

I thank God that heaven is the world of God's obedient children. Whatever else we may say of its pearly gates, golden streets, and jasper walls, heaven is heaven because children of the Most High God find they are in their normal sphere as obedient moral beings.

Dear Lord, thank You for Your patience with me as
I learn to obey You more fully in my daily walk with You.

....

....

....

....

....

....

....

....

....

....

....

Activity Is Not Enough

And he said unto them, Come ye yourselves apart. . .and rest a while.
MARK 6:31

Those who try to give warnings to the Christian church are never very popular. Still, I must voice the caution that our craze for "activity" brings very few enriching benefits into our Christian circles. Look into the churches, and you will find groups of half-saved, half-sanctified, carnal people who know more about social niceties than they do about the New Testament.

It is a fact that many of our church folks are activists—engaged in many religious journeys—but they do not seem to move up any closer to Jesus in heart and in spirit.

This modern religious emphasis on activity reminds me of the Japanese mice I have seen in the pet store windows. They are called waltzing mice—but they do not waltz. They just run continually!

Many in our churches hope to have a part in "something big and exciting." But God calls us back—back to the simplicity of the faith, back to the simplicity of Jesus Christ and His unchanging Person!

Dear Lord, help me to find some quiet moments in the midst of today's schedule to focus my thoughts on Your goodness and mercy.

Playing at Religion

Whatsoever is born of God overcometh the world.
1 JOHN 5:4

When our faith becomes obedience to our Savior, then it is true faith, indeed! The difficulty we modern Christians face is not misunderstanding the Bible, but persuading our untamed hearts to accept its plain instruction. Our problem is to get the consent of our world-loving minds to make Jesus Lord in fact, as well as in word. For it is one thing to say, "Lord, Lord," and quite another thing to obey the Lord's commandments.

We may sing "Crown Him Lord of all," and rejoice in the tones of the loud organ and the deep melody in harmonious voices, but still we have done nothing until we have left the world and set our faces toward the City of God in hard, practical reality.

The world's spirit is strong, and it can play at religion with every appearance of sincerity. It can have fits of conscience (particularly during Lent)! It will contribute to charitable causes and campaigns on behalf of the poor, but all with its own condition: "Let Christ keep His distance and never assert His lordship." This positively will not endure!

Dear Lord, I want to be an authentic follower of Jesus Christ.
I don't want to play "religious games" with my faith.

We See God's Purpose

*That. . .he might gather together in one all
things in Christ. . .in heaven, and. . .on earth.*
EPHESIANS 1:10

❦

We trust the Word of God—and the inspired revelation makes it plain to the believing Christian that all things in the universe have derived their form from Christ, the eternal Son!

We are assured that even as an architect builder gathers the necessary materials needed to fashion the structure he has designed, so God will ultimately gather all things together under one head, even Christ (see Ephesians 1:9–10).

Everything in the universe has received its meaning by the power of His Word; each has maintained its place and order through Him.

Jesus Christ is God creating!

Jesus Christ is God redeeming!

Jesus Christ is God completing and harmonizing!

Jesus Christ is God bringing together all things after the counsel of His own will!

I can only hope that as we grow and mature and delight in our faith, we are beginning to gain a new appreciation of God's great, eternal purpose!

*Your master design of the universe is perfect even though mankind has neglected Your
creation and Your desire for fellowship. I pray that by Your Spirit our churches will
become "like a mighty army" and help lead many people in the world to faith in Christ.*

Man's Wasted Potential

Depart from me, ye cursed, into everlasting fire,
prepared for the devil and his angels.
MATTHEW 25:41

God has made it plain that hell is a real place—a final abode for people who do not want to love God and serve Him!

The sadness and the tragedy of this fact are that these are human beings, all dear to God because He created them in His own image. Of nothing else in the Creation is it said that it was created in the likeness of God!

Because fallen and perishing man is still nearer to God's likeness than any other creature on earth, God offers him conversion, regeneration, and forgiveness. It was surely because of this great potential in the human personality that the eternal Word could become flesh and dwell among us.

We are assured in many ways in the scriptures that God the Creator does not waste human personality, but it is surely one of the stark tragedies of life that human personality can waste itself!

A man by his own sin may waste himself, which is to waste and lose that which on earth is most like God. The man who dies out of Christ is said to be lost, and hardly a word in our language expresses his condition with greater accuracy!

Lord, make me sensitive today to opportunities to share Your love
with someone who does not have a personal relationship with You.

We Were Outcasts, Too

As the Father hath loved me, so have I loved you.
JOHN 15:9

We confess, do we not, that we have a Christian responsibility to believe God's Word and to obey God's truth?

Then we should accept the fact that it is our task to practice the Christian virtues in the power of the Holy Spirit as we await the coming of Him who will come.

The great spiritual needs around us should drive us back to the Gospel records of the life and ministry of our Lord Jesus. When evil men crucified Jesus, killed Him, they had no power to change Him. They could not alter the Person or the personality of the Son of God. Putting Him on the cross did not drain away any of His divine affection for a lost race.

The best thing we know about our Lord and Savior is that He loves the sinner. He has always loved the outcast—and for that we should be glad, for we, too, were once outcasts! We are descended from that first man and woman who failed God and disobeyed. They were cast out of the garden, and God set in place a flaming sword to keep them from returning!

Dear heavenly Father, that You love us at all is amazing. But to think that You came down to earth to redeem us is nearly inconceivable. Such love is worthy of all my praise and obedience.

God's Highest Will

Then said he, Lo, I come to do thy will, O God.
HEBREWS 10:9

---

*L*et us consider three simple things reinforced in the Word of God for those who would discern God's highest will. First, be willing to put away known sin! Second, separate yourself from all of the attractions of the world, the flesh, and the devil!

Finally, offer yourself to your God and Savior in believing faith!

God has never yet turned away an honest, sincere person who has come to know the eternal value of the atonement and the peace that is promised through the death and resurrection of our Lord Jesus Christ.

The only person who will never be cleansed and made whole is the one who insists he or she needs no remedy. The person who comes in faith to God and confesses, "I am unclean; I am sin sick; I am blind," will find mercy and righteousness and life.

Our Lord Jesus Christ is the Savior, the Cleanser. He is the Purifier, the Healer. He is the Sight Giver and the Life Giver. He alone is the Way, the Truth, and the Life!

Dear Lord, truth seems to be in short supply in our postmodern world today.
Help me to be bold but loving in my presentation of Your truth.

....
....
....
....
....
....
....
....
....
....
....

Every Hindrance Removed

*Being justified by faith, we have peace
with God through our Lord Jesus Christ.*
ROMANS 5:1

———

There are many legal and governmental reasons why lost men and women should not go to heaven!

It should not be difficult for us to acknowledge that a holy and righteous God must run His universe according to holy laws—and we do not belong there because we have broken every one of those holy laws in some way!

Therefore, there must be an effective redemption, a justification of some kind if we are to have God and He is to have us!

Thank God, it has been done!

The New Testament language is as plain as can be—in Christ through His death and resurrection, every legal hindrance has been met and satisfied: taken away! There is nothing that can keep us from assurance except our own selves.

Let us quit trying to think our way in, to reason our way in. The only way to get in is to believe Him with our hearts forevermore!

Yes, Lord, thank You so much for providing an "effective redemption" so that we may have unbroken fellowship with You—both now and for all eternity. Praise Your holy and righteous name!

We Have It All

Seek ye first the kingdom. . .all these things shall be added unto you.
MATTHEW 6:33

How much time have you spent in your Christian life meditating on the plain instruction from our Savior?—"Seek ye first the kingdom of God, and his righteousness; and all these things shall be added unto you."

The God who has revealed Himself to needy men and women wants us to know that when we have Him, we have everything—we have all the rest!

Any of us who have experienced a life and ministry of faith can tell how the Lord has met our needs—even for food and the essentials of life.

Brethren, we ought to learn, and learn it soon, that it is much better to have God first and have God Himself, even if we have only a thin dime, than to have all the riches and all the influence in this world and not have God with it!

Let us go on to know Him and to love Him more dearly, not for His gifts and benefits, but for the pure joy of His presence. Thus we will fulfill the purpose for which He created us and redeemed us!

*Dear Lord, help me make the transition from wanting more and more "things"
to being satisfied—and overjoyed—with only Your presence in my life.*

Our Individual Worth

For Christ is the end of the law for
righteousness to every one that believeth.
ROMANS 10:4

❦

*O*ur lost race has always been prone to discount and reject the wonderful fact of the individual factor in the love of God. Far, far too many men and women in this world are convinced that God's love for the world is just one big lump—and the individual is not involved.

We have only to look around us with serious observation to confirm the fact that the devil has been successful in planting his lie that no one cares for the individual person.

Even in nature around us, there appears to be very little individual concern. The burden of concern is always for the species.

But Jesus did not preach to the multitudes as though they were a faceless crowd. He preached to them as individuals, and with a knowledge of the burdens and the needs of each one. Our Savior did not come into the world to deal with statistics!

Each of us must come with full confidence that it is a personal word God has spoken to us in Christ, that "whosoever believeth in Him shall not perish."

Lord, Your Word says that each of us is "fearfully and wonderfully made"
and that You are concerned about the one lost sheep in a flock of a hundred.
Thank You for purchasing my redemption by Your death and resurrection. I love You, Lord.

The Spirit Illuminates

Your faith should not stand in the wisdom of men, but in the power of God.
1 CORINTHIANS 2:5

When we study the New Testament record, we see plainly that Christ's conflict was with the theological rationalists of His day.

John's Gospel record is actually a long, inspired, passionately outpoured account trying to save us from evangelical rationalism—the doctrine that says the text is enough.

Divine revelation is the ground upon which we stand. The Bible is the book of God, and I stand for it with all my heart; but before I can be saved, there must be illumination, penitence, renewal, inward deliverance.

In our Christendom, we have tried to ease many people into the kingdom, but they have never been renewed within their own beings. The apostle Paul told the Corinthians that their faith should not stand in the wisdom of men but in the power of God! There is a difference.

We must insist that conversion to Christ is a miraculous act of God by the Holy Spirit— it must be wrought in the Spirit. There must be an inward illumination!

Lord, I pray for my family, neighbors, and friends who do not yet know You.
Illumine their hearts and minds by Your Holy Spirit.

Give Time to God

In his law doth he meditate day and night.
PSALM 1:2

———— ❧ ————

I have often wished that there were some way to bring modern Christians into a deeper spiritual life painlessly by short, easy lessons; but such wishes are vain. No shortcut exists!

God has not bowed to our nervous haste nor embraced the methods of our machine age. It is well that we accept the hard truth now: the man who would know God must give time to Him!

He must count no time wasted which is spent in the cultivation of His acquaintance.

He must give himself to meditation and prayer hours on end. So did the saints of old, the glorious company of the apostles, the goodly fellowship of the prophets, and the believing members of the holy Church in all generations.

And so must we if we would follow in their train!

May not the inadequacy of much of our spiritual experience be traced back to our habit of skipping through the corridors of the kingdom like little children through the marketplace, chattering about everything but pausing to learn the true value of nothing?

*Dear Lord, help me order my time so that I may
get to know You and Your Word more intimately.*

....
....
....
....
....
....
....
....
....
....

"Now It Is the Lord"

In Christ Jesus, who of God is made unto us. . .sanctification.
1 CORINTHIANS 1:30

⸺⸱⸺

*I*s it possible to become so enamored of God's good gifts that we fail to worship Him, the Giver?

Dr. Albert B. Simpson, the founder of The Christian and Missionary Alliance, invited to preach in a Bible conference in England, discovered on his arrival that he was to follow two other Bible teachers. All three had been given the same topic, "sanctification."

From the pulpit, the first speaker made clear his position that sanctification means eradication—the old carnal nature is removed. The second, a suppressionist, advised: "Sit on the lid and keep the old nature down!"

Dr. Simpson in his turn quietly told his audience that he could only present Jesus Christ Himself as God's answer.

"Jesus Christ is your Sanctifier, your all and in all! God wants you to get your eyes away from the gifts. He wants your gaze to be on the Giver—Christ Himself," he said.

This is a wonderful word for those who would worship rightly:

Once it was the blessing;
Now it is the Lord!

Father, this morning I praise You for Your holy presence in my life.
Glorify Yourself through me today.

"Be Still and Know"

Be still, and know that I am God.
PSALM 46:10

———— ❧ ————

Prayer among evangelical Christians is always in danger of degenerating into a glorified "gold rush." Almost every book on prayer deals mainly with the "get" element. How to get things we want from God occupies most of our space.

Christians should never forget that the highest kind of prayer is never the making of requests.

Prayer at its holiest moment is the entering into God to a place of such blessed union as makes miracles seem tame and remarkable answers to prayer appear something very far short of wonderful, by comparison.

We should be aware that there is a kind of school where the soul must go to learn its best eternal lessons. It is the school of silence. "Be still and know," said the psalmist (46:10).

It might well be a revelation to some Christians if they were to get completely quiet for a time—a time to listen in the silence for the deep voice of the Eternal God!

Heavenly Father, I desire my prayer time to be more than a "wish list."
Help me to spend more time listening for Your voice than making personal requests.

....
....
....
....
....
....
....
....
....
....
....
....
....

The End of the Age

All these things shall be dissolved,
what manner of persons ought ye to be?
2 PETER 3:11

———— ❦ ————

*E*verywhere around us we are experiencing a great new wave of humanity's interest in spiritism and devil worship. I must take this as one of the signs that God's age of grace and mercy is approaching the end point. It tells us that the time may be near when God proclaims: "I have seen enough of mankind's sin and rebellion. It is time for the trumpets of judgment to sound!"

If we are willing to add the appeals from the book of Revelation to the weight of the other scriptures, we discover God saying to us that the earth on which we live is not self-explanatory and certainly not self-sufficient.

Although the earth on which we spin is largely populated by a rebel race, it had a divine origin. Now God is about to enforce His claim upon it and judge those who are usurpers. He is saying that there is another and better world, another kingdom, that is always keeping an eye on the world we inhabit!

Lord, help me to be sensitive to the spiritual realm that coexists with
the physical world. Thank You that You are still on the throne of this
universe and that You are the One who holds all things together.

Soldiers of Christ

Thou therefore endure hardness,
as a good soldier of Jesus Christ.
2 TIMOTHY 2:3

It is possible to be beaten until you are numb. You can smile and praise the Lord and say, "Jesus, I my cross have taken," for a while. But then you are slowly beaten until you are numb, and you get into a sort of a rut where you cannot fight back.

Timothy had been with Paul a long time, and Paul had been in so much trouble so much of the time. Timothy was tagging along behind in the same trouble, and Paul had noticed a little temptation to be ashamed of the cross. Essentially, Paul was saying, "Don't be ashamed of the cross. Don't shrink from the affliction of the gospel. God has not given us the spirit of fear." Then in 2 Timothy 2:3 Paul said, "Endure hardship as a good soldier of Christ Jesus." It is as though he might have detected in the young man a little temptation to recoil a bit from the hard life he was called into.

Lord, teach me self-discipline, that I may be a good soldier
of Jesus Christ. Help me to be bold for the sake of Your cross.

What Is True Religion?

If they speak not according to this word,
it is because there is no light in them.
ISAIAH 8:20

To the convicted Christian there can be but one true religion. The self-converted may shy away from the bigotry and intolerance which he fears lie in an exclusive devotion to Christianity, but the wholly converted will have no such apprehensions. To him Christ is all in all, and the faith of Christ is God's last word to mankind. To him there is but one God the Father, one Lord and Savior, one faith, one baptism, one body, one Spirit, one fold, and one Shepherd. To him there is none other name under heaven given among men whereby we must be saved. For him Christ is the only way, the only truth, and the only life. For him Christ is the only wisdom, the only righteousness, the only sanctification, and the only redemption.

When, therefore, I ask the question, "Are we having a revival of true religion?" I have only one religion in mind. I mean the faith of the New Testament as held and experienced by the fathers. I mean religion of which Moses and all the prophets did write, that religion which originated in the heart of God the Father, was made effectual through the dying and resurrection of God the Son and is vitalized by God the Holy Spirit. Of this religion the Hebrew and Christian scriptures are the source book, the first and last word, to which we dare add nothing and from which we dare take nothing away.

Lord, You are my all in all, my righteousness. I pray that I will not be
caught up with religious accoutrements but that my focus will
always be on the Father, the Son, and the Holy Spirit.

....

....

....

....

....

....

....

....

Begin with God

Not as pleasing men, but God, which trieth our hearts.
1 THESSALONIANS 2:4

———⟡———

I am really sad for the great throngs of men and women who have never known the satisfaction of believing what God says about all of the good things He has created—and everything having its purpose!

This is an area in which you must begin with God. Then you begin to understand everything in its proper context. All things fit into shape and form when you begin with God!

In Christian circles, there is now an undue deference to intellectual knowledge and accomplishment. I insist that it ought to be balanced out. We appreciate the efforts and hours that go into academic progress, but we must always keep God's wisdom and God's admonitions in mind.

Search and study as we will and we discover that we have only learned fragments of truth. On the other hand, the newest Christian believer has already learned many marvelous things at the center of truth. He has met and knows God!

That is the primary issue, my brother and sister. That is why we earnestly invite men and women to become converted, taking Jesus Christ as their Savior and Lord!

Lord, I am privileged to know You—the beginning and the end of everything in this world.
Allow me to share Your truth with someone who needs to hear it today.

The Godhead—Forever One

Father, into thy hands I commend my spirit.
LUKE 23:46

⟡

When Christ Jesus died on that unholy, fly-infested cross for mankind, He never divided the Godhead! We are assured from the earliest church fathers that the Father in heaven, His eternal Son, and the Holy Ghost are forever One—inseparable, indivisible—and can never be anything else.

Not all of Nero's swords could ever cut down through the substance of the Godhead to cut off the Father from the Son.

It was Mary's son who cried out, "Why hast Thou forsaken me?" It was the human body which God had given Him. It was the sacrifice that cried—the lamb about to die! The Son of Man knew himself forsaken. God dumped that vast, filthy, slimy mass of human sin on the soul of the Savior—and then backed away.

Believe it that the ancient and timeless Deity was never separated. He was still in the bosom of the Father when He cried, "Into thy hands I commend my spirit!" (Luke 23:46).

Little wonder that we are amazed and marvel every day at the wonder of the ancient theology of the Christian Church!

Lord, sometimes Your nature is a mystery to my limited thinking. But how grateful I am that You were willing to bear my sin—and that of the whole human race—on the cross of Calvary.

Glory of the Trinity

Three that bear record in heaven, the Father, the Word,
and the Holy Ghost: and these three are one.
1 JOHN 5:7

———— ❧ ————

*T*he more I read my Bible, the more I believe in the triune God!

With the prophet Isaiah, I am stirred by the vision of the heavenly creatures, the seraphim around the throne of God, engrossed in their worship and praise.

I have often wondered why the rabbis and saints and hymnists of the olden times did not come to the knowledge of the Trinity just from the seraphims' chorus: "Holy! Holy! Holy!"

I am a Trinitarian—I believe in one God, the Father Almighty, maker of heaven and earth. I believe in one Lord Jesus Christ, Son of the Father, begotten of Him before all ages. I believe in the Holy Spirit, the Lord and Giver of life, who with the Father and the Son together is worshipped and glorified.

Isaiah was an astonished man. He could only manage this witness: "Mine eyes have seen the King" (6:5). Only the King of glory can reveal Himself to the willing spirit of a man so that an Isaiah, or any other man or woman, can say with humility but with assurance, "I know Him!"

Lord, the modern world has all but packed You into a small box and placed
You in the corner closet—accessing You only for occasional holidays or special
family events. But in reality You are a great God, and I bow before You today.

....

....

....

....

....

....

....

....

....

Preach a Whole Christ

God is faithful, by whom ye were called unto the
fellowship of his Son Jesus Christ our Lord.
1 CORINTHIANS 1:9

I reject the human insistence among us that Christ may sustain a divided relationship toward us in this life.

I am aware that this is now so commonly preached that to oppose it or object to it means that you are sticking your neck out and you had best be prepared for what comes.

But, I am forced to ask: How can we insist and teach that our Lord Jesus Christ can be our Savior without being our Lord?

How can so many continue to teach that we can be saved without any thought of obedience to our Sovereign Lord?

I am satisfied in my own heart that when a man or a woman believes on the Lord Jesus Christ, he or she must believe on the whole Lord Jesus Christ—not making any reservation! How can a teaching be justified when it encourages sinners to use Jesus as a Savior in their time of need, without owing Him obedience and allegiance?

I believe we need to return to preaching a whole Christ to our needy world!

Heavenly Father, I humbly acknowledge Your saving
grace in my life, and it is an honor to obey and serve You.

Lord of Righteousness

*But of him are ye in Christ Jesus, who of God
is made unto us wisdom, and righteousness.*
1 CORINTHIANS 1:30

———⟨⟩———

*I*n the midst of all the confusions of our day, it is important that we find out that Jesus Christ is the Lord of all righteousness and the Lord of all wisdom.

Righteousness is not a word easily acceptable to lost men and women in a lost world. Outside of the Word of God, there is no book or treatise that can give us a satisfying answer about righteousness, because the only One who is Lord of all righteousness is our Lord Jesus Christ Himself. A scepter of righteousness is the scepter of His kingdom. He is the only One in all the universe who perfectly loved righteousness and hated iniquity.

Our great High Priest and Mediator is the righteous and Holy One—Jesus Christ, our risen Lord. He is not only righteous, He is the Lord of all righteousness!

Then, there is His wisdom. The sum total of the deep and eternal wisdom of the ages lies in Jesus Christ as a treasure hidden away. All the deep purposes of God reside in Him because His perfect wisdom enables Him to plan far ahead! Thus history itself becomes the slow development of His purposes.

*Lord, I admit that my mind at times has difficulty wrapping
around the concept of Your depth of wisdom and knowledge.
I am humbled that You think of me, care for me, and love me.*

The Gospel Warning

As he reasoned of righteousness, temperance,
and judgment to come, Felix trembled.
ACTS 24:25

We who rejoice in the blessings that have come to us through the Savior need to bear in mind that the gospel is not good news only!

The message of the cross is good news indeed for the penitent, but to those who obey not the gospel, it carries an overtone of warning.

The Spirit's ministry to the impenitent world is to tell of sin and righteousness and judgment. For sinners who want to cease being willful sinners and become obedient children of God, the gospel message is one of unqualified peace, but it is by its very nature also an arbiter of the future destinies of man.

Actually, the message of the gospel may be received in either of two ways: in word only without power, or in word with power.

The truth received in power shifts the bases of life from Adam to Christ—a new and different Spirit enters the personality and makes the believing man new in every department of his being!

Loving Father, thank You that You are a patient and loving God.
I pray again for those in my community and around the world
who do not know You. Will Your Spirit convict many of them today?

....
....
....
....
....
....
....
....
....

The Eternal Verity

Jesus Christ the same yesterday, and to day, and for ever.
HEBREWS 13:8

───── ❧ ─────

There is a great deal of discussion now taking place about the lack of spiritual power in our Christian churches. What about the New Testament patterns?

Brethren, the apostolic method was to provide a foundation of good, sound biblical reasons for following the Savior, for our willingness to let the Spirit of God display the great Christian virtues in our lives.

That is why we come in faith and rejoicing to the eternal verity of Hebrews 13:8: "Jesus Christ the same yesterday, and to day, and for ever!" This proclamation gives significance to every other section of teaching and exhortation in the letter to the Hebrews. In this verse is truth that is morally and spiritually dynamic if we will exercise the faith and the will to demonstrate it in our needy world.

I think this fact, this truth that Jesus Christ wants to be known in His church as the ever-living, never-changing Lord of all, could bring back again the power and testimony of the early church!

Lord, I pray for my pastor and my church, that they will comprehend anew the truth that You are ever-living and never-changing.

We Know What We Believe

If ye continue in the faith grounded and settled. . .
not moved away from the hope of the gospel.
COLOSSIANS 1:23

The hope of the Christian Church still lies in the purity of her theology—that is, her beliefs about God and man and their relation to each other.

It is a fact that positive beliefs are not popular these days. I sense that the modern efforts to popularize the Christian faith have been extremely damaging to that faith. The purpose has been to simplify truth for the masses by using the language of the masses instead of the language of the Church. It has not succeeded but has added to rather than diminished religious confusion.

A mistaken desire to maintain a spirit of tolerance among all races and religions has produced a breed of Janus-like Christians with built-in swivels, remarkable only for their ability to turn in any direction gracefully!

Our Christian beliefs have been revealed by the inspiration of the Holy Spirit in the sacred scriptures. Everything there is clear-cut and accurate. We dare not be less than accurate in our treatment of anything so precious!

Lord, Your Word is sacred and true, even though so many people disregard and disrespect it today.
I pray that there will be an explosion of interest in the Bible during this generation.

"Automatic" Saints?

*Always bearing about in the body the dying of the Lord Jesus,
that the life also of Jesus might be made manifest.*
2 CORINTHIANS 4:10

*N*ot everyone agrees with me that full qualification for eternity is not instant or automatic or painless.

I can only hope that you are wise enough, desirous enough, and spiritual enough to face up to the truth that every day is another day of spiritual preparation, another day of testing and discipline with our heavenly destination in mind.

I hope too that you may begin to understand why many evangelical churches are in such a mess. It has become popular to preach a painless Christianity and automatic saintliness. It has become a part of our "instant" culture—"just pour a little water on it, stir mildly, pick up a gospel tract, and you are on your Christian way!"

"Lo," we are told, "this is Bible Christianity!"

"It is nothing of the sort!"

To depend upon that kind of a formula is to experience only the outer fringe, the edge of what Christianity really is. For when the new birth is real and the wonder of regeneration has taken place, then comes the lifetime of preparation with the guidance of the Holy Spirit!

*Dear Lord, I'm not interested in putting on a religious façade for people to see.
I want to make progress in becoming more like You today.*

Normal—or Nominal?

Where your treasure is, there will your heart be also.
LUKE 12:34

⁘

Is the Lord Jesus Christ your most precious treasure in the whole world? If so, count yourself among "normal" Christians, rather than among "nominal" Christians! My old dictionary gives this definition as the meaning of nominal:

Existing in name only, not real or actual; hence so small,
slight, as to be hardly worth the name.

With that as a definition, those who know they are Christians "in name only" should never make the pretense of being normal Christians. Thankfully those who are "normal" are constantly being drawn to praise and worship, charmed by the moral beauty which is found only in Jesus.

I cannot understand how anyone can profess to be a follower and a disciple of our Lord Jesus Christ and not be overwhelmed by His attributes. Those divine attributes faithfully attest that He is indeed Lord of all, completely worthy of our worship and praise!

Heavenly Father, You are the Creator of heaven and earth. You are holy and
righteous in all Your ways. You are my Treasure today and every day.

The Great Physician

When Jesus saw him. . .he saith unto him,
Wilt thou be made whole?
JOHN 5:6

If you are a discouraged and defeated Christian believer, you may have accepted the rationalization that your condition is "normal for all Christians."

You may now be content with the position that the progressive, victorious Christian life may be suitable for a few Christians—but not for you! You have been to Bible conferences; you have been to the altar—but the blessings are for someone else.

Now, that attitude on the part of Christian believers is neither modesty nor meekness. It is a chronic discouragement resulting from unbelief. It is rather like those who have been sick for so long that they no longer believe they can get well.

Jesus is still saying, as He said to the man lying by the gate at the Jerusalem pool, "Do you want to be made whole?" (see John 5:6). Jesus made him whole—because of his desire! His need was great, but he had never lapsed into that state of chronic discouragement.

Thank You, Lord, that a victorious Christian life can be the norm—even in the midst of
this chaotic, malevolent world. Fill me anew with Your Spirit, and shine through me today.

Wisdom from God

Things which are seen are temporal. . .
things which are not seen are eternal.
2 CORINTHIANS 4:18

━━━━━ ⁓ ━━━━━

The thinking of our generation often reflects a willingness to exchange a high view of God's eternity for a short-term concept called "here and now." Technology is presumed to be paramount, but the answers science gives us are short-term answers.

The scientists may be able to keep us alive for a few extra years, but believing Christians know some things that Einstein did not know!

For instance, we know why we are here. We can say why we were born. We also know what we believe about the value of things eternal.

We are thankful that we have found the promise from the God of all grace that deals with the long term and the eternal. We belong to a company of the plain people who believe the truth revealed in the Bible.

Actually, the wisest person in the world is the person who knows the most about God—the person who realizes that the answer to creation and life and eternity is a theological answer not a scientific answer!

Dear Lord, I pray that You will reveal Yourself in some small way to this
unbelieving generation, resulting in many people turning their hearts to You.

....

....

....

....

....

....

....

....

....

....

MARCH 13

The Image We Project

O come, let us worship and bow down. . . .
For he is our God.
PSALM 95:6–7

⸻

*A*re we presently missing important elements of worship in our churches? I speak of the genuine and sacred offering of ourselves as we worship the God and Father of our Lord Jesus Christ.

We must ask the question, even though we are building great churches and large congregations. We are boasting about high standards and talking about revival. But as evangelical Christian believers, are we as concerned as we should be about the image we really project to the community around us? It cannot be denied that many who profess the name of Christ still fail to show forth His love and compassion!

It should say something to us that the often-quoted Jean Paul Sartre described his turning to philosophy and hopelessness as a turning away from a secularistic church.

His indictment: "I did not recognize in the fashionable God who was taught me, Him who was waiting for my soul. I needed a creator: I was given a big businessman!"

O Lord, convict me by Your Holy Spirit if I am projecting a false impression of You to others.
Express Your love and compassion through me so that others will be attracted to You.

Worship—and Word

And the Lord make you to increase and abound in
love one toward another, and toward all men.
1 Thessalonians 3:12

I must take issue with those in the churches who insist that the worshipping saints do not get anything done but worship! Such an attitude reveals that they have not done their homework. The beautiful part of worship is that it prepares you and enables you to zero in on the important things that must be done for God.

Listen to me! Practically every great deed done in the church of Christ all the way back to the apostles was done by people blazing with the radiant worship of their God!

The great hospitals and the mental institutions have grown out of the hearts of worshipping and compassionate disciples. It is true, also, that wherever the Church has come out of her lethargy and into the tides of revival and spiritual renewal, always the worshippers were back of it.

A survey of church history will prove that it was those who were the yearning worshippers who also became the great workers and the selfless servants. If we give ourselves to God's call for worship, everyone will do more for the Savior than they are doing now!

Lord, I worship You this morning. I praise You for Your faithfulness and goodness.
Glorify Yourself today in the lives of every true worshipper around the globe.

"Tears of Joy—Amen!"

He shall baptize you with the Holy Ghost and with fire.
LUKE 3:16

***

*W*e need not be afraid of a genuine visitation of the Spirit of God!

Blaise Pascal, the famed seventeenth-century French scientist and philosopher, experienced in his lifetime a personal, overwhelming encounter with God that changed his life. Those who attended him at his death found a worn, creased paper in his clothing, close to his heart—apparently a reminder of what he had felt and sensed in God's very presence.

In Pascal's own hand it read:

> *From about half past ten at night, to about half after midnight—fire! O God of Abraham, God of Isaac, God of Jacob—not the God of philosophers or the wise. The God of Jesus Christ who can be known only in the ways of the Gospel. Security. Feeling. Peace. Joy. Tears of joy—Amen!*

Were these the expressions of a fanatic, an extremist? No; it was the ecstatic utterance of a yielded man during two awesome hours in the presence of God. The astonished Pascal could only describe the visitation in one word—"Fire!"

Dear Lord, I pray that I will experience the "fire" of Your holy presence in my life.
Burn away all the dross by Your Spirit. I want to live for You and You only.

....

....

....

....

....

....

....

....

Except Ye Repent

The rest of the men. . .repented not.
REVELATION 9:20

⁂

There are many compelling lessons to be drawn from the scriptures, and one of the clearest is that sinful and rebellious people can never be forced into repentance. The same act that may cause one person to repent and believe will cause others to hate and despise God!

The same Bible sermon that brings the person to tearful submission at an altar of prayer will send others out with pride and a resolve to have their own human way.

Students of the scriptures are aware that the Old Testament prophets and the writing apostles of New Testament times foresaw and proclaimed God's coming day of judgment—the consummate settling of accounts between the Sovereign God and His rebellious and sinful creation.

How desperately we would like to believe that in the face of coming judgment, all lost men and women will cry out to God, but such will not be the case: "The rest of the men which were not killed by these plagues yet repented not of the works of their hands. . ." (Revelation 9:20).

*Lord, I pray today that a massive number of people who do not yet know
You will turn away from their sin and receive new life in Jesus Christ.*

Response to the Word

The word of God is. . .sharper than any twoedged sword.
HEBREWS 4:12

---

*M*en and women who read and study the scriptures for their literary beauty alone have missed the whole purpose for which they were given. God's Word is not to be enjoyed as one might "enjoy" a Beethoven symphony or a poem by Wordsworth.

The reason: The Bible demands immediate action, faith, surrender, committal. Until it has secured these, it has done nothing positive for the reader, but it has increased his responsibility and deepened the judgment that must follow.

The Bible was called forth by the fall of man. It is the voice of God calling men home from the wilds of sin; it is a road map for returning prodigals. It is instruction in righteousness, light in darkness, information about God and man and life and death and heaven and hell.

Further, the destiny of each individual depends upon the response to that Voice in the Word!

Father, Your Word contains the precious words of life. I pray today that the Word of God will be proclaimed faithfully—and effectively—to people of every language, tribe, and nation.

....
....
....
....
....
....
....
....
....
....
....
....
....

The Crowd Turns Back

From that time many of his disciples went back,
and walked no more with him.
JOHN 6:66

---

*O*ur Lord Jesus Christ called men to follow Him, but He plainly taught that "no man can come unto me, except it were given unto him of my Father" (John 6:65).

It is not surprising that many of His early followers, upon hearing these words, went back and walked no more with Him. Such teaching cannot but be deeply disturbing to the natural mind. It takes from sinful men much of the power of self-determination. It cuts the ground out from under their self-help and throws them back upon the sovereign good pleasure of God—and that is precisely where they do not want to be!

These statements by our Lord run contrary to the current assumptions of popular Christianity. Men are willing to be saved by grace, but to preserve their self-esteem, they must hold that the desire to be saved originated with them.

Most Christians today seem afraid to talk about these plain words of Jesus concerning the sovereign operation of God—so they use the simple trick of ignoring them!

Dear Lord, I do not want to be counted among those who turn their backs on You.
I want to follow You, Lord. Guide me today.

Money Is Not Truth

The blessing of the LORD, it maketh rich,
and he addeth no sorrow with it.
PROVERBS 10:22

It is a fact in human history that men and women have never in any great numbers sought after truth.

The young people who stream from our halls of learning each year confess to having no more than a passing and academic interest in truth. The majority admit that they go to college only to improve their social standing and increase their earning power.

So, the average American will confess that he most wants success in his chosen field; and he wants success both for prestige and for financial security.

The ominous thing about all this is that everything men and women want can be bought with money, and it would be difficult to think of an indictment more terrible than that!

Real seekers after truth are almost as rare as albino deer! Why? Because truth is a glorious but hard master. Jesus said, "I am. . .the Truth" (John 14:6) and followed Truth straight to the cross. The Truth seeker must follow Him there, and that is the reason few men seek the Truth!

Lord, it is so easy to get wrapped up in the things of this world. Help me to find
a balance between working to provide for my family and trusting You for all our needs.

Tell the Whole Truth

In hope of eternal life, which God, that cannot lie,
promised before the world began.
TITUS 1:2

It is sad indeed to know that there are Christian leaders among us who are too timid to tell the people all the truth. They are now asking men and women to give to God only that which costs them nothing!

The contemporary moral climate does not favor a faith as tough and fibrous as that taught by our Lord and His apostles.

Christ calls men to carry His cross; we call them to have fun in His name!

He calls them to suffer; we call them to enjoy all the bourgeois comforts modern civilization affords!

He calls them to holiness; we call them to a cheap and tawdry happiness that would have been rejected with scorn by the least of the Stoic philosophers!

When will believers learn that to love righteousness it is necessary to hate sin? That to accept Christ it is necessary to reject self? That a friend of the world is an enemy of God? Let us not be shocked by the suggestion that there are disadvantages to the life in Christ!

O Lord, it is so hard for the human spirit to deny or reject itself. I pray
that Your Spirit will take hold of the steering wheel of my will today.

Pour Yourself Out

Howbeit when he, the Spirit of truth,
is come, he will guide you into all truth.
JOHN 16:13

Science declares that nature abhors a vacuum. It should be happy knowledge to us, then, that the same principle is true in the kingdom of God—when you empty yourself, God Almighty rushes in!

The Creator God who fills the universe and overflows into immensity can never be surrounded by that little thing we call our brain, our mind, our intellect. Never can we rise to face God by what we are and by what we know!

Only by love and faith are we lifted thus to know Him and adore Him!

What a happy hour it becomes when we are drawn out of ourselves, and into that vacuum rushes the blessed Presence.

How wonderful in our humanity to sense the reality of the Holy Spirit's invitation: "Pour yourself out! Give yourself to Me! Empty yourself! Bring your empty earthen vessels! Come in meekness like a child!"

Drawn out of ourselves by the Holy Spirit of God—for who knows the things of God but the Holy Spirit?

We are delivered from ourselves when we finally seek God for Himself alone!

Yes, Lord, deliver me from myself today! Help me to live for You and for others.

MARCH 22

God's Overcomers

These. . .have washed their robes,
and made them white in the blood of the Lamb.
REVELATION 7:14

I insist that if we are burdened with genuine concern, we have the responsibility of examining the true spiritual condition of men and women within the church's ranks.

We do live in a time of soft, easy Christianity. It is an era marked by a polite "nibbling" around the edges of the Word of God. There is a mind-set within present-day Christianity that supposes one should get into trouble or suffer embarrassment for Christ's sake!

My brethren, what does it mean to be loyal to Jesus Christ? To confess that Jesus Himself is more important to us than anything else in the world?

Many find it hard to understand how large numbers of Christian believers could have died for their faith in our own generation! With a sense of distant admiration, we call them simple-hearted nationals. God calls them overcomers!

Professing Christians in our North American churches can hardly comprehend so costly a price for the faith we take for granted. Material prosperity and popular acceptance have sapped the vitality of our Christian witness!

Lord, I want to be counted among Your overcomers, and I pray especially for
my brothers and sisters in Christ who profess Your name in antagonistic cultures.

Here for Our Time

*Who knoweth whether thou art come
to the kingdom for such a time as this?*
ESTHER 4:14

—◈—

Just as those who lived in the past had the privilege of being God's people of faith then, so do we in our own day! It is good to come to the understanding that while God wants us to be holy and Spirit filled, He does not expect us to look like Abraham or to play the harp like David or to have the same spiritual insights given to Paul.

All of the former heroes of the faith are dead. You are alive in your generation. A Bible proverb says that a living dog is better than a dead lion (see Ecclesiastes 9:4). You may wish to be Abraham or Isaac or Jacob, but remember they have been asleep for centuries, and you are still around!

You can witness for our Lord today! You can still pray! You can still give of your substance to help those who are in need!

In this, your own generation, give God all your love, all your devotion. You do not know what holy, happy secret God may want to whisper to your responsive heart!

*Thank You, Lord, for the encouragement of this devotional today. It is what I needed to hear.
Use me to advance Your kingdom, Lord. Whisper, and I will obey.*

"Born of God!"

By his own blood he entered in once into the holy place.
HEBREWS 9:12

I think most of us remember with assurance the words of the Charles Wesley hymn which was his own personal testimony:

> *His Spirit answers to the blood,*
> *And tells me I am born of God!*

Wesley testified here and in many other hymns to an inner illumination!

When I became a Christian, no one had to come to me and tell me what Wesley meant. That is why Jesus taught that whosoever is willing to do His will shall have a revelation in his own heart. He shall have an inward revelation that tells him he is a child of God.

Too many persons try to make Jesus Christ a convenience. They reduce Him simply to a Big Friend who will help us when we are in trouble.

That is not biblical Christianity! Jesus Christ is Lord, and when an individual comes in repentance and faith, the truth flashes in. For the first time he finds himself saying, "I will do the will of the Lord, even if I die for it!"

Lord, I pray today for friends and family who may be questioning their relationship with You. Draw them to Yourself, heavenly Father.

Conviction and Pain

Nicodemus answered and said unto him,
How can these things be?
JOHN 3:9

I consider it a good sign that some people are still asking questions like these in our churches: "What should happen in a genuine conversion to Christ?" and "What should a man or woman feel in the transaction of the new birth?"

If I am asked, my answer is this: "There ought to be a real and genuine cry of pain!"

That is why I am not impressed with the kind of evangelism that tries to invite people into the fellowship of God by signing a card. There should be a birth within, a birth from above. There should be the terror of seeing ourselves in violent contrast to the holy, holy God!

Unless we come into this place of conviction and pain concerning our sin, I am not sure how deep and real our repentance will ever be.

The man whom God will use must be undone, humble, and pliable. He must be, like the astonished Isaiah, a man who has seen the King in His beauty!

Lord, I pray that many unbelieving people in hard-to-reach nations will
realize their need for a Savior and will call upon Your holy name for their salvation.

Break with This World

Come out from among them, and be ye separate, saith the Lord.
2 CORINTHIANS 6:17

I dare to say that Christians who have genuinely come to love and trust Jesus Christ have also renounced this world and have chosen a new model after which to pattern their lives.

Further, we should say that this is the aspect of the Christian life that most people do not like. They want comfort. They want blessing. They want peace. But they recoil from this radical, revolutionary break with the world.

To follow Christ in this rough and thoroughgoing way is too much for them!

Actually, the true Christian dissents from the world because he knows that it cannot make good on its promises. As Christ's believing disciple, he is not left without a "norm" to which he seeks to be adjusted. The Lord Jesus Christ is Himself the norm, the ideally perfect model, and the worshipping soul yearns to be like Him. Indeed, the whole drive behind the Christian life is the longing to be conformed to the image of Christ!

Dear Lord, it is difficult to be a future citizen of heaven yet live and function in this present world. Help me live each day in a manner worthy of Jesus Christ (see Philippians 1:27).

The Worldly "Virus"

Let all bitterness, and wrath, and anger, and clamour. . .be put away from you.
EPHESIANS 4:31

———⊰⊱———

As Christian believers, we must stand together against some things. So, if you hear anyone saying that A. W. Tozer preaches a good deal that is negative, just smile and agree: "That is because he preaches the Bible!"

Here are some of the things we oppose: We are against the many modern idols that have been allowed to creep into the churches; we are against the "unauthorized fire" that is being offered on the altars of the Lord; we are against the modern gods that are being adopted in our sanctuaries.

We are against the world's ways and its false values. We are against the world's follies and its vain pleasures. We are against this world's greed and sinful ambitions. We are against this world's vices and its carnal habits.

We believe this spells out clearly the Bible truth of separation. God asks us to stand boldly against anything or anyone who hurts or hinders this New Testament body of Christians. Where the Church is not healed, it will wither. The Word of God is the antibiotic that alone can destroy the virus that would plague the life of the Church!

Lord, I pray that our churches will be faithful to the whole Word of God
and that churchgoers will set themselves apart from the world's ungodly values.

....
....
....
....
....
....
....
....
....

Let Fear Become Trust

Ye have not received the spirit of bondage again to fear.
ROMANS 8:15

What can we do but pray for the throngs of defiant men and women who believe that their humanistic view of life is all sufficient? They believe that they are responsible "captains" of their own souls.

The sad fact is that even while they are joining in the age-old rejection of Jesus Christ— "We will not have this Man to rule over us"—they still are beset with fears within.

The present competitive world and its selfish society have brought many new fears to the human race. I can sympathize with those troubled beings who lie awake at night worrying about the possible destruction of the race through some evil, misguided use of the world's store of nuclear weapons. The tragedy is that they have lost all sense of the sovereignty and omnipotence and faithfulness of the living God.

Although the material world has never understood it, our faith is well placed in the scriptures! Those who take God's Word seriously are convinced of an actual heavenly realm as real as this world we inhabit!

Dear Lord, thank You that You are a strong tower where we
can find shelter and protection. I choose to put my trust in You.

Our Future Rewards

Every man shall receive his own reward.
1 CORINTHIANS 3:8

———— ◆ ————

*O*ur motives in the Christian life should be both right and genuine. God is the Faithful One. We are to love Him and serve Him because He is God—not because of the gracious things He does for us or for the rewards He promises us!

However, it should be said that God does not expect us to forget or ignore the gracious future promises He has made to us. It is a glorious truth that if we believe God and honor His Word, if we walk by faith in love and obedience, there will be eternal rewards for each of us in that great coming day. The rewards will differ. Wisdom and knowledge and love reside in Him who is our God. He will make the right judgments for His people.

I for one will not be surprised if some of God's faithful people serving Him today should rise as high and shine as brightly as the heroes of faith listed in the book of Hebrews.

I say that in all truthfulness because I do not think that all of the heroes of faith are dead and gone!

Praise to the Lord from whom all blessings flow!
I worship You today, the mighty God of all creation!

Which Cross Do We Carry?

Having made peace through the blood of his cross.
COLOSSIANS 1:20

———— ❧ ————

*O*ne of the strange things under the sun is a "crossless" Christianity. The cross of Christendom is a "no cross," an ecclesiastical symbol. The cross of our Lord Jesus Christ is a place of death!

Let each one be careful which cross he carries!

Thousands turn away from Jesus Christ because they will not meet His conditions. He watches them as they go, for He loves them, but He will make no concessions.

Admit one soul into the kingdom by compromise and that kingdom is no longer secure. Christ will be Lord, or He will be Judge. Every man must decide whether he will take Him as Lord now, or face Him as Judge then!

"If any man will. . .let him. . .follow me" (Matthew 16:24). Some will rise and go after Him, but others give no heed to His voice. So the gulf opens between man and man, between those who will and those who will not.

The Man, the kindly Stranger who walked this earth, is His own proof. He will not put Himself again on trial; He will not argue. But the morning of the judgment will confirm what men in the twilight have decided!

Heavenly Father, thank You for Your patience as You wait for people to repent and turn to You. I pray that this will be a day when many will respond to Your voice calling them to follow You.

Power of the Cross

The cross. . .by whom the world is crucified
unto me, and I unto the world.
GALATIANS 6:14

———❦———

Only a person with a perfect knowledge of mankind could have dared to set forth the terms of discipleship that our Lord Jesus Christ expects of His followers. Only the Lord of men could have risked the effect of such rigorous demands: "Let him deny himself" (Matthew 16:24). Can the Lord lay down such severe rules at the door of His kingdom? He can—and He does!

If He is to save the man, He must save him from himself. It is the "himself" which has enslaved and corrupted the man. Deliverance comes only by denial of that self.

No man in his own strength can shed the chains with which self has bound him, but in the next breath the Lord reveals the source of the power which is to set the soul free: "Let him take up his cross."

The cross was an instrument of death—slaying a man was its only function. "Let him take his cross," said Jesus, and thus he will know deliverance from himself!

Dear Lord, I have much to learn about denying myself and bearing my cross daily—
especially in the midst of so many mundane activities. Have Your way with me, Lord.

The Presence of God

*The righteous shall give thanks. . .
the upright shall dwell in thy presence.*
PSALM 140:13

The spiritual giants of old were those who at some time became acutely conscious of the presence of God. They maintained that consciousness for the rest of their lives.

How otherwise can the saints and prophets be explained? How otherwise can we account for the amazing power for good they have exercised over countless generations?

Is it not that indeed they had become friends of God? Is it not that they walked in conscious communion with the real Presence and addressed their prayers to God with the artless conviction that they were truly addressing Someone actually there?

Let me say it again, for certainly it is no secret: we do God more honor in believing what He has said about Himself and coming boldly to His throne of grace than by hiding in a self-conscious humility!

Those unlikely men chosen by our Lord as His closest disciples might well have hesitated to claim friendship with Christ. But Jesus said to them, "You are my friends!"

*Lord, my prayer this morning is that I will become
"acutely conscious of the presence of God."*

God Has a Remedy

If we confess our sins, he is faithful
and just to forgive us our sins.
1 JOHN 1:9

❧

*S*eekers and inquirers have often voiced this deep question of concern: "Why does God forgive? And how does God forgive sin?"

There is plain teaching throughout the Old and New Testaments concerning God's willingness to forgive and forget. Yet there are segments of the Christian church which appear to be poorly taught concerning God's clear remedy, through the atonement of Christ, for the believer who has yielded to temptation and failed his Lord.

God knows that sin is the dark shadow standing between Him and His highest creation, man. God is more willing to remove that shadow than we are to have it removed!

He wants to forgive us—and that desire is a part of God's character. In the sacrificial death of a lamb in the Old Testament, God was telling us that one day a perfect Lamb would come to actually take away sin.

That is how and why God forgives sin now. In John's words: "We have an advocate with the Father, Jesus Christ the righteous: and he is the propitiation for our sins" (1 John 2:1–2).

I am truly thankful, Lord, for Your constant willingness
to forgive me when I stumble in my walk with You.

Spiritual Unanimity

*Finally, be ye all of one mind, having
compassion one of another, love as brethren.*
1 PETER 3:8

———— ✒ ————

The Holy Spirit knew what He was doing when He moved the apostle Peter to write to the early Christian church about the reality of being "of one mind" in their fellowship.

Peter was not asking all the brothers and sisters to settle for some kind of regulated uniformity. He was recommending a spiritual unanimity—which means that the Spirit of God making Christ real within our beings will also give us a unity in certain qualities and disposition.

Peter leaves little doubt about the fruits of genuine Christian unanimity within: "Be alike in compassion. Be alike in loving. Be alike in pity. Be alike in courtesy. Be alike in forgiving!" Then he sums it all up: "Finally, be ye all of one mind!"

God's love shed abroad in our hearts—compassion and love which can only be found in Jesus Christ—these are the only elements of true unity among men and women today!

*Lord, I want to pray for spiritual unity among all true believers
and for spiritual harmony among all Christ-honoring churches.*

Hope—or Despair?

A man can receive nothing,
except it be given him from heaven.
JOHN 3:27

⬥

John the Baptist gave his questioners a brief sentence that I have called the "hope and the despair" of mankind. He told them that "a man can receive nothing, except it be given him from heaven."

John was not referring to men's gifts. He was speaking of spiritual truth. Divine truth is of the nature of the Holy Spirit, and for that reason it can be received only by spiritual revelation.

In his New Testament letters, the apostle Paul declares again and again the inability of human reason to discover or comprehend divine truth. In that inability we see human despair.

John the Baptist said, "Except it be given him from heaven"—and this is our hope! These words do certainly mean that there is such a thing as a gift of knowing, a gift that comes from heaven. Jesus promised His disciples that the Holy Spirit of truth would come and teach them all things (see John 16:13–14).

Jesus also prayed: "I thank thee, O Father, because thou hast hid these things from the wise, and hast revealed them unto babes" (see Luke 10:21).

Lord, I pray that as I read Your Word, Your Spirit will
help me perceive its spiritual truth and apply it to my life.

The Easter Triumph

Why seek ye the living among the dead?
He is not here, but is risen.
LUKE 24:5–6

❧

I do not mind telling you that within me I find the Easter message and the reality of the Resurrection more beautiful and glorious than the Christmas scene.

Christmas tells us that Jesus was born—that He was born for the humiliation of suffering and death and atonement. But Easter is the radiant and glory-filled celebration of Christ's mighty triumph over the grave and death and hell!

When Easter comes, our voices are raised in the triumphant chorus:

> *The three sad days had quickly sped;*
> *He rises glorious from the dead!*

There is the real beauty! This is more than the beauty of color; more than the beauty of outline or form; more than the beauty of physical proportion.

In the living Christ is the perfection of all beauty; and because He lives, we too shall live in the presence of His beauty and the beauties of heaven forever!

Risen Lord, what a privilege it is to call You my Savior and King!
That you triumphed over death is both wonderful and incomprehensible.

....

....

....

....

....

....

....

....

....

Resurrection Power

Jesus came and spake unto them, saying,
All power is given unto me in heaven and in earth.
MATTHEW 28:18

―――――❦―――――

Let us be confident, Christian brethren, that our power does not lie in the manger at Bethlehem nor in the relics of the cross. True spiritual power resides in the victory of the mighty, resurrected Lord of glory, who could pronounce after spoiling death: "All power is given me in heaven and in earth."

The power of the Christian believer lies in the Savior's triumph of eternal glory!

Christ's resurrection brought about a startling change of direction for the believers. Sadness and fear and mourning marked the direction of their religion before they knew that Jesus was raised from the dead—their direction was toward the grave. When they heard the angelic witness, "He is risen, as He said," the direction immediately shifted away from the tomb—"He is risen, indeed!" If this is not the meaning of Easter, the Christian church is involved only in a shallow one-day festival each year.

Thankfully, the resurrection morning was only the beginning of a great, vast outreach that has never ended—and will not end until our Lord Jesus Christ comes back again!

Dear heavenly Father, speed the triumphant resurrection message into areas not yet
reached by the gospel. Strengthen, encourage, and equip Your servants for this awesome task.

Resurrection: A Fact

Be established in the present truth. . .
for we have not followed cunningly devised fables.
2 PETER 1:12, 16

———◆———

The resurrection of Christ and the fact of the empty tomb are not a part of this world's complex and continuing mythologies. This is not a Santa Claus tale—it is history and it is a reality!

The true Church of Jesus Christ is necessarily founded upon the belief and the truth that there was a real death, a real tomb, and a real stone!

But, thank God, there was a sovereign Father in heaven, an angel sent to roll the stone away, and a living Savior in a resurrected and glorified body, able to proclaim to His disciples, "All power is given unto me in heaven and in earth!" (Matthew 28:18).

Brethren, He died for us, but ever since the hour of the Resurrection, He has been the mighty Jesus, the mighty Christ, the mighty Lord!

Our business is to thank God with tearful reverence for the cross, but to go on to a right understanding of what the Resurrection meant both to God and to men. We understand and acknowledge that the Resurrection has placed a glorious crown upon all of Christ's sufferings!

Lord, I praise You that the resurrection of Jesus Christ is a fact and not a fable.
Because He lives, I have real purpose in this life and I can look forward to the life hereafter.

Easter—and Missions

That I may know him, and the power of his resurrection.
PHILIPPIANS 3:10

———— ❧ ————

Do we really believe that the resurrection of Jesus Christ is something more than making us the "happiest fellows in the Easter parade"?

Are we just to listen to the bright cantata and join in singing, "Up from the Grave He Arose," smell the flowers, and go home and forget it?

No, certainly not!

It is truth and a promise with a specific moral application. The Resurrection certainly commands us with all the authority of sovereign obligation—the missionary obligation!

I cannot give in to the devil's principal, deceitful tactic which makes so many Christians satisfied with an "Easter celebration" instead of experiencing the power of Christ's resurrection. It is the devil's business to keep Christians mourning and weeping with pity beside the cross instead of demonstrating that Jesus Christ is risen indeed.

When will the Christian church rise up, depending on His promise and power, and get on the offensive for the risen and ascended Savior?

Lord, Your resurrection is a call to action. No other religion can claim the power
You displayed on that first Easter morning. You are the one, true God!
Give me opportunities to tell others about Your saving power.

....
....
....
....
....
....
....
....
....

"I Will Not Forsake You!"

And, lo, I am with you alway, even unto the end of the world. Amen.
MATTHEW 28:20

---

*M*en without God suffer alone and die alone in times of war and in other circumstances of life. All alone!

But it can never be said that any true soldier of the cross of Jesus Christ, no man or woman as missionary or messenger of the Truth has ever gone out to a ministry alone!

There have been many Christian martyrs—but not one of them was on that mission field all alone. Jesus Christ keeps His promise of taking them by the hand and leading them triumphantly through to the world beyond.

We can sum it up by noting that Jesus Christ asks us only to surrender to His lordship and obey His commands. When the Spirit of God deals with our young people about their own missionary responsibility, Christ assures them of His presence and power as they prepare to go: "All power is given unto Me! I am no longer in the grave. I will protect you. I will support you. I will go ahead of you. I will give you effectiveness for your witness and ministry. Go, therefore, and make disciples of all nations—I will never leave you nor forsake you!"

Thank You, Lord, that You are very near to me and my loved ones at all times.

Leaning Toward Heresy

The mighty God, even the LORD, hath spoken. . . .
thou thoughtest that I was altogether such an one as thyself.
PSALM 50:1, 21

When large numbers of adherents in the Christian churches come to believe that God is different from what He actually is, that concept becomes heresy of the most insidious and deadly kind!

When the Christian church surrenders her once lofty concept of God and substitutes for it ideas so low, so ignoble as to be utterly unworthy, her situation is tragic indeed. Into the life and the practices of the church comes a whole new philosophy; and the sense of the divine presence and the majesty of God is no longer known.

Although "morality" is no longer a popular word in our world, it is apparent that such low and unworthy concepts of God's Person actually constitute a moral calamity for professed believers in great segments of Christianity. The records of both sacred and secular history show that low views of God will surely destroy the appeal of the Christian for all who hold them!

To all sinners, Jesus said, "You must be born again—from above!" He knew that the gods begotten in the shadowy thoughts of the fallen sons and daughters of Adam will quite naturally be no true likeness of the true and living God!

Dear Lord, prevent me from ever diminishing Your greatness. I pray that You will reveal
a glimpse of Your mighty power to all those in the world who hold You in low esteem.

To Sin Is to Rebel

Sin, when it is finished, bringeth forth death.
JAMES 1:15

$\mathscr{S}$ome of you will object to my saying this—but it is my opinion that in Christianity we have overemphasized the psychology of the lost sinner's condition.

We spend time describing the sinner's woes and the great burden he carries until we almost forget the principal fact that the sinner is actually a rebel against properly constituted authority!

That is what makes sin sin! We are rebels, we are sons of disobedience. Sin is the breaking of the Law and we are fugitives from the just laws of God while we are sinners. We are fugitives from divine judgment.

But thankfully, the plan of salvation reverses that and restores the original relationship, so that the first thing the returning sinner does is confess: "Father, I have sinned against heaven and in Thy sight, and I am no more worthy to be called Thy son. Make me as one of Thy hired servants!" (see Luke 15:21).

Thus, in repentance, we reverse that relationship and we fully submit to the Word of God and the will of God, as obedient children!

Dear Lord, You didn't come to this world to condemn but to save sinners.
I pray that Your Spirit will do His convicting work in the hearts of many seekers today.

The Transformed Life

He that taketh not his cross. . .is not worthy of me.
MATTHEW 10:38

---

*M*any of the great evangelists who have touched the world for God, including such men as Jonathan Edwards and Charles Finney, have declared that the Church is being betrayed by those who insist on Christianity being made "too easy."

Jesus laid down the terms of Christian discipleship, and there are some among us who criticize: "Those words of Jesus sound harsh and cruel."

This is where we stand: Receiving Jesus Christ into your life means that you have made an attachment to the Person of Christ that is revolutionary, in that it reverses the life and transforms it completely! It is complete in that it leaves no part of the life unaffected. It exempts no area of the life of the total man.

By faith and through grace, you have now formed an exclusive relationship with your Savior, Jesus Christ. All of your other relationships are now conditioned and determined by your one relationship to your Savior.

To receive Jesus Christ, then, is to attach ourselves in faith to His holy person, to live or die, forever! He must be first and last and all!

Lord, Your call upon my life is total. But there are times when I feel pulled in other directions that may not be pleasing to You. Give me grace and strength to keep You in first place in my life.

Running Life's Race

Let us run with patience the race that is set before us.
HEBREWS 12:1

The writer to the Hebrews gives us good New Testament counsel: "Let us run the race with patience."

The Holy Spirit here describes Christian believers as runners on the track, participants in the race which is the Christian life. He provides both strong warning and loving encouragement, for there is always the danger of losing the race, but there is also the victor's reward awaiting those who run with patience and endurance. So, there are important things each of us should know and understand about our struggles as the faithful people of God.

For instance, it is a fact that the Christian race is a contest. But in no sense is it a competition between believers or between churches! As we live the life of faith, we Christians are never to be in competition with other Christians. The Bible makes this very plain!

Christian churches are never told to carry on their proclamation of the Savior in a spirit of competition with other Jesus churches. The Holy Spirit tells us to keep our eyes on Jesus, not on others who are also running the race!

Lord Jesus, help me to keep my eyes on You as I run the race of the Christian life.

Are We Mired Down?

I know thy works, that thou art neither cold nor hot.
REVELATION 3:15

God will speak to us if we read and study and obey the Word of God! But when He does speak, we should speak back to Him in prayer and devotion. Otherwise, we are among the Christians who are mired down right where we are.

Many in our congregations have grown older and yet are not one inch farther up the mountain than on that day when the sun first arose on them in conversion. In fact, some are not even as far advanced along the way with God as they were a few years ago.

If these things are true, I can only conclude that there are "common" Christians, men and women who no longer hear the Lord speaking to them as they should.

Can they really think that this halfway Christian life is the best that we can know?

In the face of what Christ offers us, how can we settle for so little?

It is a tragedy of our time that so many are settling for less than the Lord is willing to give!

Dear Lord, sometimes my spiritual life seems like a world-class roller-coaster ride! I want to keep growing in my relationship with You, Lord.

Mediocre Christianity

I, brethren, could not speak unto you as unto spiritual, but as unto carnal.
1 CORINTHIANS 3:1

⟡

*R*ead your New Testament again and you will agree that mediocrity in the Christian life is not the highest that Jesus offers. Certainly God is not honored by our arrested spiritual development—our permanent halfway spiritual condition.

We all know that the Bible tells us that we honor God by going on to full maturity in Christ!

Why, then, do we settle for those little pleasures that tickle the saintlets and charm the fancy of the carnal?

It is because we once heard a call to take up the cross and instead of following toward the heights, we bargained with the Lord like a street huckster! We felt an urge to be spent for Christ, but instead of going on, we started asking questions. We began to bicker and bargain with God about His standards for spiritual attainment.

This is plain truth—not about unbelieving "liberals"—but about those who have been born again and who dare to ask, "Lord, what will it cost me?"

O Lord, in my heart of hearts I desire to honor You by going on to full maturity in Christ.
Help me not to be satisfied with mediocrity.

Instruct—Then Exhort

Let the word of Christ dwell in you richly. . .
teaching and admonishing one another.
COLOSSIANS 3:16

The godly men of old through whom the scriptures came to us were faithful in their exhortations to personal faith and godliness, characteristic of the early church.

The apostolic method of teaching, instructing, and encouraging was based on solid and fundamental Christian doctrine. This was Paul's method in his New Testament letters. First he gives his readers the scriptural reasons for certain Christian actions and attributes. He provides the basis and reason—then he exhorts the readers to respond appropriately.

We do not know if Paul was the human writer to the Hebrews, but the method of exhortation is like Paul's. We are assured that Christ is greater than Moses and greater than the angels and that He purchased mankind's salvation.

Then the exhortation: If all of these things are true, then we should keep on loving one another, keep on praying for one another. It is a good and gracious argument: because we have reasons for doing something, we ought to do it without delay and without reservation!

Lord, today I pray for all the biblical instruction presented by professors
in our Christian institutions and by pastors in our churches. May Your
Word be taught with Spirit-anointed clarity and power. Amen.

Not Ready for Heaven?

My meditation of him shall be sweet: I will be glad in the LORD.
PSALM 104:34

———

I can safely say on the authority of all that is revealed in the Word of God that any man or woman on this earth who is bored and turned off by worship is not ready for heaven! Now, I can almost hear someone saying, "Is Tozer getting away from justification by faith?"

I assure you that Martin Luther never believed in justification by faith more strongly than I do. But nowadays there is a deadly, automatic quality about getting saved.

This bothers me greatly: "Sinner, just put a nickel's worth of faith in the slot, pull down the lever, and take out the little card of salvation." Tuck it in your wallet and off you go—a justified believer!

But really, my brother or sister, we are brought to God and to faith and to salvation that we might worship. We do not come to God that we might be automatic Christians stamped out with a die!

God has provided His salvation that we might be, individually and personally, vibrant children of God, loving God with all our heart and worshipping Him in the beauty of holiness!

Lord, I bow before You this morning as my Lord and King.
You are deserving of all my love and praise and worship.

....
....
....
....
....
....
....
....
....
....

Knowing His Presence

Lo, I am with you always, even unto the end of the world.
MATTHEW 28:20

———— ❧ ————

Do not try to short-circuit God's plans for your discipleship and spiritual maturity here. If you and I were already prepared for heaven in the moment of our conversion, God would have taken us home instantly!

We must remember that God exists in Himself. His holy nature is such that we cannot comprehend Him with our minds. He is of a substance not shared by any other being. Hence, God can be known only as He reveals Himself!

I have found this to be a fact: every redeemed human being needs the humility of spirit that can only be brought about by the manifest presence of God.

This mysterious yet gracious Presence is the air of life eternal. It is the music of existence, the poetry of the Christian life. It is the beauty and wonder of being one of Christ's own—a sinner born again, regenerated, created anew to bring glory to God!

To live surrounded by this sense of God is not only beautiful and desirable, but it is imperative!

Lord, I am so grateful that You have revealed some of
Your nature to Your children. But I want to know You even more!

Come As You Are

Being justified by his grace. . .
heirs according to the hope of eternal life.
TITUS 3:7

Let me say this to any of you who are still trying to add up your human merits—look away in faith to the Lord of abundant mercy!

Fixing yourself over and trying to straighten yourself out will never be sufficient—you must come to Jesus as you are!

Our Lord told about two men who went up into the temple to pray. One said, "God, here I am—all fixed up. Every hair is in place!"

The other said, "O God, I just crawled in off skid row. Have mercy on me!"

God forgave the skid row bum but sent the other man away, hardened and unrepentant and unforgiven.

We come to Him just as we are but in humble repentance. When the human spirit comes to God knowing that anything it receives will be out of God's mercy, then repentance has done its proper work!

God promises to forgive and forget and to take that man into His heart and teach him that all of God's kindnesses are due to His mercy. What more can a sinner ask?

Dear Lord, You know me as I really am, yet You extended Your great
mercy toward me. Thank You for Your divine love and forgiveness.

....

....

....

....

....

....

....

....

Seeking after Truth

We have received. . .the spirit which is of God; that we
might know the things that are freely given to us of God.
1 CORINTHIANS 2:12

———◦◦◦———

We live in a mixed-up kind of world in which many people are not at all sure of what they believe or what they ought to believe.

Some churches advertise that way—you do not have to believe anything: "Just be a seeker after truth." Some actually settle for poetry, siding with Edwin Markham, who "saw his bright hand sending signals from the sun."

I, for one, never had any such signals from God. We have Bibles everywhere and the gospel is preached faithfully. Yet men and women seek God in old altars and tombs—in dark and dusty places, and finally wind up believing that God is sending signals from the sun.

Some folks get mad at me when I say that this kind of "seeking after truth" needs to be exposed. We need to double our efforts in telling the world that God is spirit and those who worship Him must worship in spirit and in truth.

It must be the Truth of God and the Spirit of God! Far from being an optional luxury in our Christian lives, the presence and the power of the Holy Spirit is a necessity!

Dear Lord, I pray that Your truth will go out into all the world with a mighty surge today.
I especially pray for this to happen in Islamic, Buddhist, and Hindu nations.

....
....
....
....
....
....
....
....
....

Spiritual Testing

Do therefore as the LORD your God hath commanded you:
ye shall not turn aside to the right hand or to the left.
DEUTERONOMY 5:32

In the scriptural accounts, there are many examples of men and women being tested, and I think it is plain that the Holy Spirit rarely tells a believer that he is about to be tested.

Abraham was being tested when the Lord asked him to take his only son up into the mountain. He thought he was being ordered. He did not know he was being tested.

Peter was unconsciously tested. Paul was tested and tried. There does come a time when we have heard enough truth and the Holy Spirit says, "Today this disciple is going to be tested."

The people of Israel in their time of testing came to Kadeshbarnea, and instead of crossing into the promised land, they said, "We will not go over!" God simply let them make their own test, and they flunked it!

Are there any among us who have an honest desire to be Christlike? We should all be aware that every day is a day of testing. Some come to their own Kadeshbarnea and turn back.

What a solemn thought: many of the persons whom God is testing will flunk the test!

Lord, tutor me by Your Spirit and help me successfully "pass"
Your times of testing. I can't do it by myself.

Glorious Contradictions

The life which I now live in the flesh I live
by the faith of the Son of God, who loved me.
GALATIANS 2:20

———❦———

God has revealed so many glorious contradictions in the lives and conduct of genuine Christian believers that it is small wonder that we are such an amazement to this world. The Christian is dead and yet he lives forever. He died to himself and yet he lives in Christ. The Christian saves his own life by losing it, and he is in danger of losing it by trying to save it.

It is strange but true that the Christian is strongest when he is weakest and weakest when he is strongest. When he gets down on his knees thinking he is weak, he is always strong.

The Christian is in least danger when he is fearful and trusting God and in the most danger when he feels the most self-confident.

He is most sinless when he feels the most sinful, and he is the most sinful when he feels the most sinless.

The Christian actually has the most when he is giving away the most; and in all of these ways, the Christian is simply putting into daily practice the teachings and example of Jesus Christ, his Savior and Lord!

Heavenly Father, the biggest contradiction is that I am a sinner and You are sinless.
Yet You have redeemed me by Your death and resurrection. I praise You, Lord.

Rejoicing in Trials

But rejoice, inasmuch as ye are partakers of Christ's sufferings.
1 PETER 4:13

The apostle Peter stated a great Christian truth in the form of an amazing paradox: The obedient Christian believer will continue to rejoice and praise God even in the midst of continuing trials and suffering in this earthly life!

God's people know that things here on this earth are not all they ought to be, but they refuse to join the worry brigade. They are too busy rejoicing in the gracious prospect of all that will take place when God fulfills His promises to His redeemed children.

This ability to rejoice is demonstrated throughout the Bible, and in the New Testament it rings forth like a silver bell!

The life of the normal believing child of God can never become a life of gloom and pessimism, for it is the Holy Spirit of God who keeps us above the kind of gloomy resignation that marks the secularism of the day.

We are still able to love the unlovely and to weep with those who weep, for in Peter's words, "When Christ's glory shall be revealed, you may be glad with exceeding joy!" (see 1 Peter 4:13).

Lord, thank You for helping me not just to cope but to rise above the difficult situations that face me at work, at home, and at church.

Confessing Our Love

He brought me to the banqueting house,
and his banner over me was love.
SONG OF SOLOMON 2:4

Consider with me the appealing Old Testament story of the beautiful young woman in the Song of Solomon. Deeply in love with the young shepherd, she is also actively sought out by the king, who demands her favor. She remains loyal to the simple shepherd, who gathers lilies and comes to seek her and calls to her through the lattice.

In many ways, this is a beautiful picture of the Lord Jesus, of His love and care for His Bride, the Church. In the scriptural account, she does turn her loved one away with simple excuses. But condemned in heart, she rises to go out and search for him. As she seeks, she is asked: "What is he above others that you should seek him?" (see 5:9).

"Oh, he is altogether lovely," she replies. "He came and called for me, and I had not the heart to go!" (see 5:16).

But at last she is able to confess, "I have found him whom my soul loveth!" (3:4).

He had been grieved but He was not far away. So it is with our Beloved—He is very near to us and He awaits our seeking!

Lord, You are "altogether lovely." Thank You for pursuing
the human race even in our state of unloveliness.

"As I Was, So I Will Be"

As I was with Moses, so I will be with thee.
JOSHUA 1:5

For all things, God is the great Antecedent! Because He is, we are and everything else is. We cannot think rightly of God until we begin to think of Him as always being there—and being there first!

Joshua had this to learn. He had been so long the servant of God's servant Moses, and had with such assurance received God's word at his mouth, that Moses and the God of Moses had become blended in his thinking, so blended that he could hardly separate the two thoughts. By association they always appeared together in his mind.

Now Moses is dead and lest the young Joshua be struck down with despair, God spoke to assure him: "As I was with Moses, so I will be with thee!"

Moses was dead, but the God of Moses still lived! Nothing had changed and nothing had been lost, for nothing of God dies when a man of God dies.

"As I was—so I will be." Only the Eternal God could say this!

Almighty God, I pray today for Christian leaders and pastors in foreign lands who need to be reminded that You are the Eternal God who faithfully stands with them in all their challenges.

APRIL 26

The Walk of Faith

Enoch walked with God. . .for God took him.
GENESIS 5:24

———— ⌘ ————

*T*here are spiritual lessons for every Christian believer in the life of godly Enoch, seventh generation from Adam through Adam's third son, Seth.

We are impressed that he could resist the devil and find fellowship with his Creator God, for he lived in a worldly society headed for destruction.

Enoch's daily walk was a walk of faith, a walk of fellowship with God. The scriptures are trying to assure us that if Enoch could live and walk with God by faith in the midst of his sinful generation, we likewise should be able to follow his example because the human race is the same and God is the same!

Beyond that, Enoch reminds us that the quality and boldness of our faith will be the measure of our preparation for the return of Jesus Christ to this earth. We walk by faith as Enoch did, and although it is now twenty centuries after Christ's sojourn on earth, we hold firmly to the New Testament promise that our risen Lord will return to earth again!

Lord, the example of Your servant Enoch is a reminder to me that it is possible to be godly in the midst of a perverse generation. Help me to remain faithful to You and Your ways, O Lord.

Enoch Escaped Death

By faith Enoch was translated that he should not see death. . .
he had this testimony, that he pleased God.
HEBREWS 11:5

The Genesis record concerning Enoch should speak to us of our own troubled times—for that is the purpose of the Word of God. It should be our concern that we hear and that we obey!

The faith and deportment of the man Enoch compose a vivid picture—a powerful object lesson—to encourage every believer in his or her faith. There is only one conclusion to be drawn—Enoch was translated into the presence of God because of his faith, and thus he escaped death!

It is my strong conviction that Enoch's experience of translation is a type, or preview, of the coming rapture of the Church, the Bride of Christ, described in the scriptures.

It is evident that there was no funeral for Enoch. Perhaps members of his family did not fully understand his walk with God, but they could answer with the facts! "He is gone! We thought he was extreme in his beliefs but now he is gone, and we are still here in a troubled world!"

Lord, some days it is especially good to know that there will be an
eternal reward for those who walk in close fellowship with You.

A Man Sent from God

Among them that are born of women there
hath not risen a greater than John the Baptist.
MATTHEW 11:11

———

The Bible record is very plain when it assures us that John the Baptist was a man sent from God.

Our generation would probably decide that such a man ought to be downright proud of the fact that God had sent him. We would urge him to write a book. Seminary leaders would line up to schedule him as guest lecturer.

Actually, John the Baptist would never have fit into the contemporary religious scene in our day—never! He did not keep his suit pressed. He was not careful about choosing words that would not offend. He did not quote beautiful passages from the poets. The doctors of psychiatry would have quick advice for him: "John, you really need to get adjusted to the times and to society!"

Adjust. That is a modern word I have come to hate. It was never an expression used to speak about human beings until we forgot that man has a soul. Now we have weird guys with mental "screwdrivers" adjusting one person a little tighter and another a little looser. John needed no adjustment. He gladly stepped down so that all eyes could turn to Jesus, the Lamb of God!

Lord, I pray that my church and other evangelical churches will exhibit
the courage and boldness of John the Baptist and point many people to Jesus Christ.

Demonstrate Your Faith

*It is the spirit that quickeneth. . .the words that
I speak unto you, they are spirit, and they are life.*
JOHN 6:63

❧

We know of many who have been deceived into believing that the learning and the memorizing of Christian doctrine is all sufficient. They actually think that somehow they are better off for having learned the doctrines of religion.

God actually asks of us what He asked of Noah long ago! "Demonstrate your faith in God in your everyday life!"

It is evident that God did not say to Noah, "I am depending on you to hold the proper orthodox doctrines. Everything will be just fine if you stand up for the right doctrines."

I have read a statement by Martin Lloyd-Jones, the English preacher and writer, in which he said: "It is perilously close to being sinful for any person to learn doctrine for doctrine's sake."

I agree with his conclusion that doctrine is always best when it is incarnated—when it is seen fleshed out in the lives of godly men and women. Our God Himself appeared at His very best when He came into our world and lived in our flesh!

*Dear Lord, enable me to demonstrate my faith in practical ways today. Remind me to
put feet to my faith when I have the inclination to hide my "light" under a stack of hay.*

Heed the Call of God

I heard the voice of the Lord, saying, Whom shall I send,
and who will go for us? Then said I, Here am I; send me.
ISAIAH 6:8

If Abraham had ever grumbled to the Lord about leaving the beggarly idols of Ur, God would have let him go back. We are free to do the will of God, but God never makes us His unwilling prisoners. God called Abraham out, God gave him the Promised Land, and God said, "Abraham, from among your posterity will come the Messiah in the fullness of time!"

This is the gracious reason why we should tell people everywhere to hear and heed the call of God—so He can lead them into everything that is good and blessed and worthwhile.

God wants to call us out into a more abundant and fruitful Christian life than we have ever known!

Lord, who am I to argue with You or to call into question Your sovereign choice?
The decision is not mine but Yours. So be it, Lord; Your will, not mine be done.

Your Devotional Life

Be strong in the Lord, and in the power of his might.
EPHESIANS 6:10

———⟡———

Too many of us object, perhaps unconsciously, to the rather evident fact that the maintenance of the devotional mood is indispensable to success in the Christian life.

And what is the devotional mood?

It is nothing else than constant awareness of God's enfolding presence, the holding of inward conversations with Christ and private worship of God in spirit and in truth!

To establish our hearts in the devotional mood, we must abide in Christ, walk in the Spirit, pray without ceasing, and meditate in the Word of God day and night. Of course, this implies separation from the world and obedience to the will of God, as we are able to understand it.

No matter how we may argue, true holiness and spiritual power are not qualities that can be once received and thereafter forgotten, as one might wind a clock or take a vitamin pill. Every advance in the spiritual life must be made against the determined resistance of the world, the flesh, and the devil!

Dear Lord, thank You for watching over me and my loved ones last night.
I look forward to spending time with You throughout the course of this day.

....

....

....

....

....

....

....

....

....

....

....

....

Practicing the Truth

Cleanse your hands. . .and purify your hearts, ye double minded.
JAMES 4:8

Christians habitually weep and pray over beautiful truth, only to draw back from that same truth when it comes to the difficult job of putting it into practice!

Actually, the average church simply does not dare to check its practices against biblical precepts. It tolerates things that are diametrically opposed to the will of God, and if the matter is pointed out to its leaders, they will defend its unscriptural practices with a casuistry equal to the verbal dodgings of the Roman moralists.

Can it be that there is no vital connection between the emotional and the volitional departments of life? Since Christ makes His appeal directly to the will, are we justified in wondering whether or not these divided souls have ever made a true commitment to the Lord? Or whether they have been inwardly renewed?

It does appear that too many Christians want to enjoy the thrill of feeling right but are not willing to endure the inconvenience of being right! Jesus Himself left a warning: "Thou hast a name that thou livest, and art dead" (Revelation 3:1).

Lord, help me to do more than pay lip service to the teaching of Your Word.
I invite Your Holy Spirit to point out any shortcomings I may be developing.

An Exclusive Attachment

*But now, after that ye. . .are known of God, how turn
ye again to the weak and beggarly elements?*
GALATIANS 4:9

I am not in the business of trying to downgrade any other believer's efforts to win souls. I am just of the opinion that we are often too casual and there are too many tricks that can be used to make soul-winning encounters completely "painless" and at "no cost" and without any "inconvenience."

Some of the unsaved with whom we deal on the "quick and easy" basis have such little preparation and are so ignorant of the plan of salvation that they would be willing to bow their heads and "accept" Buddha or Zoroaster if they thought they could get rid of us in that way.

To "accept Christ" in anything like a saving relationship is to have an attachment to the Person of Christ that is revolutionary, complete, and exclusive!

It is more than joining some group that you like. It is more than having enjoyable social fellowship with other nice people. You give your heart and life and soul to Jesus Christ—and He becomes the center of your transformed life!

*Lord, as Your followers share the gospel around the world today,
I pray that each hearer will have a clear understanding of the
consequences of the decision they will make to either accept or reject Jesus.*

A Birth from Above

Marvel not that I said unto thee, Ye must be born again.
JOHN 3:7

⸻

This may sound like heresy in some quarters, but I have come to this conclusion—that there are far too many among us who have thought that they accepted Christ, but nothing has come of it within their own lives and desires and habits!

This kind of philosophy in soul winning—the idea that it is "the easiest thing in the world to accept Jesus"—permits the man or woman to accept Christ by an impulse of the mind or of the emotions.

It allows us to gulp twice and sense an emotional feeling that has come over us, and then say, "I have accepted Christ."

These are spiritual matters about which we must be legitimately honest and in which we must seek the discernment of the Holy Spirit. These are things about which we cannot afford to be wrong; to be wrong is still to be lost and far from God.

Let us never forget that the Word of God stresses the importance of conviction and concern and repentance when it comes to conversion, spiritual regeneration, being born from above by the Spirit of God!

Lord, I pray that new believers will become firmly discipled in the Word of God
and that their lives will reflect the transformation from death to life.

....
....
....
....
....
....
....
....
....

Spiritual Confirmation

Let us draw near with a true heart in full assurance of faith.
HEBREWS 10:22

———— ❦ ————

The human personality has a right to be consciously aware of a meeting with God. There will be a spiritual confirmation, an inward knowledge or witness! This kind of confirmation and witness was taught and treasured by the great souls throughout the ages.

Conscious awareness of the presence of God! I defy any theologian or teacher to take that away from the believing church of Jesus Christ!

But be assured they will try. And I refer not just to the liberal teachers. God has given us the Bible for a reason—so it can lead us to meet God in Jesus Christ, in a clear, sharp encounter that will burn on in our hearts forever and ever.

When the Bible has led us to God and we have experienced God in the crisis of encounter, then the Bible has done its first work. That it will continue to do God's work in our Christian lives should be evident!

Dear Lord, I pray for all Christian workers who are doing the hard work of translating scripture into foreign languages. Quicken their minds and bless their work today.

The Ethics of Jesus

And ye shall be witnesses unto me.
ACTS 1:8

―――⸙―――

The teachings of Jesus belong to the Church, not to society, for in society is sin, and sin is hostility to God!

Christ did not teach that He would impose His teachings upon the fallen world. He called His disciples to Him and taught them, and everywhere throughout His teachings there is the overt or implied idea that His followers will constitute an unpopular minority group in an actively hostile world.

The divine procedure is to go into the world of fallen men, preach to them the necessity to repent and become disciples of Christ, and, after making disciples, to teach them "the ethics of Jesus," which Christ called "all things whatsoever I have commanded you" (Matthew 28:20).

The ethics of Jesus cannot be obeyed or even understood until the life of God has come to the heart of a man or woman in the miracle of the new birth.

The righteousness of the law is fulfilled in those who walk in the Spirit. Christ lives again in His redeemed followers the life He lived in Judea, for righteousness can never be divorced from its source, which is Jesus Christ Himself!

Lord, pour out Your Spirit upon our nation today, that men and women will be convicted of sin and turn their lives over to You.

....

....

....

....

....

....

....

....

....

....

May 7

Faith and Experience

O taste and see that the LORD is good.
PSALM 34:8

I insist that the effective preaching of Jesus Christ, rightly understood, will produce Christian experience in Christian believers. Moreover, if preaching does not produce spiritual experience and maturing in the believer, that preaching is not being faithful to the Christ revealed in the scriptures.

Let me say it again another way: the Christ of the Bible is not rightly known until there is an experience of Him within the believer, for our Savior and Lord offers Himself to human experience.

When Jesus says, "Come unto me, all ye that labour and are heavy laden" (Matthew 11:28), it is an invitation to a spiritual experience. He is saying, "Will you consent to come? Have you added determination to your consent? Then come; come now!"

Yes, our Lord gives Himself to us in experience. David says in Psalm 34: "O taste and see that the Lord is good." I think David said exactly what he meant.

Surely the Holy Spirit was saying through David: "You have taste buds in your soul for tasting, for experiencing spiritual things. Taste and experience that God is good!"

Lord, the great need of people within and outside our churches today is to experience the "real thing"—God in all His power and majesty and personal involvement in our lives. Help me to inspire others to "taste" You, Lord.

We Are Not All Alike

For we are his workmanship,
created in Christ Jesus unto good works.
EPHESIANS 2:10

We ought to be fully aware that in the Body of Christ we are not interested in the production of "cookie cutter" Christians.

This is a word of caution in the matter of Christian experience—there is no pattern or formula for identical Christian experiences. It is actually a tragic thing for believers to try to be exactly like each other in their Christian faith and life.

I have probably been overly cautious about testifying to my own experiences because I do not want anyone to be tempted to try to copy anything the Lord has done for me.

God has given each of us an individual temperament and distinct characteristics. Therefore it is the office of the Holy Spirit to work out as He will the details of Christian experience. They will vary with personality.

Of this we may be sure: whenever a person truly meets God in faith and commitment to the gospel, he will have a consciousness and a sharp awareness of the details of that spiritual transaction!

Lord, help me to be a faithful steward of the gifts
You have given me to use in the church.

Questions We Ask

A living sacrifice, holy, acceptable unto God,
which is your reasonable service.
ROMANS 12:1

———

I am convinced that anyone who brings up the question of consequences in the Christian life is only a mediocre and common Christian!

I have known some who were interested in the deeper life but began asking questions: "What will it cost me—in terms of time, in money, in effort, in the matter of my friendships?" Others ask of the Lord when He calls them to move forward: "Will it be safe?" This question comes out of our constant bleating about security and our everlasting desire for safety above all else.

A third question that we want Him to answer is: "Will it be convenient?"

What must our Lord think of us if His work and His witness depend upon the security and the safety and the convenience of His people? No element of sacrifice, no bother, no disturbance—so we are not getting anywhere with God!

We have stopped and pitched our tent halfway between the swamp and the peak. We are mediocre Christians.

Lord, I pray for Christians in other countries who face persecution as a routine event.
Protect and strengthen them, Father. May many come to know Christ as a result
of the testimony of believers who remain faithful to You.

....
....
....
....
....
....
....
....

Beyond Empty Profession

*Examine yourselves, whether ye be
in the faith; prove your own selves.*
2 CORINTHIANS 13:5

---

*P*reaching from the pulpit about the Christian "deeper life" does not automatically produce a deeper-life church and congregation. The profession of men and women that they believe in "the deeper Christian life" is no assurance that their fellowship is actually a deeper-life church.

The deeper spiritual life many people say they want is not a message; it is not a sermon; it is not a profession.

I am a pastor and I think I major in telling the truth. It is true that it is about time we stop coddling and apologizing for congregations that have reputations for being deeper-life churches.

The deeper spiritual life is not something just to be talked about. It is a quiet enjoyment of daily blessing and peace and victory that is lived day by day, beyond empty profession and without any two-faced circumstances!

*Lord, with Christ living in me, I have the Source of joy and victorious living.
Thank You for Your promise of daily blessing and peace. I want more of You, Lord.*

Confess Christ's Lordship

As ye have therefore received
Christ Jesus the Lord, so walk ye in him.
COLOSSIANS 2:6

I think it is a completely wrong concept in Christian circles to look upon Jesus as a kind of divine nurse to whom we can go when sin has made us sick, and after He has helped us, to say, "Good-bye, Jesus"—and go on our own way.

Suppose I go into a hospital in need of a blood transfusion. After the staff has ministered to me and given their services, do I just slip out with a cheery "good-bye"—as though I owe them nothing and it was kind of them to help me in my time of need?

That may sound far-out to you, but it draws a picture of attitudes among us today.

But the Bible never in any way gives us such a concept of salvation. Nowhere are we ever led to believe that we can use Jesus as a Savior and not own Him as our Lord. He is the Lord and as the Lord He saves us, because He has all of the offices of Savior, Christ, High Priest, and Wisdom and Righteousness and Sanctification and Redemption!

He is all of these—and all of these are embodied in Him as Christ, the Lord!

Father, You are my Savior and my Lord.
My debt to You is huge! I owe You my life.

How Do We Listen?

I will hear what God the LORD will speak. . .peace unto his people.
PSALM 85:8

───※───

The living God has spoken to lost mankind in a variety of ways. The general response among us has been, "We did not hear His voice. We did not hear anything."

John recorded in his gospel the reactions of an audience of people who heard God speak audibly. When Jesus talked of His coming death, asking God to glorify His name through it, "a voice [came] from heaven saying, I have both glorified it, and will glorify it again" (John 12:28).

And what were the reactions of the bystanders? "The people therefore, that stood by, and heard it, said that it thundered: others said, An angel spake to him" (John 12:29).

People prefer their own logic, their own powers of reason. Even when God speaks, they refuse to recognize His voice. They will not confess that God has spoken through Jesus Christ, the eternal Son. When He confronts them with their sin, they consult a psychiatrist and hope they can get their personalities "properly adjusted."

But in a coming day every knee will bow and every tongue will confess that Jesus Christ is Lord of all!

Almighty God, I am so grateful that You sent Your Son, Jesus Christ, to live among us and to show us the way of eternal life. I pray that many seekers will bow before You today.

Unclean by Comparison

And when I saw him, I fell at his feet as dead.
REVELATION 1:17

---

*I*n the Old Testament, whenever the living God revealed Himself in some way to human-kind, terror and amazement were the reactions. People saw themselves as guilty and unclean by comparison!

In the book of Revelation, the apostle John describes the overwhelming nature of his encounter with the Lord of glory. Although a believer and an apostle, John sank down in abject humility and fear when the risen, glorified Lord Jesus appeared before him on Patmos.

Our glorified Lord did not condemn John. He knew that John's weakness was the reaction to revealed divine strength. He knew that John's sense of unworthiness was the instant reaction to absolute holiness. Along with John, every redeemed human being needs the humility of spirit that can only be brought about by the manifest presence of God.

Jesus at once reassured John, stooping to place a nail-pierced hand on the prostrate apostle, and saying: "Do not be afraid. I am the Living One. I was dead, and behold I am alive for ever and ever, and I hold the keys of death and Hades" (see Revelation 1:17–18).

Lord, only through Your divine presence in my life do I have spiritual power to serve others in Your name. Fill me anew today, O Lord.

God Knows the Hypocrites

Let us not therefore judge one another any more.
ROMANS 14:13

I do not consider that it is my place as a Christian to stand around making judgments and calling other people "hypocrites."

Our Lord Jesus Christ is the only man I know who was holy and perfect enough to call the religious leaders of the day hypocrites.

I am just a man with faults and shortcomings of my own, and I must always consider myself lest I be tempted!

I preach to my own congregation about our faults and our failings, with the warning that some of our professions of blessing and victory may get into the area of "unintentional hypocrisy." Through the grace of God and the kindness of our spiritual ancestors, we may have spiritual light that some others do not have—but in all honesty, we are wretchedly far below what we should be in living up to it, day by day.

It helps us to be honest and frank and humble to know that the great God Almighty knows the secrets of every person's heart!

Lord, You know the secrets of my heart, yet You love me unconditionally.
I confess my sins to You, Lord. Forgive me when I fall.

More Than Religion

Walk worthy of God, who hath called you unto his kingdom and glory.
1 THESSALONIANS 2:12

Contrary to much that is being said and practiced in churches, true worship is not something that we "do" in the hope of appearing to be religious!

True worship must be a constant and consistent attitude or state of mind within the believer, a sustained and blessed acknowledgment of love and admiration. If we have this awareness in our own lives and experience, then it is evident that we are not just waiting for Sunday to come to church and worship.

Having been made in His image, we have within us the capacity to know God and the instinct that we should worship Him. The very moment that the Spirit of God has quickened us to His life in regeneration, our whole being senses its kinship to God and leaps up in joyous recognition!

That response within our beings—a response to the forgiveness and pardon and regeneration—signals the miracle of the heavenly birth without which we cannot see the kingdom of God. Thus the primary work of the Holy Spirit is to restore the lost soul to intimate fellowship with God through the washing of regeneration.

Lord Jesus, many people in our country and around the world are not yet born again.
I pray that Your Spirit will restore many lost souls to intimate fellowship with God today.

Holy Spirit, All Divine

It is the Spirit that beareth witness, because the Spirit is truth.
1 JOHN 5:6

───※───

I wonder if any Christian can ever show forth the transforming radiance of the love of God without a complete surrender to the indwelling Person of the Holy Spirit. Surely that was in the mind of the songwriter, as he prayed and sang:

> *Holy Ghost, with light divine,*
> *Shine upon this heart of mine;*
> *Chase the shades of night away,*
> *Turn my darkness into day.*
>
> *Holy Spirit, all divine,*
> *Dwell within this heart of mine;*
> *Cast down every idol throne,*
> *Reign supreme—and reign alone.*

Our world is filled with hatred and conflict, violence and bloodshed. Through the plan of redemption, God has dealt graciously with this global problem of hatred in the hearts of men and women. He has sent the source of love and light and radiance to the human bosom; Paul himself testifying: "The love of God is shed abroad in our hearts by the Holy Ghost which is given unto us" (Romans 5:5).

Lord, may Your divine love minister through me to a hurting person today.

....
....
....
....
....
....
....
....

Honor God's Spirit

Grieve not the holy Spirit of God,
whereby ye are sealed unto the day of redemption.
EPHESIANS 4:30

I think there are great numbers of Christian believers who ought to go home and go into their places of prayer and apologize to God for their demeaning attitudes toward the Holy Spirit of God.

Included in their numbers are Bible teachers who are guilty of leading us astray. They have dared to teach Christians that the Holy Spirit will never speak of His own person or position, as though the third Person of the Godhead may be ignored and His ministry downgraded!

Jesus said, "[When He comes] he shall not speak of himself; but whatsoever he shall hear, that shall he speak" (John 16:13).

Jesus was actually telling His disciples: The Comforter will not come to stand on His own, to speak on His own authority. He will guide you into all truth—He will speak and act on the authority of the divine Godhead: Father, Son, and Holy Spirit.

If you do not yield to and honor the Holy Spirit, your lives will not show forth the blessed fruits of the Spirit!

Lord, I pray that my life will produce the fruit
of Your Spirit today (see Galatians 5:22–23).

Responding to the Spirit

Quench not the Spirit. Hold fast that which is good.
1 THESSALONIANS 5:19, 21

————⚬————

*A*re we raising a whole generation of young men and women without any sensitivity to the voice of God's Holy Spirit?

I am on record, and I will be as long as I live, that I would rather lose a leg and hobble along throughout the rest of my life than to lose my sensitivity to God and to His voice and to spiritual things!

Oh, how I want to keep that sensitivity within me—within my soul!

I am thinking about a great throng of men and women raised in Christian homes. They have been brought up in Sunday school. They probably cut their first baby tooth on the edge of a hymnbook when the mother was not watching.

Still, to this day, they are not right with God. Some have made a kind of profession but have never been able to delight themselves in the Lord.

The reason? They have lost sensitivity to the message and the voice of God. If the Holy Spirit cannot move something within their beings every day, they are not going to be effective Christians—if they are Christians at all!

Lord, today my heart goes out to mediocre Christians who "know" the truth of the gospel but who have not experienced a personal relationship with You. Lord, will You give them a divine nudge so that they will find delight in truly knowing You?

....
....
....
....
....
....
....
....
....
....

When Pentecost Came

But ye shall receive power, after that the Holy Ghost
is come upon you: and ye shall be witnesses.
ACTS 1:8

---

*A*s we read the New Testament, we find a very simple and very plain and very forceful truth—
the Holy Spirit makes a difference!

Consider the early disciples—Jesus Himself had taught them for more than three years—
the greatest Bible school! But still He had to caution them and encourage them not to depend
on their own wisdom and strength: "Tarry ye. . .until ye be endued with power from on high"
(Luke 24:49). He promised that they would receive the Person of the Holy Spirit to carry out
His plan of world evangelization.

After Pentecost, the Spirit brought them a new and vivid consciousness of the actual presence of God. He gave them the gifts of divine joy and peace. He gave them great and continuing delight in prayer and communion with God!

Finally, we recall that before Pentecost the disciples could only ask questions. After Pentecost, throughout the record in the book of Acts, they stood in the authority of the Spirit and
answered all of the questions of the people concerning God's plan of salvation through the
crucified and risen Christ!

Lord, I pray that Your Spirit will "visit" our local churches and anoint them with
a renewed sense of urgency to become involved in Your plan of world evangelization.

....

....

....

....

....

....

....

....

....

....

MAY 20

The Promise of the Spirit

*This Jesus. . .being by the right hand of God exalted,
and having received of the Father the promise of the Holy Ghost.*
ACTS 2:32–33

The miraculous events wrought in Jerusalem by the Holy Spirit on the day of Pentecost indicated to the disciples that Jesus Christ, the Messiah Savior, had indeed taken His place at the right hand of the Majesty on high.

With Jewish critics all around, Peter lifted his voice and said that all who were in Jerusalem on that day were seeing the fulfillment of prophecy—the words of Jesus that He would send the Holy Spirit after His death and resurrection and exaltation.

"Therefore," Peter cried, "let all the house of Israel know assuredly, that God hath made that same Jesus, whom ye have crucified, both Lord and Christ" (Acts 2:36).

Many, many have failed to note Peter's Pentecostal emphasis: The important thing in God's plan was the fact that Jesus had been exalted in heaven, and that His glorification there had been the signal for the coming of the promised Holy Spirit. What a lesson! The Spirit does not have to be begged—He comes when the Savior is honored and exalted!

*Father, Your Spirit dwells in all those who receive Your gift of salvation
through faith in Jesus Christ. What a power source we possess!
Lord, awaken Your Church to this reality today, I earnestly pray!*

Geared into Things Eternal

Christ, who through the eternal
Spirit offered himself without spot to God.
HEBREWS 9:14

The coming of the Holy Spirit on the day of Pentecost was a gracious experience of fulfillment and blessing and direction for the Christian church.

It was the continuing emphasis for believers that we must live to gear ourselves into things eternal and to live the life of heaven here upon earth. We must yield our first obedience and loyalty to Jesus Christ, at any cost!

Anything we try to offer God that is less than that really is a degradation of the Christian church.

Frankly, I would rather be a member of a group that meets in a little room on a side street than to be part of a great activity that is not New Testament in its doctrine, in its spirit, in its living, in its holiness, in all of its texture and tenor. The Spirit-filled and Spirit-led congregation will be a joyful people. Beyond that, it will be useful and caring and compassionate! I do believe that the Christian church ought to be a helpful influence to the whole community!

Lord, empower the local churches in this community to reach out in
Your name with love and compassion to those who are spiritually needy.

God Is Sovereign

We are in him that is true, even in his Son Jesus Christ.
1 JOHN 5:20

---

*O*h, how I wish that I could adequately set forth the glory of the One who is worthy to be the object of our worship!

I do believe that if our new converts—the babes in Christ—could be made to see His thousand attributes and even partially comprehend His being, they would become faint with a yearning desire to worship and honor and acknowledge Him, now and forever!

I know that many discouraged Christians do not truly believe in God's sovereignty. In that case, we are not filling our role as the humble and trusting followers of God and His Christ.

And yet, that is why Christ came into our world. The old theologians called it "theanthropism"—the union of the divine and human natures in Christ. This is a great mystery, and I stand in awe before it!

The theanthropy is the mystery of God and man united in one Person—not two persons but two natures. So, the nature of God and the nature of man are united in this One who is our Lord Jesus Christ!

Lord Jesus, You are the only hope for this world. You provided the perfect plan for our redemption. Though Your supernatural being may be beyond our human comprehension, Your grace and mercy and love are worthy of all our praise.

Blame Someone Else

And the man said, The woman. . .
gave me of the tree, and I did eat.
GENESIS 3:12

In the earliest day of failure and tragedy in the garden of Eden, Adam came out of hiding, knowing full well his own guilt and shame.

Adam confessed: "We ate from the fruit of the tree that was forbidden—but it was the woman who enticed me!" (see Genesis 3:12).

When God said to Eve, "What did you do?" she said: "It was the serpent that beguiled me!" (see 3:13).

In that brief time our first parents had learned the art of laying the blame on someone else. That is one of the great, betraying evidences of sin—and we have learned it straight from our first parents. We do not accept the guilt of our sin and iniquity. We blame someone else.

If you are not the man you ought to be, you are likely to blame your wife or your ancestors. If you are not the young person you ought to be, you can always blame your parents. If you are not the wife you ought to be, you may blame your husband or perhaps the children.

Sin being what it is, we would rather lay the blame on others. We blame, blame, blame! That is why we are where we are.

Lord, help me to quickly acknowledge my sins and not try to hide them
from You—which is actually impossible to do. I want to receive
Your forgiveness and move on in my deepening relationship with You.

Unholy, Unrighteous, Unhappy

And so death passed upon all men,
for that all have sinned.
ROMANS 5:12

---

*A*ll of history and the daily newspaper testify that the human race lies in ruin—spiritually, morally, and physically.

The long parade of gods, both virtuous and obscene, and a thousand varieties of vain and meaningless religious practices declare our spiritual degeneration, while disease, old age, and death testify sadly to the completeness of our physical decay.

By nature, men and women are unholy; and by practice we are unrighteous. That we are also unhappy is of small consequence.

But it is of overwhelming importance to us that we should seek the favor of God while it is possible to find it, and that we should bring ourselves under the plenary authority of Jesus Christ in complete and voluntary obedience.

To do this is to invite trouble from a hostile world and to incur such unhappiness as may naturally follow. Add the temptation of the devil and a lifelong struggle with the flesh, and it will be obvious that we will need to defer most of our enjoyments to a more appropriate time!

Loving Father, there is nothing more important to do while we are alive than to accept
You as our Savior. I pray especially today for believers in hostile countries, that their inner
joy in knowing You will override any pain that is inflicted upon them or their families.

Bragging about God

That God in all things may be glorified through Jesus Christ,
to whom be praise and dominion.
1 PETER 4:11

———— ✦ ————

*B*asic beliefs about the Person and the nature of God have changed so much that there are among us now men and women who find it easy to brag about the benefits they receive from God—without ever a thought or a desire to know the true meaning of worship!

I have immediate reactions to such an extreme misunderstanding of the true nature of a holy and sovereign God, for I believe that the very last thing God desires is to have shallow-minded and worldly Christians bragging about Him.

Beyond that, it does not seem to be very well recognized that God's highest desire is that every one of His believing children should so love and so adore Him that we are continually in His presence, in spirit and in truth.

Something wonderful and miraculous and life changing takes place within the human soul when Jesus Christ is invited in to take His rightful place. That is what God anticipated when He wrought the plan of salvation. He intended to make worshippers out of rebels; to restore the place of worship which our first parents knew when they were created!

Lord, this morning I want to give You first place in my life all over again.
It's all about You, Lord. You deserve all my worship.

Man's View of This World

Choose you this day whom ye will serve. . .
but as for me and my house, we will serve the LORD.
JOSHUA 24:15

———◈———

*I*f you have ever given much thought to this present world in which we live, you have some idea of the power of interpretation. The world is a stable fact, quite unchanged by the passing of years, but how different is modern man's view of the world from the view our fathers held.

The world is for all of us not only what it is; it is what we believe it to be, and a tremendous load of weal or woe rides on the soundness of our interpretation!

In the earlier days, when Christianity exercised a dominant influence over American thinking, men conceded this world to be a battleground. Man, so our fathers held, had to choose sides. He could not be neutral—for him it must be life or death, heaven or hell!

In our day, the interpretation has changed completely. We are not here to fight, but to frolic! We are not in a hostile foreign land; we are at home! It now becomes the bounden duty of every Christian to reexamine his spiritual philosophy in the light of the Bible. So much depends on this that we cannot afford to be careless about it!

Lord, with Joshua I say to You today,
"But as for me and my house, we will serve the Lord."

The Humble Place

All of you be subject one to another, and be clothed with humility.
1 PETER 5:5

I have met two classes of Christians: the proud who imagine they are humble, and the humble who are afraid they are proud!

There should be another class: the self-forgetful men and women who leave the whole thing in the hands of Christ and refuse to waste any time trying to make themselves good. They will reach the goal far ahead of the rest.

The truly humble person does not expect to find virtue in himself, and when he finds none he is not disappointed. He knows that any good deed he may do is the result of God's working within him.

When this belief becomes so much a part of any man or woman that it operates as a kind of unconscious reflex, he or she is released from the burden of trying to live up to the opinion they hold of themselves. They can relax and count upon the Holy Spirit to fulfill the moral law within them.

Let us never forget that the promises of God are made to the humble: the proud man by his pride forfeits every blessing promised to the lowly heart, and from the hand of God he need expect only justice!

*Lord, it is very difficult to "put on humility" in a culture that idolizes
self-promotion and individuality. I invite You to do a work in me,
Lord, molding my life to be a useful instrument in Your hands.*

Ashamed of Sin

Verily every man at his best state is altogether vanity. . . .
Surely every man walketh in a vain shew.
PSALM 39:5–6

Brethren, I am not ashamed of this world God created—I am only ashamed of man's sin! If you could take all of man's sin out of this world, there would be nothing to be ashamed of and nothing to be afraid of.

Our apologies must be for humanity—and for our sins. I keep repeating that we have no business making excuses for God.

It is popular now to talk about Christ being a guest here. I dare to tell people that they should stop patronizing Jesus Christ!

He is not the guest here—He is the Host!

We have apologists who write books and give lectures—apologizing for the person of Christ, trying to "explain" to our generation that the Bible does not really mean "exactly" what it says. But God has revealed Himself in Jesus Christ and thus we know where we stand, believing that all things were made by Him and "without him was not any thing made that was made" (John 1:3).

Lord, in my own personal life I relinquish control
to Your Spirit within me. Slay my vanity, Lord.

A Great Moral Blunder

By the name of Jesus Christ of Nazareth, whom ye crucified. . .
This is the stone which was set at nought of you builders.
ACTS 4:10–11

Of all the people on the earth, the nation of Israel surely was the best prepared to receive the Christ of God. The children of Abraham, they were called to be a chosen people in an everlasting covenant with God, the Father.

Yet they failed to recognize Jesus as Messiah and Lord. There is no doubt that theirs was the greatest moral blunder in the history of mankind. He came to His own people, and they rejected Him!

Jesus taught frankly that He was asking His followers to throw themselves out on the resources of God. For the multitude, He was asking too much. He had come from God but they received Him not!

It seems to be a comfort to some Christians to sit back and blame and belabor the Jews, refusing to acknowledge that they have information and benefits and spiritual light that the Jews never had.

It is surely wrong for us to try to comfort our own carnal hearts by any emphasis that Israel rejected Him. If we do that, we only rebuild the sepulchres of our fathers as Jesus said!

Lord, would I have mocked You? Denied You? Ignored who You really were? I only know
that I wholeheartedly worship You today as the King of kings and Lord of lords!

Astonished Reverence

Come and hear, all ye that fear God,
and I will declare what he hath done for my soul.
PSALM 66:16

———— ❧ ————

*I*n my own being, I could not exist very long as a Christian without the inner consciousness of the presence and nearness of God! I can only keep right by keeping the fear of God on my soul and delighting in the fascinating rapture of worship.

I am sorry that the powerful sense of godly fear is a missing quality in churches today.

The fear of God is that "astonished reverence" of which the saintly Faber wrote. I would say that it may grade anywhere from its basic element—the terror of the guilty soul before a holy God—to the fascinated rapture of the worshipping saint.

There are few unqualified things in our lives, but I believe that the reverential fear of God, mixed with love and fascination and astonishment and adoration, is the most enjoyable state and the most purifying emotion the human soul can know. A true fear of God is a beautiful thing, for it is worship, it is love, it is veneration. It is a high moral happiness because God is!

Lord, our world in general has lost any sense of the fear of God.
Even some of our churches hold a small view of Your greatness.
I pray for a spiritual revival in our country, Lord.

Live Right or Die

Blessed are the dead which die in the Lord. . .
that they may rest from their labours.
REVELATION 14:13

—⟋⟍—

*W*e modern Christians seem to be a strange breed in many of our ways. We are so completely satisfied with earthly things and we enjoy our creature comforts so much that we would just rather stay on here for a long, long time!

Probably most of us do not tell God about that kind of desire when we pray. But I have made a practice of writing many of my earnest prayers to God in a little book—a book now well worn. I remind God often of what my prayers have been.

One prayer in the book—and God knows it well by this time—is an honest supplication:

O God, let me die rather than to go on day by day living wrong. I do not want to become a careless, fleshly old man. I want to be right so that I can die right! Lord, I do not want my life to be extended if it would mean that I should cease to live right and fail in my mission to glorify You all of my days!

I would rather go home right now than to live on—if living on was to be a waste of God's time and my own!

Lord, it's true that shelter and security are key human pursuits as we strive to provide for ourselves and our families. But help me find a balance between focusing too much on myself and not enough on You and Your plan for this world.

God's Grace Is Eternal

Much more the grace of God, and the gift by grace,
which is by one man, Jesus Christ, hath abounded unto many.
ROMANS 5:15

It is a typical and accepted teaching in Christian churches today that Moses and the Old Testament knew only God's law, and that Christ and the New Testament know only God's grace.

I repeat: That is the "accepted" teaching of the hour—but I also hasten to add that it is a mistaken concept, and that it was never the concept held and taught by the early Christian church fathers.

God has always been the God of all grace, and He does not change. Immutability is an attribute of God; therefore, God at all times and in all of history must act like Himself!

He is the God of all grace; therefore, the grace of God does not ebb and flow like the ocean tides. There has always been the fullness of grace in the heart of God. There is no more grace now than there was previously, and there will never be any more grace than there is now!

The flow of God's grace did not begin when Christ came to die for us. It was part of God's ancient plan of redemption and was manifested in the blood and tears and pain and death at Calvary's cross!

Lord, I am a recipient of Your abundant grace, and without it I would perish.
I pray that others will see Your grace in my life today.

....

....

....

....

....

....

....

....

....

His Cross Is My Cross

The disciple is not above his master,
nor the servant above his lord.
MATTHEW 10:24

—◦—

To take Jesus Christ into your life without reservation is to accept His friends as your friends and to know that His enemies will be your enemies! It means that we accept His rejection as our rejection. We knowingly accept His cross as our cross.

If you then find yourself in an area where Christ has no friends, you will be friendless—except for the one Friend who will stick closer than a brother. I made up my mind a long time ago. Those who declare themselves enemies of Jesus Christ must look upon me as their enemy, and I ask no quarter from them! And if they are friends of Christ, they are my friends—and I do not care what color they are or what denomination they belong to.

If the preachers would faithfully tell the people what it actually means to receive Christ and obey Him and live for Him, we would have fewer converts backsliding and foundering.

Preachers who are not faithful one day will stand before the judgment seat of Christ and answer to a faithful Savior why they betrayed His people in this way!

Lord, I pray that You will send encouragement to Your children today
who live and/or serve in an area where Christ is not formally welcome.

New Testament Roots

*For by one Spirit are we all baptized into one body. . .
and have been all made to drink into one Spirit.*
1 CORINTHIANS 12:13

———— ❧ ————

It is really a blessed thing in our Christian fellowship and in our congregations that God never asks whether it is a big church or a little church!

A young pastor, when introduced to a well-known church leader, said, "You do not know me. I am the pastor of a little rural church."

I think it was a wise reply that came from the churchman: "Young man, there are no little churches; all churches are the same size in God's sight!"

But whether large or small, it must be an assembly of believers brought together through the name of Jesus to worship in God's presence—and with the right to receive all that God bestows.

With these roots we should ask ourselves if we are truly interested in spiritual attainment as were the New Testament believers. We must confess that the spiritual temperature among us may often be lower than in the early church. But we hold to the message that those who truly honor the presence of the Savior are included in this relationship that goes back to the New Testament and to the apostles!

Lord, even small churches can be a large beacon in their communities through prayer and service. Glorify Yourself today through the good works of Your universal Church.

Spectator Christians

By love serve one another.
GALATIANS 5:13

This we have heard: "I am a born-again Christian and I am happy that my sins are forgiven and I go to church on Sunday because I like the fellowship!" We ask: "Do you not go to put yourself in the way of spiritual blessing?"

The answer: "No, I am saved and I do not need anything!"

We ask: "Have you offered to witness, to pray, to encourage, to assist, to participate in your church's life and outreach?"

The answer: "No. My church seems to get along very well without my help!"

Brethren, this "nonparticipation" kind of faith is a strange parody on Bible Christianity. Men and women who say they are believers just cancel themselves out. Is it something we have learned from the sporting events?—the great majority are spectators. They come and sit!

If there is any true spiritual life within us, God will give us a gift of some kind and the humble soul will find something to do for God!

Lord, I pray for my local church today, that many "fringe"
attendees will desire to participate in our church's life and ministry.

....
....
....
....
....
....
....
....
....
....
....

Do Things Possess Us?

Nor trust in uncertain riches, but in the living God,
who giveth us richly all things to enjoy.
1 TIMOTHY 6:17

I think a lot of people in our congregations get confused when some learned brother advises us that we must all join in a fervent fight against "materialism." If men and women do not know what materialism is, how can they be expected to join the battle?

Materialism in its crisis form occurs when men and women created in the image of God accept and look upon matter as "the ultimate"—the only reality.

The advice, "We must fight materialism," does not mean that everyone should get a sword and run after a fellow named Material and cut him down.

What it does mean is that we should start believing in the fact of God's creation and that matter is only a creature of the all-wise and ever-loving God! The believer is not deceived into believing that the physical things we know and enjoy are the ultimate end in themselves.

Dear Lord, You are the reality that so many people today fail to see.
Make me more sensitive to Your spiritual realm all around me.

Without Feeling?

Singing and making melody in your heart to the Lord.
EPHESIANS 5:19

$\mathcal{I}$ do know something of the emotional life that goes along with conversion to Jesus Christ. I came into the kingdom of God with joy, knowing that I had been forgiven.

I have had people tell me very dogmatically that they will never allow "feeling" to have any part in their spiritual life and experience.

"Too bad for you!" is my reply.

I say that because I have voiced a very real definition of what I believe true worship to be: "Worship is to feel in the heart!"

In the Christian faith, we should be able to use the word *feel* boldly and without apology. What worse thing could be said of us as the Christian Church if it can be said of us that we are a feelingless people?

I think we must agree that those of us who have been blessed within our own beings would not join in any crusade to "follow your feelings." But if there is no feeling at all in our hearts, then we are dead!

Lord, if we didn't have feelings, we'd all be like robots. Thank You for creating us as whole people—intellectually, emotionally, and spiritually. It is a joy to worship You with feeling!

Who Is Your Example?

Be thou an example. . .in word, in conversation,
in charity, in spirit, in faith, in purity.
1 TIMOTHY 4:12

The Christian churches of our day have suffered a great loss in rejecting the example of good men, choosing instead the "celebrity of the hour" for their pattern. We must agree that it is altogether unlikely that we know who our "greatest" men are. One thing is sure, however—the greatest man alive today is the best man alive today. That is not open to debate.

Spiritual virtues run deep and silent. The holy and humble man will not advertise himself nor allow others to do it for him.

The Christian who is zealous to promote the cause of Christ can begin by living in the power of God's Spirit, and so reproducing the life of Christ in the sight of men. In deep humility and without ostentation, he can let his light shine.

To sum it all up: the most effective argument for Christianity is still the good lives of those who profess it!

Lord, I pray that You will enable me to be an example of Your love
and humility in every situation today, tomorrow, and the weeks that follow.

Make God's Will Our Will

And he trembling and astonished said,
Lord, what wilt thou have me to do?
ACTS 9:6

The mystery of man's free will is far too great for us! God said to Adam and Eve: "Thou shalt not eat from this tree" (see Genesis 2:16–17). Here was a divine requirement calling for obedience on the part of those who had the power of choice and will. When they disobeyed, they usurped the right that was not theirs!

The poet Tennyson must have thought about this, for he wrote in his "In Memoriam": "Our wills are ours, we know not how; our wills are ours to make them Thine!"

"We know not how"; then Tennyson girds himself and continues, "Our wills are ours to make them Thine!"

As created beings, that is our only right—to make our wills the will of God, to make the will of God our will! God is sovereign, and we are the creatures. He is the Creator and has the right to command us with the obligation that we should obey.

It is a happy obligation, I might say, for "His yoke is easy and His burden is light"! It is important to agree that true salvation restores the right of a Creator-creature relationship, acknowledging God's right to our fellowship and communion!

Heavenly Father, intellectually it is easy to say that I want to do Your will,
but to really do so I need Your Spirit's help. Strengthen me, Lord. I am Yours.

Why Settle Down?

That ye might be filled with all the fulness of God.
EPHESIANS 3:19

———— ❧ ————

Why should a Christian "settle down" as soon as he has come to know the Lord?

I blame faulty exposition of the New Testament for stopping many Christians dead in their tracks, causing them to shrug off any suggestion that there is still spiritual advance and progress beckoning them on.

It is the position of some would-be teachers that everyone who comes into the kingdom of God by faith immediately obtains all there is of God's spiritual provision.

I believe that such a teaching is as deadly as cyanide to the individual Christian life. It kills all hope of spiritual advance and causes many believers to adopt what I call "the creed of contentment."

I am sure you agree with me that there is always real joy in the heart of the person who has become a child of God. Sound teaching of the Word will then hold out the goal of moving forward, emulating the apostle Paul's desire to become a special kind of Christian!

Lord, there are several areas in my spiritual life in which I would like to move forward.
Guide me in this process through Your Word and through Your Church.

....
....
....
....
....
....
....
....
....
....
....

False Pretenders

*When the young man heard that saying, he went
away sorrowful: for he had great possessions.*
MATTHEW 19:22

———※———

All persons who are alienated from God and outside of Christ are part and parcel of a mighty deception!

They are called upon to pretend that they can have peace of mind within and that they can be relatively happy and make a big success of their human lives if they have youth and wealth and morality and high position.

In that sense of what is going on all around us, David never had to apologize for writing that "every man is a liar"! (see Psalm 116:11). The whole human concept of success and happiness and inner peace, based upon who we are and what we have, is completely false.

The rich young ruler who came to question Jesus had wealth, morality, position, and youth. But his very first question gave the clue to his own inner emptiness of life: "What good thing should I do, that I may have eternal life?" (see Luke 18:18).

He knew very well that there is not a person alive who has eternal youth or eternal position or eternal righteousness. So, like every other man, he had to make a choice!

*Lord, make me sensitive to those within my sphere of influence whose goals for success
and happiness are based on a faulty foundation. I pray for these people, Lord,
that their eyes may be opened to the truth and that they will fully repent.*

Compromise Is Costly

I pray. . .that thou shouldest keep them from the evil.
JOHN 17:15

⁓

Christianity today is so entangled with this present world that millions never guess how radically they have missed the New Testament pattern.

Compromise is everywhere—but actually no real union between the world and the Church is possible. When the Church joins up with the world, it is the true Church no longer but only a pitiful hybrid thing, an object of smiling contempt to the world, and an abomination to the Lord!

Nothing could be clearer than the pronouncements of the scriptures on the Christian's relation to the world. The confusion which gathers around this matter results from the unwillingness of professing Christians to take the Word of the Lord seriously.

This whole thing is spiritual in its essence. A Christian is what he is not by ecclesiastical manipulation but by the new birth. He is a Christian because of a Spirit which dwells in him. Only that which is born by the Spirit is spirit, no matter how many church dignitaries work on it!

Lord, I pray that the leaders in my church will stand firmly on biblical principles when faced with social and political issues of moral importance.

Christ Made the World

God. . .hath. . .spoken unto us by his Son. . .
by whom also he made the worlds.
HEBREWS 1:1–2

———

Think about the world into which our Lord Jesus Christ came—it is actually Christ's world!

Every section of this earth that we buy and sell and kick around and take by force of arms is a part of Christ's world. He made it all, and He owns it all.

Jesus Christ, the eternal Word, made the world. He made the very atoms of which Mary was made; the atoms of which His own body was made. He made the straw in the manger upon which He was laid as a newborn baby.

Let me digress here. I hear an occasional devotional exercise on the radio, in which the participants ask: "Mary, mother of God, pray for us!" It is only right that we should express our position based on the Word of God, and the truth is that Mary is dead and she is not the "mother of God."

Mary was the mother of that tiny babe, for God in His loving and wise plan of redemption used the body of the virgin Mary as the matrix to give the eternal Son a human body. We join in giving her proper honor when we refer to her as Mary, mother of Christ.

Lord, help me and my family make the appropriate choices to be
excellent stewards of this world that You created for us to enjoy.

Loving God Only

And because iniquity shall abound, the love of many shall wax cold.
MATTHEW 24:12

———— ❦ ————

*T*he first and greatest commandment is to love God with every power of our entire being. Where love like that exists, there can be no place for a second object.

Yet popular Christianity has as one of its most effective talking points the idea that God exists to help people to get ahead in this world! The God of the poor has become the God of an affluent society. We hear that Christ no longer refuses to be a judge or a divider between money-hungry brothers. He can now be persuaded to assist the brother that has accepted Him to get the better of the brother who has not!

Whoever seeks God as a means toward desired ends will not find God. God will not be one of many treasures. His mercy and grace are infinite and His patient understanding is beyond measure, but He will not aid men in selfish striving after personal gain. If we love God as much as we should, surely we cannot dream of a loved object beyond Him which He might help us to obtain!

Lord, show me what it means to love You as You commanded—
with all my heart, soul, strength, and mind (see Luke 10:27).

No One Changes God's Law

I delight to do thy will, O my God: yea, thy law is within my heart.
PSALM 40:8

———— ❦ ————

*B*ecause we live in a period known as the age of God's grace, it has become a popular thing to declare that the Ten Commandments are no longer valid, no longer relevant in our society.

With that context it has become apparent that Christian churches are not paying attention to the Ten Commandments.

But Dwight L. Moody preached often on the commandments. John Wesley said he preached the commands of the Law to prepare the way for the gospel. R. A. Torrey told ministers if they did not preach the Law, they would have no response to the preaching of the gospel. It is the Law that shows us our need for the gospel of salvation and forgiveness!

It is accurate to say that our binding obligation is not to the Old Testament Law. As sincere Christians we are under Christ's higher law—that which is represented in His love and grace. But everything that is morally commanded in the Ten Commandments still comprises the moral principles that are the will of God for His people. God's basic moral will for His people has not changed!

Lord, I pray that in my own life I will not bristle at the idea of following Your law.
The deceit of my own heart is enough evidence to suggest that Your moral law is for my own good.

Ascription of Glory

Yet believing, ye rejoice with joy unspeakable and full of glory.
1 Peter 1:8

I am discovering that many Christians are not really comfortable with the holy attributes of God. In such cases, I am forced to wonder about the quality of their worship.

The word *holy* is much more than an adjective saying that God is a holy God. It is an ecstatic ascription of glory to the triune God. Everything that appears to be good among men and women must be discounted, for we are humans. Abraham, David and Elijah, Moses, Peter and Paul—all were good men, but each had his human flaws and weaknesses as members of Adam's race. Each had to find his own place of humble repentance. Because God knows our hearts and our intentions, He is able to restore His believing children in the faith!

So, we should be honest and confess that much of our problem in continuing fellowship with a holy God is that many Christians only repent for what they do, rather than for what they are!

*Lord, I confess before You this morning that at my very core
I am a sinner—but one who has been saved by Your grace.
I desire to please You, Father, as a child adopted into Your family.*

The Mystery in Worship

Behold, the bush burned with fire,
and the bush was not consumed.
EXODUS 3:2

⁂

Consider the experience of Moses in the desert as he beheld the fire that burned in the bush without consuming it. Moses had no hesitation in kneeling before the bush and worshipping God. Moses was not worshipping a bush; it was God and His glory dwelling in the bush whom Moses worshipped!

This is an imperfect illustration, for when the fire departed from that bush, it was a bush again.

But this Man, Christ Jesus, is eternally the Son. In the fullness of this mystery, there has never been any departure, except for that awful moment when Jesus cried, "My God, my God, why hast thou forsaken me?" (Matthew 27:46). The Father turned His back for a moment when the Son took on Himself that putrefying mass of sin and guilt, dying on the cross not for His own sin, but for ours.

The deity and the humanity never parted, and to this day, they remain united in that one Man.

When we kneel before Him and say, "My Lord and my God, Thy throne, O God, is forever and ever," we are talking to God!

Lord, I may not have seen You in a burning bush like Moses did,
but I still kneel before You and worship You as my King.

"Yet Shall He Live"

He that believeth in me, though he were dead, yet shall he live.
JOHN 11:25

This may sound strange—but it is a fact that death is not the worst thing that can happen to a believing Christian!

I can recall the first time I heard that statement, in a quiet conversation with Harry M. Shuman, for many years the president of the international Christian and Missionary Alliance.

He was a soft-spoken yet forceful man of God, rich in the wisdom of God's Word. We were talking of the serious issues of life and death. When he had something especially important to say, Dr. Shuman had an unusual way of lowering his voice and tilting his head just a bit. I can see him yet as he looked out from under his shaggy brows straight into my eyes.

"Remember, Tozer," he said, "death is not the worst thing that can happen to a person!"

For the Christian, death is a journey to the eternal world. It is a victory, a rest, a delight. I am sure my small amount of physical suffering has been mild compared to Paul's, but I feel as Paul did: "Having a desire to depart, and to be with Christ; which is far better" (Philippians 1:23).

Thank You, Lord, for offering the gift of eternal life through Your Son,
Jesus Christ. Since I have eternal life now, why should I fear death,
which for the believer is merely a journey to a much better place!

....
....
....
....
....
....
....
....
....
....

Truth Has a Soul

Neither knoweth any man the Father, save the Son,
and he to whomsoever the Son will reveal him.
MATTHEW 11:27

I believe there is a positive warning in the Gospels that a person's faith may stand in the revealed Bible text—and still be as dead as the proverbial doornail!

Consider the prayer of our Lord in Matthew 11:27: "All things are delivered unto me of my Father: and no man knoweth the Son, but the Father; neither knoweth any man the Father, save the Son, and he to whomsoever the Son will reveal him."

There is more than a body of truth—and if we do not get through to the soul of truth, we have only a dead body on our hands.

When the power of God moves in on the text and sets the sacrifice on fire, then you have genuine Christianity! We try to call that revival, but it is not revival at all. It is simply New Testament Christianity.

People who thought they were saved get saved! People who have only believed in a code now have placed their faith and trust in Christ's person. It is not any deluxe edition of Christianity—it is simply New Testament Christianity having its place!

Lord, I am grateful for the day that You called me to Yourself. I invite You
to do Your cleansing work in my soul so that I may be a more useful servant.

JUNE 19

The Conditions of Peace

He. . .came trembling, and fell down before Paul and Silas. . .
and said, Sirs, what must I do to be saved?
ACTS 16:29–30

In a world like ours, with conditions being what they are, what should a serious-minded man or woman do?

First, accept the truth concerning yourself. You do not go to a doctor to seek consolation, but to find out what is wrong and what to do about it.

Then seek the kingdom of God and His righteousness. Seek through Jesus Christ a right relationship to God and then insist upon maintaining a right relation to your fellow man.

Set about reverently and honestly to amend your doings. Magnify God, mortify the flesh, simplify your life. Take up your cross and learn of Jesus Christ, to die to this world that He may raise you up in due time.

If you will do these things in faith and love, you will know peace—the peace of God that passes all understanding.

You will know joy—the joy of resurrection. You will know, too, the comfort of the indwelling Spirit of God, for you have sought to do the will of God at any price!

Dear Lord, teach me and my family what it means to live in
this world and at the same time "die to this world" for the sake of Christ.

....

....

....

....

....

....

....

....

June 20

Our Wills Must Surrender

His servants ye are to whom ye obey; whether of
sin unto death, or of obedience unto righteousness.
ROMANS 6:16

The Christian doctrine of obedience to God and to His will is now largely neglected in modern religious circles, and many in our own congregations seem to feel that our obligation to obey has been discharged by the act of believing on Jesus Christ at the beginning of our Christian lives.

We need to remember that "the will is the seat of true religion in the soul." Nothing genuine has been done in a man or woman's life until his or her will has been surrendered in active obedience. It was disobedience that brought about the ruin of the race. It is the obedience of faith that brings us back again into the divine favor!

It needs to be said that a world of confusion results from trying to believe without obeying!

A mere passive surrender may be no surrender at all. Any real submission to the will of God must include willingness to take orders from Him from that time on.

I keep wondering whether the Lord's ministers will again give to obedience the place of prominence it occupies in the scriptures.

Lord, I pray that our churches will be moved to call their people to
an intentional, active obedience of faith and that individuals,
prompted by Your Spirit, will respond with great humility.

God Understands Us

God is love; and he that dwelleth in love dwelleth in God, and God in him.
1 JOHN 4:16

We should revel in the joy of believing that God is the sum of all patience and the true essence of kindly good will!

Because He is what He is, we please Him most, not by frantically trying to make ourselves good, but by throwing ourselves into His arms with all our imperfections and believing that He understands everything—and loves us still!

The God who desires our fellowship and communion is not hard to please, although He may be hard to satisfy. He expects from us only what He has Himself supplied. When He must chasten us, He even does this with a smile—the proud, tender smile of a Father who is bursting with pleasure over an imperfect son who is coming every day to look more and more like the One whose child he is!

This is the best of good news: God loves us for ourselves. He values our love more than He values galaxies of newly created worlds.

He remembers our frame and knows that we are dust!

Dear Lord, Your love for me—and for all people in the world—is incredible.
Thank You that even when I fail, You are my greatest Supporter.

....
....
....
....
....
....
....
....
....
....
....

Our Sovereign Lord

The most High dwelleth not in temples made with hands. . . .
Heaven is my throne, and earth is my footstool.
ACTS 7:48–49

How can you be a Christian and not be aware of the sovereignty of the God who has loved us to the death?

To be sovereign, God must be the absolute, infinite, unqualified ruler in all realms in heaven and earth and sea. To be Lord over all the creation, He must be omnipotent. He must be omniscient. He must be omnipresent.

With all that is within me, I believe that the crucified and risen and glorified Savior, Jesus Christ, is the sovereign Lord. He takes no orders from anyone. He has no counselors and no advisers. He has no secretary to the throne. He knows in the one effortless act all that can be known, and He has already lived out our tomorrows and holds the world in the palm of His hand.

That is the Lord I serve! I gladly own that I am His; glory to God! The Christ we know and serve is infinitely beyond all men and all angels and all archangels, above all principalities and powers and dominions, visible and invisible—for He is the origin of them all!

Lord, to begin to understand Your attributes is totally overwhelming.
That such an Almighty God would care so much for His creation is truly humbling.

Behind the Mask

But wilt thou know, O vain man, that faith without works is dead?
JAMES 2:20

I think it is pitiful and rather sad that about the only time you can find a fellow citizen who is not a "phony" is when he is mad. In our kind of society, most people feel that they must always be pretending, continually "putting on a front."

So, they are never their real selves until they get mad!

When Jesus faced His bitter religious enemies as recorded in John 8:47, there was no pretending, nothing staged for dramatic effect. Jesus confronted them with the words: "He that is of God heareth God's words: ye therefore hear them not, because ye are not of God!"

These were firm and severe words; His enemies answered with angry and insulting words. These men were mad; they were letting go. They had given up pretense. They were acting naturally now, showing what they were within.

As humans, we are what we do! If what we do proves us to be wrong, then it is either despair or obtaining the help we need. Jesus came to change our natures. He came to break old habits of sin, to break and conquer them!

Lord, You have a provocative way of exposing man's sinful nature.
You have a way of cutting to the core of the issue. Have Your way with me, Lord.

The Spirit's Gifts

But the manifestation of the Spirit is given to every man to profit withal.
1 CORINTHIANS 12:7

In our Christian fellowship, we must recognize that the blessed Holy Spirit of God desires to take men and women and control them, and use them as instruments through which He can express Himself in the Body of Christ.

Someone may try to give me credit for something they think I have done for God—but in actuality, God is doing it through His Holy Spirit—and using me as an instrument. There is no real sense in which we are able to do spiritual work of any kind without the Holy Spirit.

We do know that the apostle Paul said: "If any man have not the Spirit of Christ, he is none of his" (Romans 8:9). But he also exhorted those early believers not to ignore the Spirit's gifts and to "covet earnestly the best gifts" (1 Corinthians 12:31). It is still important for us to fulfill the Spirit-given functions and capabilities which are the spiritual birthright of every regenerated believer.

We should not be looking around for some other way. God has given us in His Holy Spirit every gift and power and help that we need to serve Him!

Lord, I pray that I will be a clean vessel, fit for use in Your kingdom work today.

JUNE 25

Christ Receives Sinners

Him hath God exalted with his right hand to be a Prince
and a Saviour, for to give repentance. . .and forgiveness of sins.
ACTS 5:31

———❦———

What a gracious thing for us that Jesus Christ never thinks about what we have been. He always thinks about what we are going to be!

The Savior who is our Lord cares absolutely nothing about your moral case history. He forgives it and starts from there as though you had been born one minute before.

The woman of Samaria met our Lord at the well and we ask, "Why was Jesus willing to reveal so much more about Himself in this setting than He did in other encounters during His ministry?"

You and I would never have chosen this woman with such a shadow lying across her life, but Jesus is the Christ of God, and He could sense the potential within her innermost being. He gave her the secret of His Messiahship and the secret of the nature of God. Her frankness and her humility appealed to the Savior as they talked of man's need and the true worship of God by the Spirit of God.

In Jesus' day, His critics said in scorn: "This man receives sinners!" They were right—and He lived and died and rose again to prove it. The blessed part is this: He is still receiving sinners!

Lord, I have many family, friends, and coworkers who need You as their Savior.
Will You receive them into Your family today?

....
....
....
....
....
....
....
....
....

Lord of Our Living

Who died for us, that, whether we wake or sleep,
we should live together with him.
1 THESSALONIANS 5:10

I have studied the New Testament enough to know that our Lord Jesus Christ never made the sharp distinctions between "secular" and "sacred" that we do!

I think it is wrong to place our physical necessities on one side, and put praying and singing and giving and Bible reading and testifying on the other.

When we are living for the Lord and living to please and honor Him, eating our breakfast can be just as spiritual as having our family prayers. There is no reason for a committed Christian to apologize: "Lord, I am awfully sorry but You know I have to eat now. I will be with You again just as soon as I am through."

Well, we have a better way than that in our living for God, and we see as we consider His feeding of the five thousand the meaning of His lordship. Jesus Christ is Lord—Lord of our bread and Lord of our eating and Lord of our sleeping and Lord of our working!

Brethren, our Lord is with us, sanctifying everything we do, provided it is honest and good.

Lord, today I want to be especially aware that You are the Lord of whatever I am doing.
Thank You for Your all-encompassing presence in my life.

Christ Glorified in Us

Eye hath not seen, nor ear heard. . .the things which
God hath prepared for them that love him.
1 CORINTHIANS 2:9

———⌘———

The Bible tells us that eye has not seen nor ear heard, neither has it entered into the heart of men, the things that God has laid up for those who love Him! That is why the apostle goes on to remind us that God has revealed these mysteries to us by the Holy Spirit.

Oh, if we would only stop trying to make the Holy Spirit our servant and begin to live in His life as the fish lives in the sea, we would enter into the riches of glory about which we know nothing now. Too many of us want the Holy Spirit in order to have some gift—healing or tongues or preaching or prophecy.

Yes, these have their place in that total pattern of the New Testament, but let us never pray that we may be filled with the Spirit for a secondary purpose!

Remember, God wants to fill you with His Spirit as an end in your moral life. God's purpose is that we should know Him first of all, and be lost in Him, and that we should enter into the fullness of the Spirit that the eternal Son, Jesus Christ, may be glorified in us!

O Lord, I desire to lose my life in Yours today,
so that You may be glorified in and through me.

The Spiritual Essence

By the. . .renewing of the Holy Ghost;
which he shed on us abundantly through Jesus Christ.
TITUS 3:5–6

We who are the disciples of Jesus Christ often need to be reminded that God is allowing us to live on two planes at the same time.

He lets us live in this religious plane where there are preachers and song-leaders and choirs, teachers and evangelists—and that is religion. It is actually "religion in overalls"—it is the external part of religion and it has its own place in God's work and plan.

But beyond that and superior to all of the externals in our religious experience is the spiritual essence of it all! It is that spiritual essence that I want to see enthroned in our communion and fellowship in the Church of Jesus Christ!

We need the caution that much theology, much Bible teaching, and many Bible conferences begin and end in themselves. They circle fully around themselves—but when everyone goes home, no one is any better than he was before. We sorely need this caution about holding truth that begins and ends in itself. The danger is that we teach and live so that truth is given no opportunity of moral expression!

Dear Lord, I pray today for Your blessing upon all national pastors and Bible
study leaders abroad. Bestow upon their hearts and minds a true understanding
of Your Word so that many listeners will mature in their faith.

Eternity in Our Hearts

The high and lofty One that inhabiteth eternity...
with him also that is of a contrite and humble spirit.
ISAIAH 57:15

The only reason that men and women can be saved is the fact that God has put eternity in our hearts! Man is fallen—yes! Man is lost, a sinner, and needs to be born again—yes!

But God made man in His own image and He keeps the longing after eternity and a desire after everlasting life there within the hearts of men.

What, then, is the matter with man? Like the lion in the cage, he paces back and forth and roars to the heavens before he dies.

I think this is the truth—we are disturbed because God has put everlastingness in our hearts. He has put a longing for immortality in our beings, something that demands God and heaven. Yet, we are too blind and sinful to find Him or even to look for Him!

As Christian witnesses, we must be faithful and timely in our preaching and teaching. There is a note of warning in this—telling men and women why they are lost and that if they will not repent they will certainly perish!

Lord, at times I have felt that this world is not my real home. I have a longing for things eternal. Yet, Lord, there are still so many people whose hearts are stone cold and who need to be told about Your free gift of eternal life.

Sanctify the Ordinary

Consecrate yourselves today to the LORD. . .
that he may bestow upon you a blessing this day.
EXODUS 32:29

Today more than ever we Christians need to learn how to sanctify the ordinary. This is a blasé generation. People have been overstimulated to the place where their nerves are jaded and their tastes corrupted. Natural things have been rejected to make room for things artificial. The sacred has been secularized, the holy vulgarized, and worship converted into a form of entertainment. A dopey, blear-eyed generation seeks constantly for some new excitement powerful enough to bring a thrill to its worn-out and benumbed sensibilities. So many wonders have been discovered or invented that nothing on earth is any longer wonderful. Everything is common and almost everything boring.

When the whole moral and psychological atmosphere is secular and common, how can we escape its deadly effects? How can we sanctify the ordinary and find true spiritual meaning in the common things of life? The answer has already been suggested. It is to consecrate the whole of life to Christ and begin to do everything in His name and for His sake.

Dear Lord, at the start of this new day, I consecrate my life and my work to You.
Help me find spiritual fulfillment and meaning in the routine tasks of this day. Amen.

Warning in the Gospel

He that believeth not is condemned already.
JOHN 3:18

When God warns a nation or a city, a church or a person, it is a grievous sin to ignore such warning. In conservative Christianity, we believe that the Christian message does indeed contain an element of alarm, but not all Christians believe this.

Some have been taught that the Christian gospel is "good news exclusively." They believe that the only way to explain the full meaning of the Christian gospel is to quote one verse: "Believe on the Lord Jesus, and you will be saved" (see Acts 16:31).

"That is it! That is all there is to it," they say.

They surely need to be reminded that in the use of language, it is impossible to make certain definite statements without bringing to mind that which is exactly opposite. So, when the scriptures admonish us to believe on the Lord Jesus Christ to be saved, there comes to our mind the fact of mankind's lost condition and the starkly plain message to those who do not believe: "He that believeth not is condemned already, because he hath not believed in the name of the only begotten Son of God" (John 3:18).

Lord, Your Great Commission (see Matthew 28:19–20) tells us to spread Your good news around the world. I pray especially for those involved in creative efforts to share the gospel in countries where preaching Christ is forbidden.

Critical Decisions

The LORD had said unto Abram, Get thee out of thy country. . . .
So Abram departed, as the LORD had spoken unto him.
GENESIS 12:1, 4

People have many different ideas about the most important moment of their lives on this earth. We know of many who have testified to the great importance of their own spiritual decision—the act of faith whereby they committed themselves and their entire futures to God!

I believe the Bible makes it plain that the single most critical, most important time in the life of Abraham was when he heard and answered the call of God. Unexpectedly and dramatically, God revealed Himself to Abraham and called him to be a pilgrim. It is a lesson to us that when Abraham was called, he by faith obeyed and went, even though he did not know where he was going!

I have found comfort in the doctrine of prevenient grace, which, simply stated, is the belief that before a sinner can seek God, God must first have sought him.

In Abraham's case, I believe that if he had been insensitive, he would never have heard God's voice calling him, and if Abraham had rejected God's overtures, the whole history of the world would have been vastly different—and different for the worse!

Heavenly Father, I thank You for Abraham's example: he heard
Your voice, and he obeyed. May it be so in my life as well, Lord.

Free to Be a Servant

Understanding what the will of the Lord is.
EPHESIANS 5:17

---

*E*very man in a free society must decide whether he will exploit his liberty or curtail it for moral and intelligent ends. He may take upon him the responsibility of business and a family, or he may shun all obligations and end on skid row. The tramp is freer than president or king, but his freedom is his undoing. While he lives he remains socially sterile, and when he dies he leaves nothing to make the world glad he lived.

The Christian cannot escape the peril of too much liberty. He is indeed free, but his very freedom may prove a source of real temptation to him. He is free from the chains of sin, free from the moral consequences of evil acts now forgiven, free from the curse of the law and the displeasure of God.

The ideal Christian is one who knows he is free to do as he will—and wills to be a servant. This is the path Christ took: blessed is the man who follows Him!

Thank You, Lord, for the freedom I have through Christ. I am not bound by sin or fear. Help me to use my freedom to serve You with unfettered boldness.

Only God Is Free

Stand fast therefore in the liberty
wherewith Christ hath made us free.
GALATIANS 5:1

To any human who bothers to think a bit, it should be evident that there is in our society no such thing as absolute freedom—for only God is free!

It is inherent in creaturehood that its freedom must be limited by the will of the Creator and the nature of the thing created. Freedom is liberty within bounds, liberty to obey holy laws, liberty to keep the commandments of Christ, to serve mankind, to develop to the full all the latent possibilities within our redeemed natures. True Christian liberty never sets us free to indulge our lusts or to follow our fallen impulses.

On earth, a healthy society requires that its members accept a limited freedom. Each must curtail his own liberty that all may be free, and this law runs throughout all of the created universe, including the kingdom of God.

The glory of heaven itself lies in the character of the freedom enjoyed by those who dwell therein!

Lord, today I pray for the members of the churches in my community.
Empower them (and myself) to curb their "fallen impulses"
and to be a bright beacon in the midst of a dark society.

God Touches Our Emotions

Set your affection on things above, not on things on the earth.
COLOSSIANS 3:2

I have heard people say that "only doctrine is important." Would they leave no room for Christian experience?

Consider the preaching and the example of the famed Jonathan Edwards, used so mightily by God in the Great Awakening throughout New England in the eighteenth century.

But, you say, "Jonathan Edwards was a Calvinist!"

I know—and that is my point. Edwards was acknowledged by society to have been one of the greatest intellects of his time. Yet he believed in genuine Christian experience so positively that he wrote a well-accepted book, *Religious Affections,* in defense of Christian emotion.

Charged by some that his revivals had too much emotion, Edwards stood forth and proclaimed that when men and women meet God, accepting His terms, they experience an awareness that lifts their hearts to rapture.

What higher privilege is granted to mankind on earth than to be admitted into the circle of the friends of God!

*Lord, we need only go to the scripture to see pure joy expressed by those
who have been set free from the grip of sin. I pray that others will observe
the deep inner joy that I possess because of Your presence in my life.*

God's Will: "Obey!"

If ye will not obey. . .then shall the hand of the LORD be against you.
1 SAMUEL 12:15

---

*I*ndependence is a strong human trait, so men and women everywhere bristle when anyone says, "You owe obedience!" In the natural sense, we do not take kindly to the prospect of yielding obedience to anyone.

Both Old and New Testaments of the Bible make it plain that sin is disobedience to the law of God. Paul's picture of sinners in Ephesians concludes that the wrath of God will come upon those who are "the children of disobedience" (2:2–3).

So, we live in a generation of men and women alienated from God, and who make a great case for individualism and "the right of self-determination." The individual's strong statement is this: "I belong to myself. No one has the authority to require my obedience!"

Now, if God had made us to be mere machines, we would not have the power of self-determination. He made us in His image, to be moral creatures with the power, but not the right, to choose evil. We have the right to be good. We never have the right to be bad because God, the Creator, is good. If we choose to be unholy, we are using a right that is not ours!

Lord, thank You so much for Your willingness to forgive when Your children err.
What other religion can boast such a loving and merciful God?

Discipline Is Dismissed

Follow me, and I will make you fishers of men.
And they straightway left their nets, and followed him.
MATTHEW 4:19–20

───── ❧ ─────

We live in a land noted and favored for its freedom; a country where Protestant Christianity is popular and well accepted.

I noted this to speak of one of the great spiritual dangers inherent in Protestantism, the fact that there is no discipline involved. Anyone in our churches is pretty much free to do anything he wants to do. If he does not like one church, he has only to cross the street and go to another. If he does not like the preacher, he can leave and soon be attending a church where he is quite pleased with the preacher and with the music and with the atmosphere.

You see, he is demanding Christianity without discipline. He is refusing to acknowledge that the Christian faith makes its own demands of obedience to God and humility of spirit.

When his personal desires take the upper hand, the voice of the Spirit of God is stifled and silenced. There can be only one result—the human soul will become starved and deformed!

Lord, forgive me for putting my personal desires above Your Spirit's rule in my life.
Sometimes this happens so subtly, but it always ends in frustration.
Speak to me, Lord. I'm listening with a renewed attentiveness.

....

....

....

....

....

....

....

....

....

....

Christians Indeed

*They. . .are choked with cares and riches and
pleasures of this life, and bring no fruit to perfection.*
LUKE 8:14

I believe we are mistaken in Christian life and theology when we try to add the "deeper life" to an imperfect salvation obtained through an imperfect concept of the entire matter.

Under the working of the Spirit of God through men like Finney and Wesley, no one would ever have dared to say "I am a Christian" if he had not surrendered his whole being, taking Jesus Christ as his Lord and Savior!

Today, we let them say they are saved no matter how imperfect and incomplete the transaction, with the proviso that the deeper Christian life can be "tacked on" at some time in the future.

Brethren, I believe we must put the blame on faulty teaching—teaching that is filled with self-deception.

Let us look unto Jesus our Lord—high and holy, wearing the crown, Lord of lords and King of all, having a perfect right to command full obedience from all of His saved people!

*O Lord, it is a real challenge in today's world to filter out all
the worldly "stuff" from our lives. Lord, help me to surrender the
things in my life that are hindering the production of fruit for You.*

Too Timid to Resist

Speak every man truth with his neighbour;
for we are members one of another.
EPHESIANS 4:25

The clever proponents of evil political ideologies are spending millions to make us Americans ashamed to love our country. They use every means possible to persuade our own people that there is little left worth defending and certainly nothing worth dying for.

They are building in the public mind a picture of an American as a generous, tolerant, smiling chap who loves baseball and babies, and who subscribes wholly to the doctrine of the brotherhood of man—so everything is going to be all right!

From our point of view, these concepts are having their effects on the nation's religious life, especially among Protestants.

Let a man rise to declare the unique lordship of Jesus Christ and the absolute necessity of obedience to Him, and he is at once branded as a hatemonger and a divider of men.

The devil has brainwashed large numbers of religious leaders so successfully that they are now too timid to resist him! And he, being the kind of devil he is, takes swift advantage of their cowardice, erecting altars to Baal everywhere!

Lord, I pray that You will raise up a new generation of religious and political
leaders who are full of integrity and who are not ashamed to honor You before men.

The Creator's Handiwork

The heavens declare the glory of God;
and the firmament sheweth his handywork.
PSALM 19:1

———— ❧ ————

*R*eading my Bible, I am greatly impressed by the manner in which godly men of old revealed in their writings an intense love for every natural beauty around them. They saw nature as the handiwork of an all-powerful and all-glorious Creator!

The Old Testament is a marvelous rhapsody on the creation. Start with Moses, and when you get beyond the Levitical order you will find him soaring in his acute consciousness of the presence of God in all creation.

Go to the book of Job. In the closing section you will be amazed at the sublimity of the language describing the world around us. Then go to the Psalms, with David literally dancing with ecstatic delight as he gazes out upon the wonders of God's world. Go to Isaiah, where imagery is neither fanciful nor flighty but a presentation of the wonders of creation.

In our generation, how rarely we get into a situation where we can feel the impulses of nature communicated to us. We seldom have time to lift our eyes to look at God's heaven—except when we are wondering if we should wear our boots!

Dear heavenly Father, You have created a beautiful world. Continue to reveal
Your power and presence through Your majestic creation to those who doubt Your existence.

God's Saving Grace

Noah found grace in the eyes of the LORD.
GENESIS 6:8

━━━━━━━━━━━━━━━

Grace is the goodness of God confronting human demerit. So, grace is what God is—unchanging, infinite, eternal!

This throws light on God's dealings with men and women throughout the Old Testament dispensations and history. It is certainly the truth, and a proper concept for us to hold, that no one was ever saved, no one is now saved, and no one will ever be saved except by the grace of God.

Before Moses came with the Law, men were saved only by grace. During the time of Moses, no one was saved except by grace. After Moses, before the cross, and after the cross, and during all of the dispensations, anywhere, anytime, no one was ever saved by anything but the grace of God!

We can say this with assurance because God dealt in grace with mankind looking forward to the Incarnation and the atoning death of Christ.

If God had not always operated in grace, He would have swept the sinning human race away. This, then, is the good news: God is gracious all the time, and when His grace becomes operative through our faith in Jesus Christ, then there is the new birth from above!

Thank You, Father, that by Your grace—that is, the death and resurrection of Your Son Jesus Christ—we are saved and restored to a right relationship with You.

....

....

....

....

....

....

....

....

....

....

We Are Too Comfortable

And others were tortured, not accepting deliverance;
that they might obtain a better resurrection.
HEBREWS 11:35

---

*I*s the fact that millions of Americans refuse to attend our church services only another symptom of original sin and love of moral darkness? No, I believe that explanation is too "pat" to be wholly true.

Churches cannot deny they are too comfortable, too rich, too contented! We hold the faith of our fathers, but it does not hold us. God is trying to interest us in a glorious tomorrow, and we are settling for an inglorious today. God has set eternity in our hearts; and we have chosen time instead. We are bogged down in local interests and have lost sight of eternal purposes.

It was the knowledge that they were part of God's eternal plan that imparted unquenchable enthusiasm to the early Christians. They burned with holy zeal for Christ and felt they were part of an army which the Lord was leading to ultimate conquest over all the powers of darkness!

Lord, there are many Christians in foreign lands who are persecuted for their faith.
Some are ostracized from family and friends; some are beaten and left to die.
Be especially near to these dear people today, I pray.

....

....

....

....

....

....

....

....

....

....

....

Out of Balance

If ye continue in my word, then are ye my disciples indeed.
JOHN 8:31

⁓

We must admit that in the evangelical Christian churches of our day, almost all of us are guilty of a lopsided view of the Christian life—all is made to depend upon the initial act of believing. At a given moment a decision is made for Christ, and after that everything is "automatic."

This is because of our failure to lay a scriptural emphasis in our evangelical preaching.

In our eagerness to make converts, we allow our believers to absorb the idea that they can deal with their entire responsibility once and for all by an act of believing. This is in some vague way supposed to honor grace and glorify God, whereas actually it is to make Christ the author of a grotesque, unworkable system that has no counterpart in the scriptures of Truth.

In the New Testament accounts, faith was for each believer a beginning, not an end. Believing was not a once-done act; it was more than an act. It was an attitude of heart and mind which inspired and enabled the believer to take up his cross and follow the Lamb whithersoever He went!

*Lord, the Christian life is a lifelong maturing process. And some days are
better than others! Help me to continue to progress in my walk of faith with You.*

Selfish Personal Interest

Chiefly them that walk after the flesh. . .and despise government.
Presumptuous are they, selfwilled.
2 PETER 2:10

⁂

Throughout history, the philosophers have pretty well agreed on the conclusion that selfish personal interest is the motive behind all human conduct.

The philosopher Epictetus illustrated his understanding with the fact that two dogs may romp on the lawn with every appearance of friendship until someone tosses a piece of raw meat between them. Instantly, their play turns into savage fight as each struggles to get the meat for himself. Let us not condemn the old thinker for comparing the conduct of men to animals. The Bible frequently does, and humbling as it may be to us, we humans often look bad by comparison.

If we would be wise in the wisdom of God, we must face up to the truth that men and women are not basically good: They are basically evil, and the essence of sin lies in their selfishness! Putting our own interests before the glory of God is sin in its Godward aspects, and the putting of our own interests before those of our fellow man is sin as it relates to society. By the cross, Jesus Christ demonstrated pure, selfless love in its fullest perfection. When He died, He set a crown of beauty upon a God-centered and an others-centered life!

Lord, as I begin this day, I pray that in every situation
I will put the interests of others before my own.

Repentance Is Rare

There is joy in the presence of the angels
of God over one sinner that repenteth.
LUKE 15:10

***

*H*umans, deceived by the devil and charmed by their own pride and abilities, deny that our world is a rebel province in God's universe. They deny that human society has willfully pulled loose from God's rule and the rest of God's domain.

In fact, they deny that men and women are the creation of God. They deny even that they owe any allegiance to God, their Creator!

The Bible is the record of how God deals with mankind, and we can draw but one conclusion: All people are morally obligated to repent and to ask forgiveness of God. Failing to do so, they will perish.

How rare it is in our day to hear of genuine repentance. We live amid a proud, selfish, and self-sufficient people. Even in our Christian churches there are those who want nothing more than to be known as "respectable church members"! When repentance is real and faith is genuine, the atoning death of Jesus Christ is effective for pardon and forgiveness and regeneration.

Dear Lord, the idea of people perishing—being separated from God for eternity—
is a frightening thought. Will You help today's churches grasp this dreadful fact
so that they will redouble their efforts to share the gospel with lost people?

God Needs No Pity

Who would not fear thee, O King of nations? . . .
there is none like unto thee.
JEREMIAH 10:7

I do not think I could ever worship a God who was suddenly caught off guard, unaware of circumstances in His world around me!

I could never offer myself to a God that actually needed me, brethren. If He needed me, I could not respect Him, and if I could not respect Him, I could not worship Him!

Some of our missionary appeals are getting close to that same error: that we should engage in missionary work because God needs us so badly!

The fact is that God is riding above this world and the clouds are the dust of His feet and if you do not follow Him, you will lose all and God will lose nothing. He will still be glorified in His saints and admired of all those who fear Him. To bring ourselves into a place where God will be eternally pleased with us should be the first responsible act of every man!

All of these considerations are based upon the character and worthiness of God. Not a man or woman anywhere should ever try to come to God as a gesture of pity because poor God needs you!

Heavenly Father, I am grateful that although You really don't "need" me,
You have gifted me in unique ways to be useful in Your kingdom work.

Losing the Mystery

If any man will do his will,
he shall know. . .whether it be of God.
JOHN 7:17

We may be sure we are gaining spiritually when we discover there is a sense of divine mystery running throughout all of the kingdom of God!

I am aware that there are teachers in various Christian circles who pretend to know everything about God. They will quickly answer any question you may have about God, His creation, His judgments. They end up taking the mystery out of life and the mystery out of worship. When they have done that, they have taken God out as well!

Their cleverness and glibness may well betray a lack of the divine awe within the human spirit—awe and adoration, silent and wonderful, that breathes a whisper, "O Lord God, Thou knowest!"

In Isaiah we see clearly what happens to a person in the mystery of the Presence. Overpowered within His own being, Isaiah can only confess, "I am a man of unclean lips!" (6:5). A person who has sensed what Isaiah sensed will never be able to joke again about "the Someone up there who likes me."

Lord, if we pause long enough to seriously reflect upon Your
divine nature, our finite minds will not be able to fathom the extent
of Your infinite greatness. Our God is an awesome God! Praise Him!

....

....

....

....

....

....

....

....

....

Old Things Pass Away

If any man be in Christ. . .old things are passed away;
behold, all things are become new.
2 CORINTHIANS 5:17

The New Testament is, among others things, a record of the struggle of twice-born men and women to live in a world run by the once born! That should indicate that we are not being as helpful as we ought to be when we fail to instruct the new Christian, that one who is "a babe in Christ," that our Lord told His earliest disciples, "In the world ye shall have tribulation" (John 16:33).

The apostle Paul knew what he was talking about when he told Christian believers, "All that will live godly in Christ Jesus shall suffer persecution" (2 Timothy 3:12).

Take the example of a person recently converted to Christ. His inner witness is clear and up to the light he has; he is beginning to live as he believes a Christian should. But this new world is altogether different from the one he has just left. Standards, values, objectives, methods—all are different. Many solid pillars upon which he had previously leaned without question are now seen to be made of chalk and ready to crumble.

There will be tears, but there will be joy and peace with the continuing discovery that in Christ, indeed, "old things pass away and all things become new" (see 2 Corinthians 5:17).

Lord, sometimes it's convenient to hide my faith when I am in the company of non-Christians.
Help me take a stand for Christ even if I'm in the midst of a hostile situation.

Obedience Is Better

Leaving the principles of the doctrine of Christ,
let us go on unto perfection.
HEBREWS 6:1

The writer to the Hebrews long ago pointed out that some professed Christians were marking time and getting nowhere! They had had opportunity to grow—but they had not grown. They had had sufficient time to mature, yet they were still babes.

So, he plainly exhorted them to leave their meaningless religious round and press on to perfection.

It is possible to have motion without progress, and this describes much of the activity among Christians today. It is simply lost motion! It boils down to this—it is possible that we may attend church for a lifetime and be none the better for it. I think we can say that most Christians have no clear end toward which they are striving. On the endless religious merry-go-round they continue to waste time and energy.

A Christian cannot hope for the true manifestation of God while he lives in a state of disobedience. Let a man refuse to obey God on some clear point, and the rest of his religious activity will be wasted. The instructed and obedient Christian will yield to God as the clay yields to the potter and will relish every moment in church!

Lord, help me to clearly understand Your calling and purpose for my life.
I don't want to spin my wheels; I want to serve You effectively.

The Family of God

I bow my knees unto the Father of our Lord Jesus Christ,
of whom the whole family in heaven and earth is named.
EPHESIANS 3:14–15

There is an important message for the believing family of God in the Bible: next to God Himself we need each other most!

God's ideal is a fellowship of faith, a Christian community. He never intended that salvation should be received and enjoyed by the individual apart from the larger company of believers. With that, it also needs to be said that to live within the religious family does not mean that we must approve everything that is done there.

But God has so created us that we need each other. We may and should go into our closet and pray in secret, but when the prayer is ended we should go back to our people. That is where we belong.

No one is wise enough to live alone, nor good enough nor strong enough. From our brethren we can learn how to do things and sometimes also we can learn how not to do them!

Our Lord who is the Great Shepherd has said that we are the sheep of His pasture and it is in our nature to live with the flock. Best of all, the Shepherd always stays with His flock!

Lord, I pray that the fellowship in our local churches will be strong and pure.
Draw us together in unity, that we may truly honor Your name throughout our community.

Is Your Line Busy?

I heard the voice of the Lord, saying, Whom shall I send...
Then said I, Here am I; send me.
ISAIAH 6:8

❧

The gospel invitation is offered freely to one and all, but many are too preoccupied to hear or heed. They never allow God's call to become a reason for decision. As a result, they live out their entire lives insisting that they never heard any call from God!

The answer to that is plain. God has been trying to get through to them, but engrossed in a host of worldly pursuits, their line is always busy.

The world around us wants to put us in the same straitjacket that would have kept Abraham in Ur of the Chaldees.

"We will talk to you about religion" is the seemingly kindly offer people give us today. But then they add the disclaimer: "Just do not make religion personal." Most people seem to have come to terms with an acceptance of religion if it does not have the cross of Christ within it!

But when God calls men and women to the belief that Christ has given us the only way to God through His death and atonement, their faith will be an offense to the world. It was so in Abraham's day, and it is so in our day!

Lord, I want to keep my channels of communication
open so I will be ready to hear Your voice speaking to me.

Our Godly Conversation

Then they that feared the LORD spake often one to another:
and the LORD hearkened, and heard it.
MALACHI 3:16

$\mathscr{I}$ have met Christians who were so intent upon winning souls to Christ that they would not talk to you about anything but God and His goodness!

Such a man was the Canadian Robert Jaffray, one of our early pioneer missionaries. His family owned the Toronto *Globe and Mail,* and as a young Christian he was disinherited because he chose to follow God's call to China rather than join the family business.

That good godly man spent his lifetime in China and the South Pacific, searching for the lost—and winning them! He was always reading maps and daring to go to the most difficult places, in spite of physical weaknesses and diabetic handicap. He sought out and lived among the poor and miserable, always praying to God, "Let my people go!"

When on furlough, he could not sit and talk about common things. Always his thoughts went back to God and missions and winning the lost. I am reminded of Malachi, who said, "They that feared the LORD spake often one to another: and the LORD hearkened" (3:16).

Thank You, Father, for caring in a special way for all the overseas
Christian workers who are serving You abroad today.

The Reality of Pride

The fear of the LORD is to hate evil:
pride, and arrogancy, and the evil way. . .do I hate.
PROVERBS 8:13

---

*L*et me warn you of the danger and the bigotry of human pride. You will find it everywhere in the world, and it will feast on almost anything that will make it fat!

I have come to the conclusion that many people I have met are not ever going to get right with God because they have determined that they simply will not humble themselves, ever!

Pride is an awesome quality in mankind, not only in Jesus' day, but in ours as well.

I heard a newscast in which one of India's highest officials was trying to deny a report that Christian missionaries were being hindered in their work in India. He said, "We are not hindering the propagation of the Christian doctrine in India. In fact, we understand that there have actually been a few people of low caste who have believed the Christian teaching."

Oh, the rising pride in his voice as he made the statement. The helpless and the hopeless in the lowest caste—he was not going to get in their way if they wanted to believe in Christ.

Yes, the bigotry of human pride is everywhere!

Lord, sometimes pride has a way of sneaking up on me so slowly
and naturally that I don't recognize it. You have my permission,
Lord, to root out the pride in the dark corners of my being.

Two-Way Traffic

Straightway the father of the child cried out, and said with tears,
Lord, I believe; help thou mine unbelief.
MARK 9:24

In the uncertainty of our times, the traffic between faith and unbelief is tragically heavy, as the scriptures declared it would be. But we may encourage our hearts with the knowledge that the traffic does not always move in the direction of unbelief—sometimes it moves the other way!

Every now and then the cheering news comes of some "liberal" who gets sick to his stomach of the mixture of applied psychology and cheap poetry, and comes home like the prodigal to the Father's house. It is true that the movement from orthodoxy to liberalism is usually slow; almost too slow to be perceived. I have never heard of a single instance where any person accepted modernism as a result of a spiritual experience.

But the movement back to faith is likely to be sudden, often explosive. A man or woman is converted to Christ by a sudden encounter with God and spiritual things!

The simple fact that the believer always experiences something and the unbeliever never does should tell us a great deal. Only the true Christian is sure the sun has risen!

Lord, there are many people in this community and around the
world who are standing at the crossroads of life, not knowing
which way to turn. Will You steer them in the right direction today?

"Unfair! Unfair!"

*He was oppressed, and he was afflicted, yet he opened
not his mouth. . .neither was any deceit in his mouth.*
ISAIAH 53:7, 9

Christians who understand the true meaning of Christ's cross will never whine about being treated unfairly. Whether or not they are given fair treatment will never enter their heads. They know they have been called to follow Christ, and certainly the Savior did not receive anything approaching fair treatment from mankind.

In language the word *unfair* seems altogether innocent, but it indicates an inner attitude that has no place among Christians.

The man who cries "Unfair!" is not a victorious man. He is inwardly defeated and in self-defense appeals to the referee to note that he has been fouled. This gives him an alibi when they carry him out on a stretcher and saves his face while his bruises heal.

It is a certainty that Christians will suffer wrongs; but if they take them in good spirit and without complaint, they have conquered their enemy. They remember that Jesus was reviled—but any thought of His shouting for fair play simply cannot be entertained by the reverent heart!

*Lord, remind me to think of Your example whenever I am
tempted to complain that "life is unfair." You suffered the
greatest injustice of all; yet You remained silent.*

The Prophetic Voice

Speak every man truth. . .that which is good to the use of edifying,
that it may minister grace unto the hearers.
EPHESIANS 4:25, 29

The Christian minister cannot deny that God has called him to be a prophet to his own generation, for the Church is God's witness to each generation and its ministers are its voice. Through them, the voice of God becomes vocal!

The true minister, therefore, should know what he means when he says that he preaches "the truth." It is not enough that the man of God preach truth—suppose he recites the multiplication table? That is also truth. A church can wither as surely under the ministry of soulless Bible exposition as it can where no Bible is given at all. To be effective, the message must be alive—it must alarm, arouse, challenge; it must be God's present voice to a particular people.

To preach the truth, the prophet must be under the constant sway of the Holy Spirit. He must be driven to God for wisdom. Otherwise, he will not pierce the conscience of each listener as if the message had been directed to him or her alone. Further, it is necessary that the man of God know the people's hearts better than they themselves do!

Dear Lord, I pray that You will do a work in the hearts
of the Christian young men of this generation. Challenge them
to be Spirit-filled dispensers of the truth from our church pulpits.

God Needs No Adjectives

I will mention the lovingkindnesses of the LORD, and the praises
of the LORD, according to all that the LORD hath bestowed on us.
ISAIAH 63:7

We do not need any enlarging adjectives when we speak of God, or of His love or mercy. God Almighty fills the universe and overfills it because it is His character—infinite and unlimited!

We do not need to say God's "great" love, although we do say it. We do not need to say God's "abundant" mercy, although we do say it. I expect we say it to cheer and elevate our own thoughts of God, not to infer that there is any degree in the mercy of God.

Our adjectives can be useful only when we talk about earthly things—when we refer to the great love of a man for his family, or of a man's fabulous wealth.

But when we are speaking of God, there can be no such measuring point. When we speak of the riches of God, we must include all the riches there are! God is not less rich or more rich—He is rich! He holds all things in His being!

So it is with mercy. God is not less merciful or more merciful. Thankfully, He is full of mercy. Whatever God is, He is that in the fullness of unlimited grace!

Heavenly Father, the depth and breadth of Your attributes are beyond
human measure and comprehension. God, there is no other god like You!

A Worldwide Body

For the body is not one member, but many. . . .
Now ye are the body of Christ, and members in particular.
1 CORINTHIANS 12:14, 27

———✦———

*S*tating it in the most simple terms, the Christian Church, called to be the Body of Christ on earth, is the assembly of redeemed saints.

We meet in local congregations and assemblies, yet we know that we are not an end in ourselves. If we are going to be what we ought to be in the local church, we must come to think of ourselves as a part of something more expansive, something larger that God is doing throughout the world.

There is an important sense here in which we find that we "belong"—belonging to something that is worthy and valuable, and something that is going to last forever!

These are considerations concerning the whole Church, the Body of Christ, and the fact that in our local congregation we have the joyful sense of belonging to an amazing fellowship throughout the world. Every believing church has a part with us and we a part with them.

Brethren, the Church must have the enabling and the power of the Holy Spirit and the glow of the Shekinah glory—God within us. For then, even lacking everything else, you still have a true church!

Lord, this morning I pray for my sisters and brothers in Christ around the world.
Encourage them and empower them to do good works in Your name today.

....

....

....

....

....

....

....

....

....

....

July 29

Making Christ Wait

*If any man. . .consent not to wholesome words, even the words
of our Lord Jesus Christ. . .he is proud, knowing nothing.*
1 TIMOTHY 6:3–4

⟡

First I become indignant and then I become sad when a person to whom I am trying to give spiritual counsel tells me: "Well, I am trying to make up my mind whether or not I should accept Christ."

This scene is taking place in our society over and over again, as proud Adamic sinners argue within themselves: "I don't know whether I should accept Christ or not." So, in this view, our poor Lord Christ stands hat in hand, shifting from one foot to the other, looking for a job—wondering whether He will be accepted!

Is it possible that we proud humans do not know that the Christ we are putting off is the eternal Son, the Lord who made the heavens and the earth and all things that are therein? He is indeed the One, the Mighty One!

Thankfully, He has promised to receive us, poor and sinful though we be. But the idea that we can make Him stand while we render the verdict of whether He is worthy is a frightful calumny—and we ought to get rid of it!

*Dear Lord, thank You for Your wonderful promise to receive us just
as we are—warts and all. You are entirely trustworthy, Lord.*

Our Love for God

Let us not love in word, neither in tongue; but in deed and in truth.
1 JOHN 3:18

The taking over of the romantic love ideal into our relation to God has been extremely injurious to our Christian lives. The idea that we should "fall in love" with God is ignoble, unscriptural, unworthy of us, and certainly does no honor to the Most High God!

We do not come to love God by a sudden emotional visitation. Love for God results from repentance, amendment of life, and a fixed determination to love Him. Then as God moves more perfectly into the focus of our hearts, our love for Him may indeed rise and swell within us till like a flood it sweeps everything before it.

But we should not wait for this intensity of feeling. We are not responsible to feel but we are responsible to love, and true spiritual love begins in the will.

We should set our hearts to love God supremely, however cold or hard they may seem to be, and go on to confirm our love by happy and careful obedience to His Word.

Enjoyable emotions are sure to follow!

Heavenly Father, I confess that I have a hard time "loving" the unlovely
people of this world. Teach me more about true spiritual love, Father.

Jesus Will Come

And sware by him that liveth for ever and ever. . .
that there should be time no longer.
REVELATION 10:6

We are living in a period when God waits in grace and mercy. In His faithfulness, God is calling out a people for His name—those who will in faith cast their lot with Jesus Christ! Then, at a time known only to God, the end of this age will come, and Jesus Christ will return to earth for His own believing people—His Church.

The event is certain—the timing is uncertain. When the mighty angel of Revelation shouts his signal and raises his hand heavenward, it will be eternally too late for unrepentant sinners.

When the time comes in heaven for that announcement, three worlds will hear it. Heaven will hear it, with full agreement that the time of judgment has indeed come. The underworld of hell will hear the shout, and there will be fright. And on earth, the saints, the believing Body of Christ, will hear it and be glad! Meanwhile, the Church is not simply a religious institution. It is an assembly of redeemed sinners, men and women called and commissioned to spread Christ's gospel to the ends of the earth.

Lord, while I look forward to Your return to restore justice and order to this
fallen world, my heart is burdened for my friends and loved ones who haven't
accepted You yet. Lord, I pray that each one will yield to Your Spirit.

Just Plain Faithful

The things that thou hast heard. . .commit thou to faithful men.
2 TIMOTHY 2:2

———

I realize that faithfulness is not a very dramatic subject and that many among us in the Christian faith would like to do something with more dash and more flair than just being faithful. While some are just concerned about getting their picture in the paper, I thank God for every loyal and faithful Christian who has only one recognition in mind, and that is to hear their Lord say in that Great Day to come: "Well done, thou good and faithful servant. . .enter thou into the joy of thy lord!" (Matthew 25:21).

It is plain truth that faithfulness and goodness are at the root of much of the consistent fruit bearing among the witnessing children of God! Throughout the Bible the Lord has always placed a great premium on the faithfulness of those who love Him and serve Him.

Noah was faithful in his day. Abraham was faithful in his day. Moses was faithful in his day. And what do we need to say about the faithfulness of our Savior, Jesus Christ? The devil was there with his lies. The world threatened Him all around. But Christ was faithful to His Father and to us!

Are we willing to learn from the Holy Spirit how to be faithful and loving, unselfish and Christlike?

Lord, great is Your faithfulness! I pray that You will enable me to be marked
by faithfulness in my walk with You—just like Noah, Abraham, and Moses.

God Would Stir Us

Blessed are they which do hunger and thirst after righteousness.
MATTHEW 5:6

---

*T*here is no way that any of us can talk ourselves into getting a "longing for God." Spiritual desire and hunger must come from God Himself! It cannot be whipped up.

As a grown boy, I tried selling peanuts, popcorn, chewing gum, candy, and books on the old Vicksburg and Pacific railroad. I did not sell enough to become any great success, but I recall that we often tried to stir up some desire for our wares among the passengers. We would go through the coaches and give each person a few salted peanuts. No one seemed to want to buy on the first trip through, but when we came back, nearly everyone who had tasted was ready to buy. This was a common trick on the trains.

But it is a different story when we consider the spiritual life. No one but God through His Spirit is able to stir up spiritual desire among us. Those who have accepted a common state of spiritual living and have no deep desire for Him will never be stirred by human means.

Lord, Your Word says, "Taste and see that the LORD is good" (Psalm 34:8).
I desire to grow closer to You, Lord. I don't want to merely sustain
a distant relationship with an unknowable God.

Thank God for Conviction

A man hath joy by the answer of his mouth:
and a word spoken in due season, how good is it!
PROVERBS 15:23

⸺ ✦ ⸺

*M*odern mankind can go anywhere, do everything, and be completely curious about the universe. But only a rare person now and then is curious enough to want to know God.

We do not thank God enough for seeking us and finding us and making it possible for us to say to His invitation: "Jesus, I come!"

I have meditated often on the Holy Spirit's quiet dealing with the heart of this untaught lad when I was only seventeen. We had a neighbor—I only knew him as "Mr. Holman"—and I had heard that he was a Christian.

One day we happened to be walking on the sidewalk together, and he said, "I am glad to have a chance to talk with you. I have been wondering if you are a Christian?"

I told him, "No, I am not a Christian. But I thank you for asking and I am going to give it some serious thought."

After that, I heard a man preaching on a street corner. He quoted Jesus' invitation, "Come unto Me," and the sinner's prayer, "Lord have mercy on me!" Those were the two things that bumped me into the kingdom of God. Sometimes it takes a very little word to stir an unnoticed desire for God and His truth!

Lord, I pray that today I will take advantage of opportunities
to ask someone about the status of his spiritual life.

Enjoying God Forever

My sheep hear my voice. . .and they shall never perish.
JOHN 10:27–28

———

I should be illuminating to us that the difference between unbelief and faith, between man's point of view and God's, often comes to light as the believer faces death.

We are told that when John Wesley was dying, he tried to sing but his voice was nearly gone. Although his own theology was Arminian, he was trying to sing the words of an old Calvinist hymn:

> *I will praise my Maker while I've breath,*
> *And when my soul is lost in death,*
> *Praise shall employ my nobler powers.*

That is at least one reason why I cannot get all heated up about contending for one theological position over another.

If Isaac Watts, a Calvinist, could write such praise to God and John Wesley, an Arminian, could sing it with yearning in his last moments, why should I allow anyone to force me to confess, "I don't know which I am!"

I was created and redeemed that I should worship Him and enjoy Him forever. That is the primary issue in our Christian walk!

> *Lord, when it's time for me to pass from this life to the next,*
> *I pray that it will be a glorious transition from praising You in*
> *this life to that of worshipping You face to face in Your holy presence.*

....

....

....

....

....

....

Giving Christ His Place

That every tongue should confess that Jesus
Christ is Lord, to the glory of God the Father.
PHILIPPIANS 2:11

Christianity at large and the Church, generally speaking, are afflicted with a dread, lingering illness that shows itself daily in the apathy and spiritual paralysis of its members.

How can it be otherwise when twentieth-century Christians refuse to acknowledge the sharp moral antithesis that God Himself has set between the Church, as the Body of Christ, and this present world with its own human systems?

The differences between the churchly world and the followers of the Lamb are so basic that they can never be reconciled or negotiated. God has never promised His believing people that they would become a popular majority in this earthly scene.

I wonder how many believers would join me in a clear-cut manifesto to our times? I want it to be a declaration of our intentions to restore Christ to the place that is rightfully His in our personal lives, in our family situations, and in the fellowship of the churches that bear His name.

Are we willing to demonstrate the standards of godliness and biblical holiness as a rebuke to this wicked and perverse generation?

Lord, though the Church and the world often collide, I pray that
each member of the Body of Christ will be so full of integrity that
many unsaved people in the world will be pointed to Jesus Christ.

Christ Does Not Change

Jesus came and spake unto them. . .
All power is given unto me in heaven and in earth.
MATTHEW 28:18

———

*Y*ou will have to prove it to me if you are among those who claim that Jesus Christ refuses to do for you something that He has done for any other of His disciples!

I address this to all of those who insist that the gifts of the Spirit ended when the last apostle died. They have never furnished chapter and verse for their position.

When some men beat the cover off their Bible to demonstrate how they stand for the Word of God, they should be reminded that they are only standing by their own interpretation!

I find nothing in the Bible that says the Lord has changed. He has the same love, the same grace, the same mercy, the same power, the same desires for the blessings of His children.

Why can we not claim all that God has promised for His redeemed people? What a sad condition for Christians who are in the Church of the mighty Redeemer and Deliverer, who is eternally the Victor, the Rock of Ages. Let us never forget that Jesus Christ is the same yesterday, today, and forever! (see Hebrews 13:8).

Almighty God, I thank You and praise You that You are the same yesterday, today, and forever. This means that You are exactly the same God who personally led the children of Israel in the desert wilderness. Thank You, Lord, for Your patience and guidance in my life today.

God—Acting Like God

The only begotten Son, which is in the bosom
of the Father, he hath declared him.
JOHN 1:18

When Jesus walked and taught in Galilee two thousand years ago, many asked, "Who is that Man?"

The Bible's answer is clear: That Man walking in Galilee was God, acting like God! It was God, limited deliberately, having crossed the wide, mysterious gulf between God and not God, between God and creature. No man had seen God at any time.

In John 1:18, the English translators have said, "The only begotten Son. . .hath declared him." Other versions skirt around it, doing everything to try to say what the Holy Spirit said, but when we have used up our words and synonyms, we still have not said all that God revealed when He said, "Nobody has ever looked at God, but when Jesus Christ came He showed us what God is like" (paraphrase of John 1:18).

He has revealed Him—He has shown us what God is like!

He has declared Him! He has set Him forth! He has revealed Him!

He is in the Father's bosom. It is stated in present, perpetual tense, the language of continuation. Therefore, when Jesus hung on the cross, He did not leave the bosom of the Father!

Lord Jesus, that You are the Son of God is the bedrock of our faith.
Thank You for revealing what God is like during Your brief sojourn on earth.

Christ, the Blessed One

Take my yoke upon you, and learn of me. . . .
For my yoke is easy, and my burden is light.
MATTHEW 11:29–30

I feel great sorrow for those who read the Sermon on the Mount and then conclude that Jesus was providing a word picture of men and women comprising the human race. In this world, we find nothing approaching the virtues of which Jesus spoke in the Beatitudes.

Instead of poverty of spirit, we find the rankest kind of pride. Instead of mourners, we find pleasure seekers.

Instead of meekness, we find only arrogance, and instead of hunger after righteousness, we hear men saying, "I am rich, and increased with goods, and have need of nothing" (Revelation 3:17).

Instead of mercy, we find cruelty. Instead of purity of heart, we encounter corrupt imaginings. Instead of peacemakers, we find men quarrelsome and resentful, fighting back with every weapon at their command.

Jesus said He came to release us from our sad heritage of sin. Blessed is the sinner who finds that Christ's words are the Truth itself, that He is the Blessed One who came from above to confer blessedness upon mankind!

Thank You, Father, for Your open-armed invitation for Your
children to cast all of their worldly cares upon You.
Lord, teach me how to trust You more deeply.

A Heavenly Fragrance

To the end he may stablish your hearts unblameable in holiness. . .
at the coming of our Lord Jesus Christ.
1 THESSALONIANS 3:13

I have been affected in my own heart and life by reading the testimonies and commentaries of humble men of God whom I consider to be among the great souls of Christian church history. From them I have learned that the word and idea of holiness as originally used in the Hebrew did not have, first of all, the moral connotation.

The original root of the word *holy* was of something beyond, something strange and mysterious and awe inspiring. When we consider the holiness of God, we talk about something heavenly, full of awe, mysterious, and fear inspiring. This is supreme when it relates to God, but it is also marked in men of God and deepens as men become more like God.

It is a sense of awareness of the other world, a mysterious quality and difference that has come to rest upon some men and women—that is a holiness. When those persons with this special quality and mysterious presence are morally right and walking in all the holy ways of God, and carrying without even knowing it the fragrance of a kingdom that is supreme above the kingdoms of this world, I am ready to accept that as being of God and from God!

Heavenly Father, You are full of awe and wonder. Yet You are the majestic Creator
of the universe who wants to connect with His creation in an intimate manner.
Why would anyone choose not to worship You as the supreme Giver of life?

Chosen in Him

He hath chosen us in him before the foundation of the world,
that we should be holy and without blame.
EPHESIANS 1:4

I have been told that sometimes when I preach I really worry the Calvinists, but I want to make a point here, and I take the chance of worrying my brethren in the Arminian persuasion.

The recorded acts of Creation in the beginning were not God's first activity. God had been occupied before that, for He must have been engaged in choosing and foreordaining before the foundation of the world!

Paul told the Ephesian Christians: "[God] hath chosen us in him before the foundation of the world, that we should be holy and without blame before him in love" (1:4).

Can I explain how God could have chosen us before the creation of the world? Can I explain the eternal nature of God, the uncreated Being? Can I explain a time when there was only God—no matter, no law, no motion, no relation and no space, no time and no beings, only God?

God was there, and God is not a void! He is the triune God, and He is all there is. Before the Creation He was already busy with eternal mercies and a redemptive plan for a mankind not yet created!

Merciful God, as I reflect upon Your eternal goodness, I am amazed once again
at Your resoluteness to save a wayward world at such a great expense—Your only Son.

....
....
....
....
....
....
....
....
....
....

Spiritual Suffocation

Where sin abounded, grace did much more abound.
ROMANS 5:20

---

*H*ow can I illustrate man's proneness to spiritual suffocation?

I have read that mining companies used to take live caged birds deep into the mines to detect the presence of dangerous gases. If there was a high concentration of poison, the bird would quickly fall down and die in the bottom of the cage.

I consider a bird a miracle created by God—a wonder with wings, created to soar over green meadows and breathe the sweet air of the heavens. But take him underground where there is black damp and pollution and he quickly dies of suffocation!

You can apply that also to the soul of man!

God created man a living soul and intended him to rise and mount up into the eternities and live with God. There is in each of us a longing after immortality. But sin has ruined us. We have listened to that serpent, the devil. We have gone down into the isolated, dark, poison-infested pockets of the world, and lost men are dying everywhere of spiritual suffocation!

Lord, the Bible says that you have "crowned [man] with glory and honour" (Psalm 8:5).
Yet so often we don't act like we deserve that status. We are self-centered and fickle.
Lord, cause a revival by Your Spirit and enable us to "soar" as You intended.

We Can Afford to Die

For here have we no continuing city, but we seek one to come.
HEBREWS 13:14

---

*B*rethren, it is a fact indeed that we will never fully realize in our earthly life what it means to be coheirs with Christ! The apostles have made it quite plain that all of the eternal implications of our heavenly inheritance will not be known to us until we see Christ face-to-face in a future time.

I have said that only a Christian has the right and can afford to die! But if we believers were as spiritual as we ought to be, we might be looking to our "home going" with a great deal more pleasure and anticipation than we do.

I say also that if we are true believers in the second advent of our Savior, we will be anticipating His return with yearning. Common sense, the perspective of history, the testimony of the saints, reason, and the Bible—all agree with one voice that He may come before we die.

The Christian believer whose faith and hope are in Jesus Christ alone knows that he may die before the Lord comes. If he dies, he is better off, for Paul said, "It is far better that I go to be with the Lord" (see Philippians 1:23).

You've placed eternity in our hearts, Lord. Therefore, You've created
us with a built-in desire to live with You in heaven. I pray that
all my family members will come to know You before it's too late.

How Do We Know Him?

I know whom I have believed.
2 TIMOTHY 1:12

I must ask this question in the context of today's modern Christianity: "Is it not true that for most of us who call ourselves Christians there is no real experience?"

We have substituted theological ideas for an arresting encounter; we are full of religious notions, but our great weakness is that for our hearts there is no one there!

Whatever else it embraces, true Christian experience must always include a genuine encounter with God. Without this, religion is but a shadow, a reflection of reality, a cheap copy of an original once enjoyed by someone else of whom we have heard.

It cannot but be a major tragedy in the life of any man or woman to live in a church from childhood to old age and know nothing more real than some synthetic god compounded of theology and logic, but having no eyes to see, no ears to hear—and no heart to love!

O Lord, I pray for the people in churches who may think they are Christians because they were raised in a religious environment. What a tragedy it would be if these men and women are not truly saved. Lord, I pray for each one, that they will receive Christ into their hearts.

....

....

....

....

....

....

....

....

....

....

....

Our Inner Sights

The eyes of your understanding being enlightened;
that ye may know what is the hope of his calling.
EPHESIANS 1:18

———

Revival and blessing come to the church when we stop looking at a picture of God and look at God Himself! Revival comes when, no longer satisfied to know about a God in history, we meet the conditions of finding Him in living, personal experience.

Conversely, revival cannot come if we are far removed from God. It cannot come if, instead of hearing His voice, we are content with only an echo!

Put those deficiencies together and you have the reason why we are dissatisfied and empty. You have the reason why there is so little of vivid, vibrant joy in the things of God.

I hold fast to the opinion that our God is ever trying to reveal Himself to us. There is no way for sinful men and women to find their way into God's presence unless He reveals Himself and appears to us. I do not mean that God is trying to appear to our physical eyesight. Rather, He is trying to appear to the eye of our soul through an inner consciousness. Never apologize for your inner eyes! They are the real eyes for discerning the nature of issues important to God.

Lord, there are so many difficult but important decisions
to make in life. Sharpen the eyes of my inner soul to be able
to discern Your presence and guidance in my life.

....
....
....
....
....
....
....
....
....

Blessedness to Come

*We have a building of God, an house not
made with hands, eternal in the heavens.*
2 CORINTHIANS 5:1

———⚬———

*A*lot of people talk about going to heaven in spite of the feeble hope popular religion affords.
Any valid hope of a state of blessedness beyond the incident of death must be in the goodness of God and in the work of atonement accomplished for us by Jesus Christ on the cross.

The deep, deep love of God is the fountain out of which flows our future beatitude; and the grace of God in Christ is the channel by which it reaches us. The cross of Christ creates a moral situation where every attribute of God is on the side of the returning sinner.

The true Christian may safely look forward to a future state that is as happy as perfect love wills it to be. Because love cannot desire for its object anything less than the fullest possible measure of enjoyment for the longest possible time, it is virtually beyond our power to conceive of a future as consistently delightful as that which Christ is preparing for us.

And who is to say what is possible with God?

*Loving Lord, though we are the objects of Your perfect love, it is a safe
guess to say that we are only partially aware of the benefits You desire
to bestow upon us. Thank You, Father, for Your unfailing, overflowing love.*

"Frozen" Unbelief

Take heed, brethren, lest there be
in any of you an evil heart of unbelief.
HEBREWS 3:12

Study the life of faithful Noah and you will know what he would say if he could come and counsel you today: "Whenever you hear God's truth," he would say, "you will go either in the direction you are moved, or you will just wait.

"If you wait, you will find that the next time you hear the truth, it will not move you quite as much. The next time, it will move you less—and the time will come when that truth will not move you at all!"

We need that message in our generation, for there is a distressing kind of "frozen" unbelief all around us. Men and women are paying little heed to any of God's warning signals.

As a farm boy, I learned the lesson of little chicks—an easy prey for hawks overhead. The mother hen heard the high-pitched cry of the soaring hawk and gave her own special "cluck cluck" of warning. Her chicks scampered to her side and soon she had them all tucked safely under her feathers.

Thank God, there is a true faith that is not ashamed to move in the direction of the Ark of safety!

Lord, I pray that today I will be especially alert to God's truth and
that I will take any appropriate action that is impressed upon my spirit.

Let Us Move Forward

That ye might be filled with all the fulness of God.
EPHESIANS 3:19

———— ❧ ————

The apostle Paul's greatest desire was to always move forward in the knowledge and blessing of God. But some modern Bible teachers now call that kind of hunger and thirsting fanaticism, instead of desire for spiritual maturity.

These teachers assure the new Christian: "You are now complete in Christ. Just relax and be glad that there is nothing more you will ever need."

With great desire Paul wrote: "That I may win Christ" (Philippians 3:8)—and yet he already had Christ! With obvious longing he said: "[That I may] be found in Him" (3:9)—and yet he was already in Him!

Paul humbly and intensely breathed his great desire: "That I may know Him" (3:10)—even though he already knew Him!

Because he did not want to stand still, Paul testified: "I follow after; I press toward the mark. I am striving to lay hold of that for which Christ laid hold on me!" (see 3:12).

It is very plain that the apostle had no other desire than to be completely available to God. Many of us refuse to follow his example!

Dear Lord, my prayer this morning is that You will satisfy my hunger
to know You more and that You will use me to help advance Your kingdom.

God's Eternal Work

The creature itself also shall be delivered from the bondage of corruption.
ROMANS 8:21

Is it possible that some of our brothers and sisters in Christ have forgotten that even though we are Christians, we live day by day in unredeemed physical bodies?

Yes, brethren, this is orthodox Christian theology, given to us by the apostle Paul in these words: "Even though we have the firstfruits of the Spirit, we groan within ourselves, waiting for the redemption of the body" (see Romans 8:23). These bodies of ours will be redeemed, for that is the promise of God. But in this life they are not yet actually redeemed. That is why we cannot do God's eternal work ourselves, for only the Holy Spirit of God can bring about His eternal purposes.

If we are to successfully engage in the Christian witness God expects of us while we are here on this earth, we must consciously know and experience the indwelling illumination of the Holy Spirit of God. We must depend upon His gifts and His enduement and His anointing if we hope to cope with the universal blight which is upon mankind.

Lord, Your Word says that "the spirit is willing, but the flesh is weak"
(Matthew 26:41). I know from personal experience that I need the
power of Your indwelling Spirit to overcome the influence of the flesh.

God Far Away

Am I a God at hand, saith the LORD, and not a God afar off? . . .
Do not I fill heaven and earth?
JEREMIAH 23:23–24

I remember the words of a little song I heard when I was young about God's presence: "Far Away Beyond the Starlit Sky." That is really where mankind has placed God. He is far away, out there somewhere beyond the starlit sky.

As men and women in this world, we are prone to think of God's presence in terms of space, as we understand it. We think in terms of light-years or meters or miles or fathoms. We think of God as dwelling in space—which He does not! God is not contained in heaven and earth as some seem to think.

God in His person and His attributes fills heaven and earth exactly as the ocean fills a bucket which is submerged in the ocean depths.

Why, then, does man say, "God is far, far away!"? Because of the complete dissimilarity between the nature of the holy God and the perverted nature of sinful man!

Heavenly Father, I praise You that You are not distant and detached from Your creation. Thank You that we can know You through Your Word and through prayer and fellowship with You.

Christian "Shrinkage"

Be ye. . .followers of God, as dear children;
and walk in love as Christ also hath loved us.
EPHESIANS 5:1–2

Why should we have to accept the idea held in some Christian circles that new converts will soon lose their first zeal and settle down to a life of dull religious routine? I believe that I carry the welfare of the saints in my heart, and it disturbs me that some Christians are satisfied to accept the title of "dead average."

What happens? Can it be that the person who has held a joyful conversion becomes enamored of his experience, failing to keep his eyes fixed on the Lord?

Only engrossment with God can maintain perpetual spiritual enthusiasm because only God can supply everlasting novelty. In God every moment is new and nothing ever gets old. Of things religious we may become tired, even prayer may weary us; but God never!

Brothers and sisters, nothing can preserve the sweet savor of our first experience except to be preoccupied with God Himself! Let the new convert know that if he would grow instead of shrink, he must spend his nights and his days in communion with the triune God!

Lord, I pray this morning that the activities of the day ahead will be
anything but routine as I converse with You. I pray that I will experience
spiritual enthusiasm as I live in the light of Your constant presence.

....
....
....
....
....
....
....
....
....

Testing Our Faith

That ye may be sincere and without offence till the day of Christ.
PHILIPPIANS 1:10

———❦———

*A*ny belief that does not command the daily walk of the one who holds it is not a real belief: it is a pseudobelief only!

I think it might shock some of us profoundly if we were suddenly brought face-to-face with our beliefs and forced to test them in the fores of practical living. How many professing Christians boast in the Lord but watch carefully that they never get caught fully depending on Him? Pseudofaith always arranges a way out to serve in case God "fails."

What we need very badly these days is a company of Christians prepared to trust God as completely now as they must do at the last day! For each of us, the time is surely coming when we shall all have nothing but God! To the men of pseudofaith, that is a terrifying thought!

For true faith, it is either God or total collapse, and not since Adam first stood up on the earth has God failed anyone who trusted Him! We can prove our faith by our committal to it—and in no other way!

*Dear Lord, I love my country, but it can be difficult even for some Christians
to trust fully in God when we are raised to be self-sufficient and self-reliant. I pray
that our nation will humble itself and return to its forgotten motto: "In God we trust."*

....

....

....

....

....

....

....

....

....

....

God Gives Assurance

But ye, beloved, building up yourselves on your most holy faith. . .
keep yourselves in the love of God.
JUDE 20–21

Moral sanity requires that we settle this most important matter first of all: settling our personal and saving relation with God!

In some Christian groups, there are believers who actually make fun of Christians in other groups who occasionally arise and sing the words of an old hymn, "Do I love the Lord, or no?" No serious-minded person should ever laugh at any man or woman, who knowing that death is only three jumps ahead, contemplates: "My God, do I really know Thee or not? Have I been mistaken in meaningless religious connection? My God, what must I do to be saved?"

Many of us better start asking questions today. We know that we had better not try to stand on our own reputation.

There is nothing in the whole world of greater meaning than to come back into the family of God by faith and through His grace! There is no joy that can be compared to that which God gives when He forgives us, cleanses us, restores and saves us, and assures us that the gift of God is indeed eternal life, to as many as will believe! (see Romans 6:23).

Lord, thank You for Your forgiveness and for the free gift of eternal life.
Though it is a free gift, it was very costly for You. Thank You, Father.

Christ's Eternal Glory

We beheld his glory, the glory as of the only begotten of the Father.
JOHN 1:14

The apostle John speaks for all when he writes of the eternal Son and reminds us that "we beheld his glory." John was speaking of much more than the glory of Christ's wondrous works. Every part of nature had to yield to Him and His authority. Everything our Lord did was meaningful in the display of His eternal glory.

But we may be sure that John had a much greater glory in mind than the gracious and wonderful acts of healing and help.

It was the very person and character of Jesus that was glorious. It was not only what He did—but what He was. What He was in His person primary!

Brethren, there can be no argument about Jesus Christ's glory—it lay in the fact that He was perfect love in a loveless world; that He was perfect purity in an impure world; and that He was perfect meekness in a harsh and quarrelsome world. Patience in suffering, unquenchable life, and God's grace and truth were in the eternal Word, as well.

This is the divine and eternal glory that earth's most famous and capable personalities can never attain!

*Lord, we get so bogged down with our life's responsibilities that we often
miss out on the kind of revelation that John had of Jesus Christ's glory.
I want to slow down, Lord, to experience more of Your eternal glory.*

Heir to All Creation

God. . .hath. . .spoken unto us by his Son,
whom he hath appointed heir of all things.
HEBREWS 1:1–2

In this life, we are experiencing only unfinished segments of God's great eternal plan. Certainly we are not able to comprehend fully the glory that will be ours in that future day when leaning on the arm of our heavenly Bridegroom we are led into the presence of the Father in heaven with exceeding joy!

The writer to the Hebrews has tried to help us in the proper exercise of our faith, with the amazing statement that our Lord Jesus Christ is the heir of all things in God's far-flung creation. All things created have been ordered and laid out so they become the garment of deity and the universal living expression of Himself to this world!

What does "heir of all things" really mean? It includes angels, seraphim, cherubim, ransomed men and women of all ages, matter, mind, law, spirit, value, meaning. It includes life and events on varied levels of being—and God's great interest embraces them all!

Surely God has left nothing to chance in His creative scheme—whether it be the tiniest blade of grass or the mightiest galaxy in the distant heavens above!

Lord of the harvest, there are still people in this world who have never heard the name of Jesus.
Nor, therefore, have they heard that He will be the rightful "heir of all things." I pray that Your
Spirit will hasten the sending of the gospel to the remaining unreached peoples of the world.

Satan's Stratagem

For we have not followed cunningly devised fables.
2 PETER 1:16

———⟡———

It is amazing that Satan's wiliest stratagem against Christian believers is to use our virtues against us! Perhaps it is more amazing that he often does this with great success.

By means of temptation to sin, he strikes at our personal lives; by working through our virtues, he gets at the whole community of believers and unfits it for its own defense.

To capture a city an enemy must first weaken or destroy its resistance. The Church will never fall as long as she resists. This the devil knows; consequently he uses any stratagem to neutralize her resistance.

Satan first creates a maudlin, inaccurate concept of Christ as soft, smiling, and tolerant. He reminds us that Christ, as a lamb brought to slaughter, opened not His mouth—and suggests that we do likewise. Then if we notice his foot in the door and rise to oppose him, he appeals to our desire to be Christlike. "Love everybody and all will be well," he urges.

The shepherd, taken in by this sweet talk, is afraid to use his club, and the wolf gets the sheep!

Lord, I pray that You will help my church resist any tactic
used by Satan designed to weaken or dilute the testimony of
the church in our community. We want to lift up Your name.

Prayer—and God's Spirit

We know not what we should pray for as we ought:
but the Spirit itself maketh intercession for us.
ROMANS 8:26

Probably none of us really knows as much about prayer as we should—but as students of the Word of God, we may agree that only the Spirit can pray effectively.

The idea has been expressed that "wrestling in prayer" is always a good thing, but that is by no means true. Extreme religious "exercises" may be undergone with no higher motive than to get our own way!

The spiritual quality of a prayer is determined not by its intensity but by its origin. In evaluating prayer we should inquire who is doing the praying—our determined hearts, or the Holy Spirit? If the prayer originates with the Spirit, then the wrestling can be beautiful and wonderful; but if we are the victims of our own overheated desires, our praying can be as carnal as any other act.

Consider Jacob's wrestling: "A man wrestled with him till daybreak" (see Genesis 32:24). But when Jacob had been beaten upon, he cried, "I will not let you go unless you bless me!" (see 32:26). That wrestling was of divine origin, and the blessed results are known to every Bible student!

Lord, Your way is the best way. Our way is fraught with selfish intentions.
Help me and my family to have pure motives whenever we pray to You.

....

....

....

....

....

....

....

....

....

Men Who Do Not Pray

The fire shall try every man's work of what sort it is.
1 CORINTHIANS 3:13

———◦———

The indications are all around us in Christianity that we are greatly in need of worshippers.

We have a lot of men who are willing to sit on our church boards but have no desire for spiritual joy and radiance and who never show up for the church prayer meeting!

It has always seemed to me to be a frightful incongruity that men who do not pray and do not worship are nevertheless running many of the churches and ultimately determining the direction they will take.

It hits very close to our own situation, perhaps, but we should confess that in many "good churches" we let the women do the praying and let the men do the voting!

God calls us to worship, but in many instances we are majoring in entertainment, just running a poor second to the theater. This is where we are, even in evangelical churches. Yet God's first call to us is for the offering of true worship!

Lord, just as You taught Your disciples how to pray, I ask that during
this current generation there will be a Spirit-led prayer revival in
all our churches. What a spiritual power surge that would create!

Trust—Not Adjust

Your life is hid with Christ in God.
COLOSSIANS 3:3

We ought to recognize one of the great problems in our modern Christianity: those who come to Christ probably have their minds made up that to stay sane they must remain "adjusted" to society around them.

This notion has been drilled into them from their playpen, and it never occurs to them to question it. There is a "norm" out there somewhere to which they must conform, and that norm is above criticism. Their success and happiness depend upon how well they adjust to it; and Christianity, though it may add something to it, must never disagree with the main idea!

This is the popular notion in the world: "To be happy, adjust to the social norm!" The problem is that the idea will not hold up under examination. The world does not know where it is going; it has not found life's highest good; it is instead puzzled, frightened, and frustrated.

Thankfully, it was to this kind of world Jesus came. He died for its sin and now lives for the salvation of all who will repudiate it!

Dear Lord, the world seems to be in an irreversible downward spiral. There is no time to be wishy-washy about my faith. Lord, keep me focused on You and Your purposes for the sake of the gospel.

More Than Consolation

Blessed is the man. . .his delight is in the law of the LORD.
PSALM 1:1–2

It is my judgment that too many of us go to church on Sunday for the same reason that a child climbs into its mother's arms after a fall or a bump or a fright—the child wants consolation!

We have fallen upon times when religion is mostly for consolation—for we are in the grip of the cult of peace. We want to relax and have the great God Almighty pat our heads and comfort us with peace of mind, peace of heart, peace of soul. This has become religion!

According to my Bible, there should be a people of God, a people called of God and subjected to a spiritual experience by God. Then they are to learn to walk in the way of Truth and the way of the scripture, producing the righteous fruit of the child of God no matter what world conditions may be.

But there is a great misunderstanding among us. Too many tend to think that we get the flower and the fragrance and the fruit of the Spirit by some kind of magical shortcut, instead of by cultivation. Meanwhile, our neighbors are waiting to see the likeness of Christ in our daily lives!

Lord, I don't want to be known as a Sunday-only Christian. I want my
faith in You to be obvious to my family, coworkers, and neighbors.
I pray that others will see the fruit of Your presence in my life today.

Human Psychology

God hath chosen the weak things of the world
to confound the things which are mighty.
1 CORINTHIANS 1:27

———— ❦ ————

To meet the kind of temptations and enemies confronting us in this world, it is not enough for us to stick out our chins, inflate our chests, and mutter the old refrain, "Never say die!"

Since I have been a Christian, I have had a negative reaction to that kind of human psychology. I do not mind saying that my favorite hymns are not those that exhort me to flex my biceps and tell the world where to get off! That is not my philosophy because it would put my confidence in the wrong place. If my faith, my belief, my confidence are in myself, then they cannot at the same time be resting in God!

The Bible tells us to believe in God and put our trust in Him. It warns us against having any confidence in the flesh. So I do not want some voice exhorting me to "Rise up, O man of God; go forth to face the foe"—and all of that. I would rather go to a place of prayer, meet God there, and then let Him face the world for me.

We rest our case completely on God—then our experiences proceed by faith, through faith, and in faith! Our victory must be God's victory first!

Dear Lord, the devotional this morning is a good reminder to me to
always go to You in prayer—first! I need to learn to wait upon You for
Your divine wisdom and guidance before I take any blundering steps.

The Halfway Christian Life

If any man serve me, him will my Father honour.
JOHN 12:26

The word *mediocre* comes from two Latin words and literally means "halfway to the peak." This makes it an apt description of the progress of many Christians. They are halfway up to the peak. They are not halfway to heaven but halfway up to where they ought to be, halfway between the valley and the peak. They are morally above the hardened sinner but they are spiritually beneath the shining saint.

Many have settled down right there, and the tragedy is that years ago some of you said, "I am not going to fail God. I am going to push my way up the mountain until I am at the top of the peak, at the highest possible point of experience with God in this mortal life!"

But you have done nothing about it. If anything, you have lost spiritual ground since that day. You are now a halfway Christian! You are lukewarm, neither hot nor cold. You are halfway up to the peak, halfway to where you could have been if you had pressed on.

Do we really think that this halfway Christian life is the best that Christ offers—the best that we can know? In the face of what Christ offers us, how can we settle for so little?

Dear Lord, when I meet You at the gate of heaven, I don't want my name to be listed under the column entitled: "Halfway Christians." I want You next to me, encouraging and exhorting me, as we scale the peak together.

....
....
....
....
....
....
....
....
....

Confidence in God

If our heart condemn us not, then have we confidence toward God.
1 JOHN 3:21

⸻

This is surely one of the great realizations that can come to us in the Christian life—we can put our complete confidence in the God who has revealed Himself to us!

It was a gracious day in my early Christian experience when I realized that it was not in God's character to pounce upon me in judgment. He knows that we are dust, and as our God He is loving and patient toward us.

If it were true that the Lord would put the Christian on the shelf every time he failed or blundered or did something wrong, I would have been a piece of statuary by this time!

It is surely true that God will bring judgment when judgment is necessary, but the scriptures say that judgment is God's strange work. Where there is a lifetime of rebellion, hardened unbeliefs and love of sin, judgment will come.

But God watches over us for spiritual growth and maturity, trying to teach us the necessity for fully trusting Him and coming to the place of complete distrust of ourselves. We have met God and can now say with Paul, "That the excellency of the power may be of God, and not of us" (2 Corinthians 4:7).

Lord, in this world there are not many "sure" things. But You,
O Lord, are 100 percent unchangeable. Your love is unfailing
toward us. Your patience is undying. I praise You, Lord.

....
....
....
....
....
....
....
....
....

Attributes of God

And there appeared unto them cloven tongues
like as of fire, and it sat upon each of them.
ACTS 2:3

What a broad world in which to roam; what an expansive sea in which to swim—and I speak of the God and Father of our Lord Jesus Christ! He is eternal, which means He is wholly independent of time. Time began in Him and will end in Him.

He is immutable, which means that He has never changed and can never change in any smallest measure. Being perfect, He cannot become more perfect. If He were to become less perfect, He would be less than God.

He is omniscient, which means that He knows in one free and effortless act all matter, all spirit, all relationships, all events. He is; and none of the limiting terms of creatures can apply to Him. Love and mercy and righteousness are His, and holiness so ineffable that no comparisons or figures will avail to express it.

In the pillar of fire, He dwelt. The fire that glowed in the "holy place" was called the Shekinah, the Presence. Then when the Old gave way to the New, He came at Pentecost as a fiery flame and rested upon each disciple!

What a day it will be, Lord, when Your children see You in all Your
glory and share in Your eternal riches. While we wait for
Your return, Father, help us to remain faithful to You.

....
....
....
....
....
....
....
....
....

Holiness Not an Option

*He that in these things serveth Christ
is acceptable to God, and approved of men.*
ROMANS 14:18

———— ❧ ————

*M*any believers in our day seem to consider the expression of true Christian holiness to be just a matter of personal option: "I have looked it over and considered it, but I don't buy it!"

But the apostle Peter clearly exhorts every Christian to holiness of life and conversation: God's children ought to be holy because God Himself is holy! I am of the opinion that New Testament Christians do not have the privilege of ignoring such apostolic injunctions.

There is something basically wrong with our Christianity and our spirituality if we can carelessly presume that if we do not like a biblical doctrine and choose to ignore it, there is no harm done. God has never instructed us that we should weigh His desires for us and His commandments to us in the balance of our own judgments—and then decide what we want to do about them.

We have the power within us to reject God's instruction—but where else shall we go? If we turn away from the authority of God's Word, to whose authority do we yield?

*Dear Lord, I truly desire to obey all of Your commandments. Yet in my
flesh I sometimes waver and fall short of Your holy standard. Forgive me,
Lord. Empower me by Your Spirit to gain victory over my weak areas.*

....
....
....
....
....
....
....
....

"Be Thou Exalted"

Be thou exalted, O God, above the heavens;
let thy glory be above all the earth.
PSALM 57:5

❧

*E*ssentially, God's gracious plan of salvation was wrought to bring about the restoration of a right relationship between men and women and their Creator.

The disobedience and fall of Adam and Eve destroyed the proper Creator-creature relation, in which, unknown to them, their true happiness lay.

Many of us are interested in walking with God and pleasing God and resting in the promises of God. We have discovered that such a life on this earth begins with a complete change in relationship between God and the sinner—a conscious and experienced change affecting the sinner's whole nature.

The atonement in Jesus' blood makes such a change judicially possible, and the working of the Holy Spirit makes it emotionally satisfying.

We must begin with God—and God must be the center of all we are and all we do. "Be thou exalted" is plainly the language of victorious spiritual experience and central to the life of God in the soul!

Heavenly Father, throughout this day my praise for You will continually be on my lips.
I am so grateful that You did not turn Your back on the human race when Adam and Eve
disobeyed You. Instead, You already had a plan for redemption in mind! Bless Your name!

....

....

....

....

....

....

....

....

....

Meekness and Rest

Blessed are the meek: for they shall inherit the earth.
MATTHEW 5:5

Jesus calls us to His rest, and meekness is His method! But, we may be assured, the meek man is not a human mouse afflicted with a sense of his own inferiority.

Rather, he may be in his moral life as bold as a lion and as strong as Samson, but he has stopped being fooled about himself. He has accepted God's estimate of his own life.

He knows that he is as weak and helpless as God has declared him to be. Paradoxically, he knows at the same time that he is, in the sight of God, of more importance than angels. In himself, nothing! In God, everything!

The truly meek man rests perfectly content to allow God to place His own values. He will be patient to wait for the day when everything will get its proper price tag and real worth will come into its own—when the righteous shall shine forth in the kingdom of their Father!

Having attained a place of soul rest, he is willing to wait for the coming of that day!

Lord, sometimes I get very upset at the injustices I see all around me. I don't want to appear obnoxious or angry in my encounters with others. Season my life with Your grace, Lord. You set the highest example for us to follow.

Weak in Discipleship

*Let us go forth therefore unto him
without the camp, bearing his reproach.*
HEBREWS 13:13

The absence of the concept of discipleship from present-day Christianity leaves a vacuum which men and women instinctively try to fill with a variety of substitutes.

One is a kind of pietism—an enjoyable feeling of affection for the person of our Lord, which is valued for itself and is wholly unrelated to cross bearing.

Another substitute is literalism—which manifests itself among us by insisting on keeping the letter of the Word while ignoring its spirit. It habitually fails to apprehend the inward meaning of Christ's words and contents itself with external compliance with the text.

A third substitute surely is zealous religious activity. "Working for Christ" has today been accepted as the ultimate test of godliness among all but a few evangelical Christians. Christ has become a project to be promoted or a cause to be served, instead of a Lord to be obeyed! To avoid the snare of unauthorized substitution, I recommend careful and prayerful study of the lordship of Christ and the discipleship of the believer!

*Dear Lord, I pray that there will be a growing interest in our
churches to implement training strategies that will help believers
take their relationship with Christ to a new, higher level.*

A Lower Level

O God, thou hast taught me from my youth:
and hitherto have I declared thy wondrous works.
PSALM 71:17

There are leaders and there are churches within the Christianity of our day who will surely answer for their failure to apply the disciplines of the New Testament to the present generation of young people.

Much of Christianity today does not hold to the necessity for disciplines in the Christian life. If we have any of God's concerns in our hearts, we must grieve over the lack of spirituality in the lives of great segments of professing Christian young people.

It is not my calling to assess blame. It is part of my Christian calling to proclaim the fact that no one, young or old, has the right to come to Jesus Christ and stake out their own conditions and terms.

Segments of Christianity have made every possible concession in efforts to win young people to Christ; but instead of converting them to Christ, they have "converted" Christianity to them. Too often they have come down to the modern level—playing, teasing, coaxing, and entertaining. In essence, they have been saying to them, "We will do everything as you want it," instead of giving them Christ's insistent word, "Take up your cross!"

O Lord, our young people are the future members and leaders of our
churches. To the degree that we teach them the ways of the Lord, they will
either be vibrant or weak believers. Lord, don't let us forsake our youth!

What Do We Love?

But we all. . .are changed into the same image from
glory to glory, even as by the Spirit of the Lord.
2 CORINTHIANS 3:18

---

*G*od wants us to recognize that human nature is in a formative state and that it is being changed into the image of the thing it loves.

Men and women are being molded by their affinities, shaped by their affections, and powerfully transformed by the artistry of their loves. In the unregenerate world of Adam, this produces, day by day, tragedies of cosmic proportions!

For His own children, our heavenly Father has provided right moral objects for admiration and love. They are not God but they are nearest to God; we cannot love Him without loving them.

I speak of His righteousness; and the heart drawn to righteousness will be repulsed in the same degree by iniquity. I speak of wisdom, and we admire the Hebrew prophets, who refused to divorce wisdom from righteousness.

I speak also of truth as another object of our Christian love. Our Lord Jesus Christ said, "I am the truth," and in so saying He joined truth to the Deity in inseparable union. Thus, to love God is to love the truth!

Father, help us to love Your entire Being—not just a few favorite attributes like Your grace and mercy and goodness. Enable us also to love Your attributes of holiness and justness.

The World Is Scared

Look up, and lift up your heads; for your redemption draweth nigh.
LUKE 21:28

⸻

A fear-stricken church cannot help a scared world; and it needs to be said that surely a fear-ridden Christian has never examined his or her defense!

No one can blame humans for being afraid. Beyond the continuing times of crisis and terror and violence, God has also warned that the world is in a baptism of fire, sooner or later. God has declared this by the voice of all of the holy prophets since time began—there is no escaping it!

Bible-reading Christians should be the last persons on earth to give way to hysteria. We have been given a prophetic preview of all those things that are to come to pass upon the earth. Can anything take us unaware?

We who are in God's secret place of safety must begin to talk and act like it! We, above all who dwell on the earth, should be calm, hopeful, buoyant, and cheerful. We will never convince the scared world that there is peace and assurance at the cross if we continue to exhibit the same fears as those who make no profession of Christianity!

Lord, I pray that Your peace will show through my behavior today.
Give me an opportunity to help someone who is dealing with fear or pain.

God's Exhortation

As he which hath called you is holy,
so be ye holy in all manner of conversation.
1 PETER 1:15

What is the apostle Peter saying to us in relaying to us God's exhortation: "Be ye holy as I am holy, and because I am holy"?

First is our own responsibility to bring our spiritual lives into line so that God may settle upon us with the Holy Spirit—with that quality of the Wonderful and the Mysterious and the Divine.

This is not something that can be humanly cultivated. This is something that we will not even be conscious we have. It is this quality of humility invaded by the presence of God which the church of our day lacks.

Oh, that we might yearn for the knowledge and presence of God in our lives from moment to moment, so that without human cultivation and without toilsome seeking, there would come upon us this enduement, this sweet and radiant fragrance that gives meaning to our witness!

I am willing to confess in humility that we need this in our day.

Dear Lord, if we seriously desired to be "holy," the only way we could do so
is through the empowerment of the Holy Spirit. By our own efforts, this would
not be possible, for the Bible says, "No one is righteous" (see Romans 3:10).

God's Validation

*Our gospel came not unto you in word only, but also
in power, and in the Holy Ghost, and in much assurance.*
1 THESSALONIANS 1:5

———

One marked characteristic of modern evangelicalism is its lack of assurance, resulting in a pathetic search for external evidence to corroborate its faith. It sets out bravely to declare its trust in Christ but is shortly overawed by the counter declarations of science and philosophy, and before long it is looking about for some collateral evidence to restore its confidence.

The faith of the Christian must rest upon Christ Himself. He is the mystery of godliness, a miracle, and emergence of the Deity into time and space for a reason and a purpose. He is complete in Himself and gains nothing from any human philosophy.

The New Testament points to Christ and says God now commands all men everywhere to repent: because He has appointed a day in which He will judge the world in righteousness by that Man He has ordained! Our assurance is the fact that He raised Him from the dead. In that, God validated forever the claims of Christ. He is who He said He was and what He said He was. So, Christ is enough! To have Him and nothing else is to be rich beyond all conceiving.

*Lord, it seems that mankind always wants to make something more
complex than it really is. Help us to be satisfied with simple faith in Jesus only!*

Our Unworthy Attitudes

God is greatly to be feared in the assembly of the saints,
and to be had in reverence of all them that are about him.
PSALM 89:7

Being a Christian does not exempt any of us from the necessity of self-examination, the necessity of dealing with injuries and unworthy mental attitudes.

I speak particularly of the attitudes and habits of many men and women who gather with us regularly as we come into the house of God to worship and pray.

Actually, as Christian men and women, we do have an appointment to meet with the King of kings and the Lord of lords. Just think of the preparations we would make if we suddenly had an invitation to meet the president of the United States in the White House.

But how many of us are lacking in respect and reverence when we come into the Christian church? Among us there are thoughtless tendencies to tell jokes on the way into church; to sit in the pews and let our minds rove about like sparrows; to daydream about where we have been and where we are going.

There is a great need for us to pray for grace that will improve our mental attitudes when we gather to honor our Savior and God!

Heavenly Father, I pray that I will never insult You by treating
You too casually when I go to church to worship You.

God-Hungry Souls

But we preach Christ crucified, unto the Jews
a stumblingblock, and unto the Greeks foolishness.
1 CORINTHIANS 1:23

———— ❧ ————

The Greek philosopher Pythagoras divided men into three classes:

1. seekers after knowledge;
2. seekers after honor;
3. seekers after gain.

I wonder why he failed to notice two other classes: those who are not seeking anything and those who are seekers after God.

Let us add them to his list:

4. Seekers after nothing. These are the human vegetables who live by their glands and their instincts. I refer to the millions of normal persons who have allowed their magnificent intellectual equipment to wither away from lack of exercise. Their reading matter is the sports page and the comic section; their music is whatever is popular and handy—and loud!

5. Seekers after God. I am thinking of men and women who are God-hungry souls though their numbers may not be large. By nature they are no better than the rest of mankind, and by practice they have sometimes been worse. The one sign of their divine election is their insatiable thirst after the Source of their being. Thank the Lord for seekers after God, and their destiny lies in the hand of the One who gave His only begotten Son to die for the life of the world!

Dear Lord, I want to be known among my family and
friends as a God-seeker. My destiny belongs to You, O Lord.

....
....
....
....
....
....
....
....

Longing to See Jesus

Behold, I come quickly: hold that fast
which thou hast, that no man take thy crown.
REVELATION 3:11

There is no doubt in my mind that millions of Christians in our day yearn within themselves to be ready to see the Lord Jesus when He appears. These are the saints of God who have a real understanding that what our Lord Jesus Christ is to us in our personal lives, moment by moment, is more important than merely dwelling on "what He did for us"!

I say this because a great segment of Christian theology emphasizes the "utility" of the cross on which Jesus died, rather than the Person who died on that cross for our sins.

Because of that view, many really have no emotional yearning for the return of Jesus. The best hope they know is a kind of intellectual, theological hope. But an intellectual knowledge of what the New Testament teaches about the return of Christ is surely a poor substitute for a love-inflamed desire to look on His face!

While we await Him, our Lord expects us to love one another, to worship Him together, and to send this gracious gospel to the ends of the earth.

Lord Jesus, what You did on the cross for us is mind-staggering,
but to know that the "story" doesn't end there is cause for great exulting!
I know that You are risen, because You live in me today!

Humility—and Worship

Humble yourselves therefore under the mighty hand of God.
1 PETER 5:6

---

*R*eal worship is, among other things, a feeling about the Lord God! It is in our hearts, and we must be willing to express it in an appropriate manner.

We can express our worship to God in many ways. But if we love the Lord and are led by His Holy Spirit, our worship will always bring a delighted sense of admiring awe and a sincere humility on our part.

There must be humility in the heart of the person who would worship God in spirit and in truth. So, the proud and lofty man or woman cannot worship God any more acceptably than can the proud devil himself!

Unfortunately, many of us are strictly "Santa Claus Christians." We need to go on from an elementary kind of love, in which we think of God as putting up a kind of Christmas tree and putting all our gifts underneath. We need, rather, to be delighted in the presence of utter, infinite excellence!

Such worship will have the ingredient of fascination, the personality captured by the presence of God!

*Father, I pray for many of our churches today that think of worship
as a mode of entertainment. O God, help these churches to stop focusing
on their own pleasures and lead them to delight in You alone.*

Heavenly Wisdom

For the LORD giveth wisdom: out of his mouth
cometh knowledge and understanding.
PROVERBS 2:6

The writer of the Proverbs in the Old Testament taught that true spiritual knowledge is the result of a visitation of heavenly wisdom. It is a kind of baptism of the Spirit of Truth that comes to God-fearing men and women. This wisdom is always associated with righteousness and humility; it is never found apart from godliness and true holiness of life.

We need to learn and declare again the ministry of wisdom from above. It is apparent that we cannot know God by the logic of reason. Through reason we can only know about God. The deeper mysteries of God remain hidden to us until we have received illumination from above. We were created with a capacity to know spiritual things—that potential died when Adam and Eve sinned. Thus, "dead in sin" is a description of that part of our being in which we should be able to know God in conscious awareness.

Christ's atoning death enabled our Lord and Savior to take God the Father with one hand and man with the other and introduce us. Jesus enables us to find God very quickly!

Thank You, Father, that You provided a way—the only way—to bring sinful people back into a right relationship with You. That one way is through faith in Jesus Christ. Thank You, Lord, that You did not leave us lost and hopeless.

Guilty Silence

*Peter and John answered. . . We cannot but
speak the things which we have seen and heard.*
ACTS 4:19–20

———————

*I*n this unfriendly world, is our Christian deportment too fearful and cowardly? Is this generation guilty of the sin of silence?

The Bible has much to say in praise of prudence, but it has nothing but condemnation for the coward! It is also plainly taught in the New Testament that the soul that is too timid to own and confess Christ before men will be denied before the Father in heaven.

It is apparent that Christian men and women are not speaking out as they should when the Enemy stalks into the very sanctuary and pollutes the holy place! Fun and frolic, films and fiction, Hollywood ideals and religious entertainment, big-business techniques and cheap worldly philosophies now overrun the sanctuary. The grieved Holy Spirit broods over the chaos but no light breaks forth.

Could it be that too many of God's true children—and especially the preachers—are sinning against God by guilty silence? Those who do speak up on the side of Truth will pay a price for their boldness, but the results will be worth it!

*Lord, I pray for Hollywood filmmakers, secular businessmen, and unscrupulous
politicians. Impress upon each one their need for a Savior—and then
help them to change the world through their godly influence.*

Fun and Religion

Thou therefore endure hardness. . .
if we suffer, we shall also reign with him.
2 TIMOTHY 2:3, 12

———✦———

History reveals that times of suffering for the Christian Church have also been times of looking upward. Tribulation has always sobered God's people and encouraged them to look for and yearn after the return of their Lord.

Our present preoccupation with the world may be a warning of bitter days to come. God will wean us from the earth some way—the easy way if possible, the hard way if necessary. It is up to us!

It is apparent that many now think Christianity is jolly good fun—another and higher form of entertainment; because Christ has done all the suffering. He has shed all the tears. He has carried all the crosses. So, we have but to enjoy the benefits of His heartbreak!

The "work of Christ" has been stressed until it has eclipsed the Person of Christ. We need to reexamine much of popular fundamentalist theology which emphasizes the utility of the cross, rather than the beauty of the One who died on that cross.

Merciful Father, I pray today for the silent heroes who faithfully serve
Jesus throughout the 10/40 Window in the face of extreme pressure.

....

....

....

....

....

....

....

....

....

....

He Is Our Victory

Therefore glorify God in your body,
and in your spirit, which are God's.
1 CORINTHIANS 6:20

———— ❦ ————

We will never be delivered from the pride of our own selfish condition until we allow the Holy Spirit of God to demonstrate God's own victory within us.

I have had disobedient believers assure me: "But, Mr. Tozer, I already know that I am bad. I am a believer in total depravity!" My reply: it is possible to be a confirmed believer in total depravity and still be as proud as Lucifer; to still trust in yourself in such a way that the face of God is hidden and you are kept from spiritual victory.

Our concern here is not with theological depravity. There is no argument with the fact that as soon as we are big enough to sin, we go directly into the business of sinning! But God is trying to reveal by His Holy Spirit the utter weakness of the child of God who is still putting his trust in himself.

Why does it take us so long to put our complete trust in God? He has made it so simple, so rewarding to yield what we are to Him!

Lord, enable me to yield myself fully to You so that I will experience
spiritual victory. Excise any remnant of pride and self-reliance in my life.

God Has the Answers

LORD, make me to know. . .the measure
of my days. . .that I may know how frail I am.
PSALM 39:4

We can all learn something from David's prayer—for none of us has all of the answers! David had come through the trying experiences of life and was now unsure about the things he once thought he knew. In the autumn of his life, I think David was a more relaxed man and more dependent on the divine answers.

I found a lesson in this for myself and I pass it on.

Some time ago I preached for a week in Rochester, New York. At the conclusion and before the benediction, the chairman of the congregation told the audience: "We have enough time for questions. Mr. Tozer will answer any questions you have."

This was news to me, so I got up and said: "Mr. Chairman, you are twenty-five years too late! Twenty-five years ago I could have answered questions on almost any subject, but now I beg to be excused!"

In our Christian life and experience, it is a blessed thing to find out that we do not have to know everything after all!

Lord, instead of getting simpler, life seems to get more complex year after year. I need
Your divine help to sort out the confusion, Lord. Thank You that I can trust in You—always.

Love Not This World

*The god of this world hath blinded
the minds of them which believe not.*
2 CORINTHIANS 4:4

———⚬———

*O*ur Lord Jesus Christ drew a sharp line between the kingdom of God and this present world. He has instructed us that no one can be at the same time a lover of both!

The apostles stood together in the New Testament teachings that it is necessary for a person to turn the back upon the world and have no fellowship with it.

What, then, is this world against which we are warned?

It is the familiar world of human society. No Christian need fail to recognize it, providing he wants to know what it is. Here are a few of its marks of identification:

1. Unbelief. To have fellowship with those who live in unbelief is the love of the world. Religion without the Son of God is worldly religion.
2. Impenitence. The worldling shrugs off his sin and continues in it. The Christian mourns over his sin and is comforted.
3. Godless philosophies. Men and women of this world accept the sufficiency of this world and make no provision for any other, esteeming earth above heaven.
4. Externalism. The man of the earth lives only for the world around him—he has no kingdom within him!

*Lord, I pray specifically that You will undo what the god of this world has done—
that is, blinded the minds of unbelievers. Then, once they are unblinded, I pray that Your
Spirit will do its work of convicting the consciences of sinners everywhere. Foil the Evil One!*

....

....

....

....

....

....

God's Beneficiary

To an inheritance incorruptible,
and undefiled, and that fadeth not away.
1 PETER 1:4

———— ❧ ————

*T*he Holy Spirit has made it plain throughout the scriptures that generally whatever God does becomes a means toward something else that He is planning to do.

Therefore, when God elects a man or woman, it does not mean that he or she can sit down and at ease announce: "I have arrived! Put a period there and write 'finis' across my experience!"

No, of course not! God begets us into His provision, and that which is still before us always is greater than that which is behind us.

Peter was not using figures of speech. He said plainly his persecuted brethren were believers in Jesus Christ, elect and begotten! The electing and the begetting were means leading into a hope and an inheritance—the true Christian believer is actually the beneficiary of God!

This is not a figure—not just a poetic phrase. It is openly taught from Genesis to Revelation that God, being who He is, His beneficences are infinite and limitless!

Gracious Father, by Your grace I am saved. But I know so many people who are
living in the shadow of their own sin—and they don't even realize it! Lord,
commission people from our numerous churches to go and tell lost people about Jesus.

....
....
....
....
....
....
....
....
....
....
....
....

Decision! Decision!

*We then, as workers together with him, beseech
you also that ye receive not the grace of God in vain.*
2 CORINTHIANS 6:1

I believe there must be great throngs of men and women who keep on assuring themselves that they will "make it" into the kingdom of God by a kind of heavenly osmosis! They have a fond hope that there is a kind of unconscious "leaking through" of their personalities into the walls of the kingdom.

That is a vain hope. No one ever comes to God by an automatic or unconscious process; it does not happen that way at all!

The individual man or woman must make the choice—and on that point we must be dogmatic. We have the Book, the Word of God. We know that God has revealed Himself through the giving of Jesus Christ, the eternal Son. We know that the saving message is the gospel—the good news of our Lord Jesus Christ.

There is no way that God can come to us and forgive us and restore us to the position of son or daughter until we consciously let Him! This is an authentic experience of the grace and mercy of God—we have made our decision!

*Lord, I pray that pastors in our churches will make it clear from their
pulpits that in order to be saved, people must acknowledge their sin before
God and receive Jesus Christ as their Savior and Lord of their new life.*

Our Daily Problems

There hath no temptation taken you but such
as is common to man: but God is faithful.
1 CORINTHIANS 10:13

Christian believers are wrongly taught if they believe that the Christian life is a guarantee against human trials and problems. If they believe that, they have mistaken earth for heaven and expect conditions here below which can never be realized until we reach the better world above.

There is a sense in which God makes no difference between the saint and the sinner. He makes His sun to rise on the evil and on the good, and He sends rain on the just and the unjust (Matthew 5:45). It is strange that we rarely notice the other side of this truth: that God also visits His children with the usual problems common to all the sons of men.

If we cannot remove our problems, then we must pray for grace to endure them without murmuring. We will learn too that problems patiently endured will work for our spiritual perfecting. Think of our Lord and Savior—He was surrounded by enemies from the moment of His birth. They constituted a real and lasting problem which He simply had to endure for the period of His earthly life. He escaped it only by dying!

Lord, I pray for Your strength to carry me through the problems I will be facing today.
Thank You that Your Spirit is a "resident" Helper in my life.

We Trust God's Plan

And cried with a loud voice, saying, Salvation to our
God which sitteth upon the throne, and unto the Lamb.
REVELATION 7:10

We who believe in God's faithfulness and in the inspired scriptures are certain that the world's redemption does not lie in the hands of mankind. I cannot tell you how glad I am that this is at least one thing that we humans cannot bungle!

The plan of salvation and the day of consummation that is coming are in God's eternal plan. The power in redemption is God's power. Only the worthy Lamb of God could die in our place. This is God's way of doing things, not our way!

Millions have feared the threat of worldwide communism with silly, frightened people declaring they would "rather be Red than dead!" But communism cannot prevail because it is raised in a materialistic teaching that there is no God, no Christ, no heaven, and no hell. Communism cannot prevail because our God in heaven has His plan and program, not just for this earth, but for all of His vast created universe.

There is no human being and no human philosophy or force able to wrest dominion from our living God. Are we being faithful in our witness and warning of the wrath of the Lamb—the crucified, resurrected, outraged Lamb of God?

Lord, one day Your plan is going to trump every false religion
and man-made philosophy. What a glorious, exciting day that will be!

Root of Bitterness

Looking diligently. . .lest any root of bitterness springing up trouble you.
HEBREWS 12:15

———— ❦ ————

*I*t is on record that Charles Spurgeon made this comment about a man who was well-known for his bitter and resentful spirit: "May the grass grow green on his grave when he dies, for nothing ever grew around him while he lived!"

The sad and depressing bitter soul will compile a list of slights at which it takes offense and will watch over itself like a mother bear over her cubs. And the figure is apt, for the resentful heart is always surly and suspicious like a she-bear!

In our Christian fellowship, what can be more depressing than to find a professed Christian defending his or her supposed rights and bitterly resisting any attempt to violate them? Such a Christian has never accepted the way of the cross. The sweet graces of meekness and humility are unknown to that person. Every day he or she grows harder and more acrimonious, trying to defend reputation, right, ministry, against imagined foes.

Is there a cure for this? Yes! The cure is to die to self and rise with Christ into newness of life!

Lord, if there is any unpleasantness or bitterness inside me,
please eradicate it so that my immature behavior will not
be a stumbling block to those who are seeking You.

No Place for Fantasy

I. . .am persuaded that he is able to keep that which
I have committed unto him against that day.
2 TIMOTHY 1:12

Let me tell you about the true Christian, the Bible Christian, and his view of this troubled and uncertain world in which he lives.

He is not the worldly-wise, smiling optimist who draws his comfort from a denial of the facts or bases his hopes on false expectation of peaceful intentions among nations.

Rather, he is of all men the truest realist. He will have nothing to do with fantasy—he wants to know the facts—and he does not hesitate to face up to any truth wherever he finds it.

He knows the world is lost on a wide area, and that the Christian alone knows the way to the desired haven. For in the Bible, and there only, is found the chart to tell us where we are in this rough and unknown ocean.

He knows that the day when Christians should meekly apologize is over; that they can get the world's attention not by trying to compromise and please, but by boldly declaring the truth of divine revelation with the affirmative signature, "Thus saith the Lord!"

Lord, I pray that Your Word will penetrate the minds and
hearts of many unbelievers today. There's no time to wait.

Why Be Artificial?

Except ye. . .become as little children,
ye shall not enter into the kingdom of heaven.
MATTHEW 18:3

Christian men and women who have sincerely knelt at the feet of Jesus and have surrendered themselves to His meekness have found a comforting and satisfying place of rest. They have discovered that we do not have to worry about what people think of us—as long as God is pleased!

We are no longer plagued with the heavy burden of artificiality. Think of the millions who live in secret fear that someday they will be careless and by chance an enemy or a friend will be allowed to peep into their poor, empty souls. Bright people are tense and alert in fear that they may be trapped into saying something common or stupid.

It is plain to see that the heart of the artificial worldling is breaking under the burden, under the weight of pretense and pride.

To men and women everywhere, Jesus says, "Come unto Me, and I will give you rest!" He offers His grace and His mercy—blessed relief that comes when we accept ourselves for what we are and cease to pretend!

Thank You, Lord, that I can come to You exactly as I am
and that You accept me completely. You are a loving, safe haven.

What We Shall Be

For whom he did foreknow, he also did
predestinate to be conformed to the image of his Son.
ROMANS 8:29

———— ❦ ————

We must take a high view of what God has done for us in consummating the plan of salvation for a lost race!

The supreme work of Christ in redemption is not just to save us from hell, but to restore us to Godlikeness again. Paul has confirmed this in Romans 8:29, "Whom he did foreknow, he also did predestinate to be conformed to the image of his Son."

While perfect restoration to the divine image awaits the day of Christ's appearing, the work of restoration is going on now. There is a slow but steady transmutation of the base metal of human nature into the gold of Godlikeness effected by the faith-filled gaze of the soul at the glory of God—the face of Jesus Christ!

We have already moved from what we were to what we are, and we are now moving toward what we shall be. To become like God is and must be the supreme goal of all moral creatures!

Lord, there are days when I feel I am losing ground in my spiritual growth.
Help me today to move closer to the image of God's Son.

Why Do Birds Sing?

And God created. . .every winged fowl after his kind:
and God saw that it was good.
GENESIS 1:21

———— ❧ ————

I am thankful I have found a promise from the God of all grace that deals with the "long term" and the eternal. I belong to a body of plain people who believe the truth revealed in the Bible. These are the people who believe that God in the beginning made the heavens and the earth and all things that are therein.

Yes, these plain, believing people will tell you that God created the flowers to be beautiful and the birds to sing, so that men and women could enjoy them. We believe that God made the birds to warble and harmonize as though they were tuned to a harp.

But the scientist disagrees, saying, "It is simply biological. The bird sings only to attract a mate."

Actually, the God who made the birds is the Chief Musician of the universe. He made the harps in those little throats and said, "Go and sing!" Thankfully, the birds obeyed, and they have been singing and praising God ever since they were created!

I praise You, Lord, for the beautiful world You created for Your enjoyment and ours.
I pray that Your Spirit will move in the hearts of scientists and physicists who
recognize the earthly wonders but who refuse to believe in a Creator God.

"I Will Arise and Go"

I will arise and go to my father,
and will say unto him, Father, I have sinned.
LUKE 15:18

When Jesus told the story of the Prodigal Son, He was giving our lost society a graphic picture of more than a willful son or a backslidden man.

Years ago I spent time alone with God in prayer and supplication, asking the Spirit of God to aid me in the comprehension of the parable of the Prodigal Son. I have relied upon the understanding which I believe God gave me.

I believe the Prodigal Son is God's clear-cut picture to us of the entire human race that went out to the pigsty in Adam—and came back to the Father in Christ!

The most telling part of the parable is the fact that the errant son "came to himself"—and that speaks to us of the reality and necessity of repentance. He could repent and turn and seek forgiveness because he knew that his Father had not changed. He knew the character of his Father. Except for that knowledge, he could never have said: "I will arise and go to my Father!"

Brethren, all of us who have come back to God by faith in our Lord Jesus Christ have found, as did the prodigal, that the Father in heaven has not changed at all!

I praise You, Lord, that nothing about You has changed. And nothing that has happened in this world has caught You by surprise. You are our faithful, loving, and just Father.

Unwilling to Yield

Yield yourselves unto God,
as those that are alive from the dead.
ROMANS 6:13

———

I know there are people who hear me preach regularly who will never consider changing their way of living. They will go "underground" before they will do that!

Our situation is not an isolated case. There are millions of men and women with an understanding of the revelation of God in Jesus Christ, who are still not willing to receive and commit themselves to Him whom the very angels and stars and rivers receive. They hesitate and they delay because they know God is asking the abdication of their own selfish little kingdom and interests.

This is the tragedy of mankind, my brethren! We have rejected Him from our lives because we must have our own way. But until Jesus Christ is sincerely received, there can be no knowledge of salvation, nor any understanding of the things of God.

The little, selfish, sinful man rejects the Son of God. While he is still enumerating the things he deserves, the Son of God stands outside.

My brethren, I repeat: this is the great tragedy of mankind!

Dear Lord, we all know of some people in our lives who are aware of the truth of the gospel but who choose to live apart from God. I pray that Your Spirit will cause each of these people to feel an overwhelming sense of dread concerning their future destiny.

....
....
....
....
....
....
....
....
....

A Christian Virtue

Let brotherly love continue.
HEBREWS 13:1

———⟡———

I am being very frank about this and I hope I am being helpful: do not ever say you are not right with God because you like some people better than others!

I believe you can be right with God and still not like the way some people behave. It is easy to love those who are friendly; others rub us the wrong way or perhaps they cut us down.

The writer to the Hebrews has appealed to us as Christian believers to "let brotherly love continue"—in other words, "never stop loving one another in the Lord."

Here is what I have found: It is possible to love people in the Lord even though you may not like their boorish or distasteful human traits. We still love them for Jesus' sake!

Yes, I believe you can be right with God and still not like the way some people behave. Our admonition is to love them in a larger and more comprehensive way because we are all one in Christ Jesus. This kind of love is indeed a Christian virtue!

Father, help me to love people for Jesus' sake even
when they do or say things that annoy or hurt me.

....
....
....
....
....
....
....
....
....
....
....

"Toward the Mark"

Forgetting those things which are behind. . .I press toward the mark.
PHILIPPIANS 3:13–14

———— ❧ ————

*I*t is one of the devil's oldest tricks to discourage Christian believers by causing them to look back at what they once were. It is indeed the enemy of our souls who makes us forget that we are never at the end of God's love.

No one will make progress with God until the eyes are lifted to the faithfulness of God and we stop looking at ourselves!

Our instructions in the New Testament all add up to the necessity of looking forward in faith—and not spending our time looking back or just looking within.

Brethren, our Lord is more than able to take care of our past. He pardons instantly and forgives completely, and His blood makes us worthy!

The goodness of God is infinitely more wonderful than we will ever be able to comprehend. If the "root of the matter" is in you and you are born again, God is prepared to start with you where you are!

Thank You, Lord, that we can never reach the end of Your love for us.
Your love, like all Your attributes, is never-ending.

The Winsome Saints

Being filled with the fruits of righteousness, which are by Jesus Christ.
PHILIPPIANS 1:11

———— ❧ ————

*M*uch of Christianity overlooks the fact that if we are led by the Spirit of God and if we show forth the love of God this world needs, we become the "winsome saints."

The strange and wonderful thing about it is that truly winsome and loving saints do not even know about their attractiveness. The great saints of the past did not know they were great saints. If someone had told them, they would not have believed it, but those around them knew that Jesus was living His life in them.

I think we join the winsome saints when God's purposes in Christ become clear to us. We join them when we begin to worship God because He is who He is! Brethren, God is not a charity case—He is not some frustrated foreman who cannot find enough help.

Let us remember that God has never actually needed any of us—not one! But we pretend that He does, and we make a big thing of it when someone agrees "to work for the Lord."

God is trying to call us back to that for which He created us—to worship and to enjoy Him forever!

Thank You, Lord, for the faithful men and women who have gone before us.
Thank You for the example of their lives that delighted in having close fellowship with You.

Failure of Religion

Having a form of godliness,
but denying the power thereof.
2 TIMOTHY 3:5

---

*M*illions of men and women refuse to face up to the fact that religion, in and of itself, is not enough for the sinner's need.

It is amazing how many things religious people want to do to you. They can start with infant baptism and end up with the last rites when you are 108 years old—and all of that time they will manipulate you, maul you, and sweet massage your soul. When it is all done, you are just what you were. You are just a decorated and massaged sinner—a sinner who did not eat meat, or on the other hand, a sinner who did eat fish!

When religion has done all it can, you are still a sinner who either went to church or did not go to church. Religion can put us on the roll and educate us and train us and instruct us. But after all that, there is still something within our beings that cries, "Eternity is in my heart and I have not found anything to satisfy it!"

Only our Lord Jesus Christ is enough to satisfy the eternal longing in our souls.

Lord, deepening my relationship with You is more important
than my involvement in "religious traditions" that have
nothing to do with my eternal destiny. I love You, Lord Jesus.

Striving for Numbers

Whatsoever things are true, whatsoever
things are honest. . .think on these things.
PHILIPPIANS 4:8

———————

*I*n Christian circles today, the church that can show an impressive quantitative growth is frankly envied and imitated by other ambitious churches. Numbers, size, and amounts seem to be very nearly all that matters—with a corresponding lack of emphasis on quality!

This is the age of the Laodiceans. The great goddess, Numbers, is worshipped with fervent devotion, and all things religious are brought before her for examination. Her Old Testament is the financial report, and her New Testament is the membership roll. To these she appeals as the test of spiritual growth and the proof of success or failure in most Christian endeavors.

A little acquaintance with the Bible should show this up for the heresy it is. To judge anything spiritual by statistics is to judge by something other than scriptural judgment. Yet this is being done every day by ministers, church boards, and denominational leaders. And hardly anyone seems to notice the deep and dangerous error!

Lord, I pray this morning for the pastor and elders of my church,
that their chief desire will be to invite the Holy Spirit of God
into our church to do His refining work in the lives of our people.

OCTOBER 8

"Someone" Is There

Seek the LORD, and his strength: seek his face evermore.
PSALM 105:4

———

Wherever faith has proved itself to be real, it has inevitably had upon it a sense of the "present" God. The holy scriptures possess in marked degree this feeling of actual encounter with a real Person.

The men and women of the Bible talked with God. They spoke to Him and heard Him speak in words they could understand. With Him they held person-to-person converse, and a sense of shining reality is upon their words and deeds.

This sense of "Someone there" filled the members of the early Christian church with abiding wonder. The solemn delight which those early disciples knew sprang straight from the conviction that there was One in the midst of them—they were in the very presence of God!

This sense of "Someone" there makes religion invulnerable to critical attack. It secures the mind against collapse under the battering of the enemy. Those who worship the God who is present may ignore the objection of unbelieving men!

*Lord, as I go out into the world today, may Your presence be
very real in my life. Thank You for always being there for me.*

Everyday Worship

Their heart is far from me. . .in vain they do worship me.
MATTHEW 15:8–9

---

*I*t is my experience that the totality of our Christian lives—our entire attitude as persons—must be toward the worship of God!

If you do not know the presence of God in your office, your factory, your home, then God is not in the church you attend either!

I became a Christian when I was a young man working in a tire factory in Akron, Ohio. I remember my work there—but I remember my worship there too! I had plenty of worshipful tears in my eyes. No one ever asked me about them, but I would not have hesitated to explain them.

You can learn to use certain skills until they are automatic. I became so skillful that I could do my work and then I could worship God even while my hands were busy.

If the love of God is in us and the Spirit of God is breathing praise within us, all the musical instruments in heaven are suddenly playing in full support! Even our thoughts become a sanctuary in which God can dwell.

Dear Lord, I pray that Your Spirit will so fill me today
that my heart and mind will overflow in praise to You.

Misusing the Bible

Which they. . .wrest, as they do also the other
scriptures, unto their own destruction.
2 PETER 3:16

❦

I believe that everything in the Bible is true, but to attempt to make the Bible a textbook for science is to misunderstand it completely and tragically!

It has become a fairly popular practice for Bible teachers to claim to find in the scriptures confirmation of almost every recent discovery made by science. Apparently no one noticed that the scientist had to find it before the Bible teacher could, and it never seemed to occur to anyone to wonder why, if it was there in the Bible in such plain sight, it took several thousand years and the help of science before anyone saw it.

In recent years, the Bible has been "recommended" for many other purposes from the one for which it was written. The purpose of the Bible is to bring men to Christ, to make them holy and prepare them for heaven. Any manipulation of the scriptures to make them speak peace to the natural man is evil and can only lead to ruin!

Thank You, Lord, for providing—and preserving—the Word of God
through successive generations. I pray that it will get more exposure
in our churches and through creative media formats reach more people.

....

....

....

....

....

....

....

....

....

....

Game of Pious Words

If any man offend not in word, the same is a perfect man,
and able also to bridle the whole body.
JAMES 3:2

Do you realize that most men play at religion as they play at games? Religion itself being of all games the one most universally played.

The Church has its "fields" and its "rules" and its equipment for playing the game of pious words. It has its devotees, both laymen and professionals, who support the game with their money and encourage it with their presence, but who are no different in life or character from many who take no interest in religion at all.

As an athlete uses a ball, so do many of us use words—words spoken and words sung, words written and words uttered in prayer. We throw them swiftly across the field; we learn to handle them with dexterity and grace—and gain as our reward the applause of those who have enjoyed the game. In the games men play there are no moral roots. It is a pleasant activity which changes nothing and settles nothing, at last.

Sadly, in the religious game of pious words, after the pleasant meeting no one is basically any different from what he had been before!

Lord, I pray that the words I speak and the songs I sing will be
acceptable to You. My faith is too important to me to play religious games.

....
....
....
....
....
....
....
....

Light—and Shadows

Charity suffereth long, and is kind.
1 CORINTHIANS 13:4

———— ❧ ————

a person once called me to ask this question: "Mr. Tozer, do you think a person who is really a Christian can hurt another Christian?" There is no easy answer—but I had to reply: "Yes, I think so."

Why is it that a man can be on his knees one day, praying earnestly, and the next day be guilty of offending or injuring another Christian? I think it is because we are halfway between heaven and hell. It is because the light—and the shadows—fall upon us.

The best answer is that we are being saved out of all these contradictions we find in our lifetime. Perhaps on this earth we will never be able to comprehend fully the awful, terrible price the Lord of all beauty paid to gain our redemption—to save His people from the ugliness of sin.

If you do not know Him and worship Him, if you do not long to reside where He is, if you have never known wonder and ecstasy in your soul because of His crucifixion and resurrection, your claim of Christianity has little foundation!

Lord, I know that I hurt some people in the past with the words I used. I can see now that I was immature at that time. Help me to continue to grow in Your grace, Lord.

The Realities of Heaven

Let not your heart be troubled. . .
I go to prepare a place for you.
JOHN 14:1–2

---

*M*uch of the secularism and rationalism of our times dismisses the Christian view and teaching about heaven as "nothing more than hopeful thinking."

But the Christian's promised hope of future blessedness is founded upon the fullest and plainest revelations of the Old and New Testaments. That it accords with the most sacred yearnings of the human breast does not weaken it, but serves rather to confirm the truth of it, because the One who made the heart might be expected also to make provision for the fulfillment of its deepest longings.

God's promises are made to the Christian believer, who generally has difficulty picturing himself as inheriting such bliss as the scriptures describe. The reason is not hard to discover, for the most godly Christian is the one who knows himself best, and no one who knows himself will believe that he deserves anything better than hell. But even justice is on his side, for it is written, "If we confess our sins, [God] is faithful and just to forgive us our sins, and to cleanse us from all unrighteousness" (1 John 1:9).

Dear Lord, thank You that so many of Your promises in scripture have already come true—
especially the advent of Your Son, Jesus. You are a faithful, holy God in whom there is no
guile or deceit. Your promise of heaven is just as real as the promise of a Savior. Bless You!

OCTOBER 14

God at the Center

He built there an altar, and called the place
Elbethel: because there God appeared unto him.
GENESIS 35:7

———————

After Jacob's first memorable encounter with God in the wilderness, he called the place Bethel, which means "the house of God." Many years later, after he had suffered and sinned and repented, and discovered the worthlessness of all earthly things, he renamed the place, El-beth-el; literally "the God of the house of God."

Thus Jacob had shifted his emphasis from the sacred place to the God he had met there. God Himself now took the center of his interest.

We need to consider that many Christians never get beyond Beth-el. God is in their thoughts but He has not been given first place. Faithfulness to the local church is a good thing; but when the church becomes so large and important that it hides God from our eyes, it may become a good thing wrongly used.

Always God must be first—and we ought never forget that the church was never intended to substitute for God! What is our primary interest? Is it Beth-el or El-beth-el? Is it my church or my Lord? Is it my creed or my Christ?

> *Father God, I want You to have first place in my life and in the lives of the*
> *people in my local church. Help us to focus on You so that we can enjoy Your*
> *presence wherever we are—at church, at home, in the office, or on vacation.*

Resources That Endure

I wish above all things that thou mayest prosper
and be in health, even as thy soul prospereth.
3 JOHN 2

The people of this world have always fussed and argued over this world's resources—hope for life, health, financial prosperity, international peace, and a set of favorable circumstances. These resources are good in their own way, but they have a fatal defect—they are uncertain and transitory! Today we have them; tomorrow they are gone.

It is this way with all earthly things since sin came to upset the beautiful order of nature and made the human race victims of chance and change.

We desire for all of God's children a full measure of every safe and pure blessing that the earth and sky might unite to bring them. But if in the sovereign will of God things go against us, what do we have left? If life and health are placed in jeopardy, what about our everlasting resources?

If the world's foundations crumble, we still have God and in Him we have everything essential to our ransomed beings forever! We have Christ, who died for us; we have the scriptures, which can never fail; we have the faithful Holy Spirit. If worst comes to worst here below, we have our Father's house and our Father's welcome!

Lord, Your Word says that everything we have belongs to You
(see 1 Chronicles 29:16). You own my possessions; You own me!
Enable me and my family to loosely grip the things of this world.

Child of Two Worlds

Jesus answered, My kingdom is not of this world.
JOHN 18:36

In the kingdom of God, the surest way to lose something is to try to protect it, and the best way to keep it is to let it go. This was the word of our Lord Jesus Christ: "If any man will come after me, let him deny himself, and take up his cross" (Luke 9:23).

Christ turned from the fallen world of Adam and spoke about another world altogether, a world where Adam's philosophy is invalid and his technique inoperative. He spoke of the kingdom of God whose laws are exactly opposite to those of the kingdom of men.

So, the true Christian is a child of two worlds. He lives among fallen men, but when he is regenerated, he is called to live according to the laws and principles that underlie the new kingdom. He may, then, find himself trying to live a heavenly life after an earthly pattern—and this is what Paul called "carnal" living. That is why it is vitally important to move up into the life of the Spirit of God. Give up your earthly "treasures" and the Lord will keep them for you unto life eternal!

O Lord, help me to elevate my living today into the life of the Spirit of God.
Some days that is just not easy to do! Sustain me today, Lord, when I grow spiritually weak.

A Sacred Gift of Seeing

Your young men shall see visions,
and your old men shall dream dreams.
ACTS 2:17

As God created us, we all have to some degree the power to imagine. That imagination is of great value in the service of God may be denied by some persons who have erroneously confused the word *imagination* with the word *imaginary*.

The gospel of Jesus Christ has no truck with things imaginary. The most realistic book in the world is the Bible. God is real. Men are real and so is sin and so are death and hell! The presence of God is not imaginary; neither is prayer the indulgence of a delightful fancy.

The value of the cleansed imagination in the sphere of religion lies in its power to perceive in natural things shadows of things spiritual. A purified and Spirit-controlled imagination is the sacred gift of seeing—the ability to peer beyond the veil and gaze with astonished wonder upon the beauties and mysteries of things holy and eternal.

The stodgy pedestrian mind does no credit to Christianity!

Lord, thank You for the vision You gave to John, which is recorded
in the book of Revelation. What a beautiful picture of heaven
he describes! Such a view makes this earthly pilgrimage tolerable.

Man's Empty Promises

*For when they shall say, Peace and safety;
then sudden destruction cometh upon them.*
1 THESSALONIANS 5:3

———⚬———

*W*e have listened throughout our lifetime to the continuing promises of peace and progress made by the educators and the legislators and the scientists, but so far they have failed to make good on any of them.

Perhaps it is an ironic thought that fallen men, though they cannot fulfill their promises, are always able to make good on their threats!

Well, true peace is a gift of God and today it is found only in the minds of innocent children and in the hearts of trustful Christian believers. Only Jesus could say: "My peace I give unto you. . . . Let not your heart be troubled; neither let it be afraid!" (see John 14:27).

Surely the "great" of this world have underestimated the wisdom of the Christian, after all. When the Day of the Lord comes, he may stand like Abraham above the burning plain and watch the smoke rising from the cities that forgot God. The Christian will steal a quick look at Calvary and know that this judgment is past!

*Thank You, Lord, for Your Spirit who apportions to our souls a kind of
"peace which passeth all understanding" (Philippians 4:7). Only You can
provide that kind of peace in a world dominated by war and conflict.*

A Libel Against God

He that believeth not God hath made him a liar.
1 JOHN 5:10

Human sin began with loss of faith in God! When our mother Eve listened to Satan's sly innuendos against the character of God, she began to entertain a doubt of His integrity—and right there the doors were opened to the incoming of every possible evil, and darkness settled upon the world.

Relationship between moral beings is by confidence, and confidence rests upon character, which is a guarantee of conduct. God is a being of supreme moral excellence, possessing in infinite perfection all the qualities that constitute holy character. He deserves and invites the unreserved confidence of every moral creature, including man. Any proper relation to Him must be by confidence—that is, faith.

Idolatry is the supreme sin, and unbelief is the child of idolatry. Both are libels on the Most High and Most Holy. John wrote: "He that believeth not God hath made him a liar" (1 John 5:10). A God who would lie is a God without character.

Repentance is a man's sincere apology for distrusting God for so long, and faith is throwing oneself upon Christ in complete confidence. Thus by faith reconciliation is achieved between God and man!

Heavenly Father, I have complete trust and confidence in
Your ability to always make the best choices for my life.

OCTOBER 20

Doting on the Past

In an acceptable time have I heard thee,
and in a day of salvation have I helped thee.
ISAIAH 49:8

I always get an uneasy feeling when I find myself with people who have nothing to discuss but the glories of the days that are past!

Why are we not willing to believe what the Bible tells us? The Christian's great future is before him. Therefore, the whole direction of the Christian's look should be forward.

It is a fact that we should ponder soberly that so many Christians seem to have their future already behind them! Their glory is behind them. The only future they have is their past. They are always bringing around the cold ashes of yesterday's burned-out campfire!

Even their testimony, if they give it, reveals their backward look. Their downcast look betrays that they are facing in the wrong direction.

We should take Paul for an example here. I think he occasionally took a quick, happy backward look just to remind himself of the grace and goodness of God enjoyed by the maturing believers in their Savior, Jesus Christ!

Lord, I look forward to the day when people from every nation will turn
away from their sin and false religions to confess You as their Savior
and Lord. How can You use me to fulfill Your plan, Father?

Faith and Prayer

The effectual fervent prayer of a righteous man availeth much.
JAMES 5:16

In Hebrews we find a long list of benefits which faith brings to its possessor: justification, deliverance, fruitfulness, endurance, victory over enemies, courage, strength, and even resurrection from the dead.

Then, everything that is attributed thus to faith might with equal truth be attributed to prayer, for faith and true prayer are like two sides of the same coin—they are inseparable!

Men may, and often do, pray without faith (though this is not true prayer), but it is not thinkable that men should have faith and not pray.

Whatever God can do, faith can do, and whatever faith can do, prayer can do when it is offered in faith.

It should not be considered strange, then, that an invitation to prayer is an invitation to omnipotence, for prayer engages the Omnipresent God and brings Him into our human affairs. According to the Bible, we have because we ask or we have not because we ask not. It does not take much wisdom to discover our next move. Is it not to pray and pray again and again until the answer comes? Let us not fail the world and disappoint God by failing to pray!

*Heavenly Father, thank You that You are a God who welcomes
dialogue with His children! My prayer this morning is that You
will build Your Church in significant ways around the world today.*

Problems and Pressures

Who shall separate us from the love of Christ? shall tribulation,
or distress, or persecution, or famine, or nakedness, or peril, or sword?
ROMANS 8:35

---

*J*esus did not promise any of us that consistent Christian living would be easy!

He did not promise a release from daily problems and pressures. He did not promise to take us to our heavenly home on a fluffy pink cloud!

We live our lives in the knowledge of the grace of God, but we dare not forget that our Lord came to die for us and to express the never-changing moral and redemptive will of God for His people.

Before we condemn the Jews of Bible history for their failures, we must be sure that we are not overlooking spiritual and moral shortcomings of our own!

As Christian believers, you and I must be careful about the reasons we give for not heeding God's Word and God's warning from heaven.

Have we taken His grace seriously enough that we have sought forgiveness for spiritual carelessness, indifference, and apathy?

I praise You, Lord, that You have equipped Your true followers to live a moral
life in an immoral world. Help me make each day count for Your kingdom, Lord.

The Lonely Human

The joy of our heart is ceased. . .woe unto us, that we have sinned!
LAMENTATIONS 5:15–16

———❦———

There is a strange contradiction in human nature all around us: the fact that a person can reek with pride, display a swollen ego, and strut like a peacock—and yet be the loneliest and most miserable person in the world!

We find these people everywhere—pretending and playing a game. Deep within their beings, they are almost overwhelmed by their great loneliness, by their sense of being orphans in the final scheme of things.

The result of this strange, aching human sense of loneliness and cosmic orphanage is the inward, groping question: "What good is it to be a human being? No one cares about me!"

In the garden, Eve believed Satan's lie—the lie that God was not concerned about her and that God had no emotional connection with her life and being. This is where the unregenerate person is in today's world.

It is only sin and defeat that can bring this sense of orphanage, this sense of having been put out of the father's house, and the feeling that follows when the house is burned down and the father is dead.

Lord, it is a joy and privilege to be counted among Your children on earth.
But there are many who remain on the outside, where it is dark and cold and
lonely. I pray for Your Spirit to draw many lost souls to join Your family today.

Postponing Obedience

Believe on the Lord Jesus Christ, and thou shalt be saved.
ACTS 16:31

A notable heresy has come into being throughout our evangelical Christian circles—the widely accepted concept that we humans can choose to accept Christ only because we need Him as Savior, and that we have the right to postpone our obedience to Him as long as we want to!

The truth is that salvation apart from obedience is unknown in the sacred scriptures. Peter makes it plain that we are "elect according to the foreknowledge of God the Father, through sanctification of the Spirit, unto obedience" (1 Peter 1:2).

It seems most important to me that Peter speaks of his fellow Christians as "obedient children" (vs. 14). He knew their spirituality—he was not just giving them an exhortation to be obedient.

The entire Bible teaches that true obedience to God and His Christ is one of the toughest requirements in the Christian life. Actually, salvation without obedience is a self-contradicting impossibility!

Humans do not want to admit it, but the apostle Paul wrote to the Romans long ago that "by one man's disobedience" came the downfall of the human race (see Romans 5:19).

Dear Lord, I pray today for all the "nominal" Christians in our churches who are straddling the fence of faith. I pray that Your Spirit will impress upon them the need to become fully devoted followers of Christ who will become actively engaged in the battle for men's souls.

Humans Judge the Lord?

But in vain they do worship me,
teaching for doctrines the commandments of men.
MATTHEW 15:9

It is a fact that God made us to worship Him, and if we had not fallen with Adam and Eve, worship would have been the most natural thing for us.

Sinning was not the natural thing for Adam and Eve, but they disobeyed and fell, losing their privilege of perfect fellowship with God, the Creator. Sin is the unnatural thing; it was never intended by God to be our nature.

Men and women who are out of fellowship with God, the Creator, still have an instinct toward some practice of worship. In most of our "civilized" circles, the practice of picking out what we like to worship and rejecting what we do not like is widespread.

This has opened up an entire new field for applied psychology and humanism under a variety of religious disguises. Thus, men and women set themselves as judges of what the Lord has said—and so they stand with pride and judge the Lord.

In the Bible, God takes the matter of worship out of the hands of men and puts it in the hands of the Holy Spirit. It is impossible to worship God without the impartation of the Holy Spirit!

I worship You this morning, Lord, for Your uncontainable power and love.
Let my life be a constant song of praise dedicated to You today and always.

Cheap Religion

Neither will I offer burnt offerings unto the
LORD my God of that which doth cost me nothing.
2 SAMUEL 24:24

What passes for Christianity in our day is cheap religion! To listen to the current concepts of Christianity, we would conclude it is little more than bits of beautiful poetry, a man-made bouquet of fragrant flowers, a kindly smile for our neighbor, and a couple of good deeds on behalf of a brother or sister.

When I consider some of the elements now offered in Christianity as acceptable religion, I have to restrain myself lest I speak too disapprovingly. I fear my words would be so strong that I would have to repent of them! And I read in the scriptures that there are some things God does not want us to say even about the devil.

What do we find surfacing in much of our Christian fellowship? The complaint that God takes a long time to work out His will. We do not want to take the time to plow and cultivate. We want the fruit and the harvest right away. We do not want to be engaged in any spiritual battle that takes us into the long night. We want the morning light right now!

We do not want the cross—we are more interested in the crown!

Lord, help me to be satisfied with Your timetable concerning certain issues in my life.
You are the sovereign God who is never late! Your divine timing is impeccable!

Brotherhood of the Redeemed

To them gave he power to become the sons of God.
JOHN 1:12

———— ❧ ————

*A*nyone making even a quick review of Genesis will discover that God has told us more about His presence in creation and in history than about the details of human civilization.

We believe that eternity dwells in the Person of God and that the material universe came into being through God's creation.

The first man and woman in the human race were created. They failed in their initial encounter with Satan, our archenemy. Following that, the Genesis record becomes a narrative of human failure against the abiding backdrop of God's faithfulness.

God Himself, through the Holy Spirit, points out a universal problem: The natural brotherhood of human beings is a sinful brotherhood. It is the brotherhood of all who are spiritually lost.

But the Bible has good news. It is the revelation of a new brotherhood, the brotherhood of the redeemed! We know it in our time as the believing Church of our Lord Jesus Christ in all nations. It is a new brotherhood among men based on regeneration—and restoration!

Merciful God, I pray today for the thousands of men and women who are
shackled by the chains of sin. Set them free today, Lord, by Your Sprit.
Accept them as members of the "brotherhood of the redeemed."

....
....
....
....
....
....
....
....
....
....
....
....
....
....
....
....

God Is on Our Side

*Let them be confounded and consumed
that are adversaries to my soul.*
PSALM 71:13

---

*I*t was a gracious revelation to my human spirit when I discovered that the Word of God was actually on my side, operating in my behalf!

I was reading Psalm 71 and I came to this amazing statement: "Thou hast given commandment to save me"! (71:3). My heart has been warmed with that realization ever since. I believe that the Word of the living God has gone throughout all the earth to save me and keep me! Let the theological experts raise their eyebrows—I do not care! The living Word has charged Himself with responsibility to forgive, to cleanse, and to keep me!

Let us not be guilty of underrating the Word of God operating on our behalf. I dare to say that there is not an uncontrolled stroke or force anywhere in all of God's mighty universe that can take eternal life away from a trusting, believing, obedient child of God.

Let us thank God for the Word! It is living and powerful and sharper than any two-edged sword (see Hebrews 4:12)!

*Lord, it is so obvious that the truth of Your Word, which is alive and powerful,
is one of the keys to world evangelization. Help me and other Christians to
spread Your Word among our personal spheres of influence.*

"Top Side of the Soul"

To open their eyes, and to turn them from darkness to light,
and from the power of Satan unto God.
ACTS 26:18

———❦———

*I*t is certainly a reality in our day that too few men and women are willing to keep the "top side" of their souls open to God and to His light from heaven.

You may wonder about such expression as the "top side" of the soul, but I do think it is in line with Bible teaching, and certainly in line with all Christian experience.

The heart and soul are open to God in some people's lives but certainly not in others.

We should be aware that man's forgiveness is not always like God's. When a man makes a mistake and has to be forgiven, the shadow may still hang over him among his fellows.

But when God forgives, He begins the new page right away. Then when the devil runs up and says, "What about his past?" God replies, "What past? He has been forgiven!"

Now, I think that kind of forgiveness and justification and acceptance with God depends upon a person's willingness to keep the "top side" of the soul open to God and His saving grace!

Dear Lord, there are people at work and in my community whose
hearts are not open to Your offer of forgiveness. I pray that
each one will open his soul to God to receive His saving grace.

....
....
....
....
....
....
....
....
....
....

The Day of the Lord

These shall make war with the Lamb, and the Lamb shall overcome them.
REVELATION 17:14

The human race has always been quick to blame the world's disasters, floods, famines, plagues on natural causes. But in the end of the age, when the final judgments of God begin to fall, how long will it be until people confess that there is another real, though invisible, force in operation?

Truly the wrath of God will leave no hiding place for sinning, alienated men and women!

John, in the Revelation, speaks of the mighty trumpets that will sound and the woes that will descend upon the earth. In my own view, I link these events to the dramatic period throughout the earth when the antichrist has prevailed by deception and force.

When God is finally ready to refine and restore the earth, everyone in heaven and on earth and in hell will know that no human laboratory could compound the fire that will be poured out on the earth. God has promised that He will not hide His wrath forever. He is prepared to speak in supernatural manifestations in that coming Day of the Lord!

Lord, it is no consolation that in the final judgment the wrath of God will be poured out upon unsaved men and women. That the Day of Judgment will surely take place should motivate us to be relentless in sharing the gospel with lost people.

When You Come to the Lord's Table

Ye do shew the Lord's death till he come.
1 CORINTHIANS 11:26

⁓

God still seeks humble, cleansed, and trusting hearts through which to reveal His divine power and grace and life. A professional botanist from the university can describe the acacia bush of the desert better than Moses could ever do—but God is still looking for the humble souls who are not satisfied until God speaks with the divine fire in the bush.

A research scientist could be employed to stand and tell us more about the elements and properties found in bread and wine than the apostles ever knew. But this is our danger: We may have lost the light and warmth of the presence of God, and we may have only bread and wine. The fire will have gone from the bush, and the glory will not be in our act of Communion and fellowship.

Heavenly Father, I pray that my heart will be prepared by
Your Holy Spirit each time I come to the Communion table—
lest the table of our Lord should become a common and careless thing.

A Career—and Christ

*A certain woman named Lydia. . .of the city
of Thyatira. . .whose heart the Lord opened. . .*
ACTS 16:14

---

*I*t is a beautiful New Testament story that tells us of Lydia of Philippi, a career woman in her own right, long before there were laws and proclamations to set women free.

A seller of purple, Lydia traveled to the market of her day, and undoubtedly she had found freedom and satisfaction in that era when women were not counted at all.

But Lydia heard the apostle Paul tell of the death and resurrection of Jesus Christ, and the Lord opened her heart. In Christ she found an eternal answer, which career and position had never been able to give.

Now, about conditions today. Our society has set women free to be just as bad as the men—and just as miserable. We have set them free to swear and curse and to set their own morals. Politically, women are now free to vote just as blindly as the men do. But I hope women today will find what Lydia found: that their careers will lack the word *eternal* until they find their answer in the eternal Christ, our Lord Jesus!

*Lord Jesus, there are many women in our own country and around the world who
are being abused and belittled. Some are trapped in desperate situations and
cannot escape. Free them, Lord—physically, emotionally, and spiritually.*

Rejoice—or Grumble

Ye greatly rejoice, though. . .ye are in
heaviness through manifold temptations.
1 PETER 1:6

I think all of us meet Christian men and women who always seem to look on the gloomy side and are never able to do anything with life's problems but grumble about them! I meet them often and when I do, I wonder: "Can these people be reading and trusting the same Bible I have been reading?"

The apostle Peter wrote to the tempted, suffering, and persecuted believers in his day and noted with thanksgiving that they could rejoice because they counted God's promises and provisions greater than their trials!

We do live in a sinful and imperfect world, and as believers in Christ we acknowledge that perfection is a relative thing now—and God has not really completed a thing with us, as yet!

Peter testified that the persecuted and suffering Christians of his day were looking, in faith, to a future state of things immeasurably better than that which they knew, and that state of things would be perfect and complete!

Lord, I pray that today, regardless of the difficulties I may face,
I will be in a perpetual state of rejoicing because of Your
promise of a hope and a future (see Jeremiah 29:11).

Is the Church Weary?

In this the children of God are manifest.
1 JOHN 3:10

———

*A*s Christian believers, we stand together in the evangelical faith—the historical faith of our fathers. Yet, we must confess that many congregations seem bogged down with moral boredom and life weariness.

The church is tired, discouraged, and unastonished—Christ seems to belong to yesterday.

The prophetic teachers have projected everything into the dim future where it is beyond our reach—unavailable! They have dispensationalized us into a state of spiritual poverty—and they have left us there!

But regardless of such teachers, the course of spiritual victory is clear; let us trust what the Word of God continues to say to us!

The scriptures are open and plain. Jesus Christ is our Savior and Lord. He is our great High Priest, alive and ministering for us today. His person, His power, and His grace are the same—without change, yesterday, today, and forever!

Lord, Your Church is the only hope for this world. My prayer is that the Church will continue to aggressively pursue the fight against evil in this present age.

Claim Your Inheritance

That thou mayest prosper and be in health,
even as thy soul prospereth.
3 John 2

Did you know that it is possible for a Christian believer to live day after day, clutching the book of Ephesians, and still not realize that he is spiritually lean and hungry?

If a pastor or evangelist suggests that this person could be in a more prosperous spiritual state, his reaction may be bristling: "Am I not accepted in the Beloved? Is not God my Father, and am I not an heir with God?"

Holding the text of the will is not enough. It is necessary to come into the possession of the riches. Suppose a rich man dies, leaving a will which passes on all of his millions to his only son. That boy borrows the text of the will from the attorney and carries it around with him. He is satisfied with the text of the will, but it has never been properly executed. Thus the son has never presented his legitimate claims to the inheritance.

He may be going around ragged, hungry, and weak. In actual experience he has received nothing. He simply holds the text of his father's will!

Lord, teach me by Your Holy Spirit how I may
grow more Christlike in my spiritual walk.

Worthy—or Unworthy?

And to know the love of Christ, which passeth knowledge.
Ephesians 3:19

———

The love of Jesus is so inclusive that it knows no boundaries. At the point where we stop loving and caring, Jesus is still there—loving and caring! The question may be asked: "How does the living Christ feel today about the sinful men and women who walk our streets?"

There is only one answer: He loves them!

We may be righteously indignant about the things they do. We may be disgusted with their actions and their ways. We are often ready to condemn and turn away from them.

But Jesus keeps on loving them! It is His unchanging nature to love and seek the lost. He said many times when He was on earth, "I have come to help the needy. The well do not need a doctor—but the sick need attention and love."

We are prone to look at the needy and measure them: "Let us determine if they are worthy of our help." During all of His ministry, I do not think Jesus ever helped a "worthy" person. He only asked, "What is your need? Do you need My help?"

Dear Lord Jesus, thank You for Your unconditional love for all mankind.
I pray that lost men and women everywhere will acknowledge
their sin problem and give their hearts to Jesus.

I Choose to Worship

Not a novice, lest being lifted up with pride
he fall into the condemnation of the devil.
1 TIMOTHY 3:6

Strange things are happening all around us in Christian circles because we are not truly worshippers. For instance, any untrained, unprepared, unspiritual empty rattletrap of a person can start something "religious" and find plenty of followers who will listen and promote it! Beyond that, it may become very evident that he or she had never heard from God in the first place.

All of the examples we have in the Bible illustrate that glad and devoted and reverent worship is the normal employment of human beings. Every glimpse that is given us of heaven and of God's created beings is always a glimpse of worship and rejoicing and praise—because God is who He is!

Because we are not truly worshippers, we spend a lot of time in the churches just spinning our wheels—making a noise but not getting anywhere.

What are we going to do about this awesome, beautiful worship that God calls for? I would rather worship God than do any other thing I know of in all this wide world!

Lord, just as You evicted the money changers from the Temple, I pray that
You will cleanse churches from their self-centered, empty attempts at worshipping You.

A Moral Pronouncement

Thy word is a lamp unto my feet, and a light unto
my path. . . . I will keep thy righteous judgments.
PSALM 119:105–106

What is God saying to His human creation in our day and time? In brief, He is saying, "Jesus Christ is My beloved Son. Hear Him!"

Why is there rejection? Why do men and women fail to listen?

Because God's message in Jesus is a moral pronouncement. Men and women do not wish to be under the authority of the moral Word of God!

For centuries, God spoke in many ways. He inspired holy men to write portions of the message in a book. People do not like it, so they try their best to avoid it because God has made it the final test of all morality, the final test of all Christian ethics.

God, being one in His nature, is always able to say the same thing to everyone who hears Him. Christian believers must know that any understanding of the Word of God must come from the same Spirit who provided the inspiration!

I am eager, Lord, to continue to learn from Your Word. Open my heart and mind that I might understand and act according to Your moral authority. I want to be obedient to Your will.

Mysticism Plus Theology

Holy men of God spake as they
were moved by the Holy Ghost.
2 PETER 1:21

Christian preachers and ministers ought to acknowledge, publicly and with humility, their great indebtedness to the apostles John and Paul. Study the Gospel of John and you will concur with me that John is surely the mystic of the New Testament!

Explore the epistles of the apostle Paul and you will also concur with the assessment that Paul is surely the theologian of the New Testament!

John and Paul were completely immersed in love and adoration for Jesus, the Christ, the eternal Son and the Savior of the world. So we may say that Paul is the instrument and John is the music!

God Himself was able to pour into the great mind and spirit of Paul the basic doctrines of the New Testament. But in John, God found harp-like qualities to sound forth devotion and praise.

Paul, then, is the theologian who lays foundations. John does not really soar any higher than Paul—but he sings just a bit more sweetly! It is not amazing, really, that there is much mysticism in Paul's theology and much theology in John's mysticism!

Lord, the theological principles expressed in the New Testament writings are life-transforming!
I pray for all the Christian Bible schools and seminaries around the world, that they will
faithfully and accurately present the Word of God to a new generation of Christian workers.

....

....

....

....

....

....

....

....

Prayers: Too Late

For the great day of his wrath is come;
and who shall be able to stand?
REVELATION 6:17

———— ✎ ————

John, in the sixth chapter of Revelation, describes the most tragic, unavailing prayer meeting in the world's history!

Cries and groans, shouts and demands, moans and whispers—all will be heard in that coming Day of the Lord when the forces of judgment are released. Even the mountains and the islands will be removed from their places.

But by then, the prayers and cries of sinful men and women will be too little and too late!

All of the great men of the earth, all the important people, all who have mistakenly put their trust and hope in purely human abilities will join those crying out in guilt. They will call on the crumbling rocks and mountains to fall on them to hide them from the wrath of God.

I am among those who believe that the judgments of God are certain. We do not know the day nor the hour. But God is indeed going to shake the earth as it has never been shaken before, and He will turn it over to the Worthy One to whom it belongs—Jesus Christ!

Lord, what if today were the day of Your return? It is a sobering thought. So many people will be caught unaware. They will not be prepared. Lord, show me some practical ways that I can point unsaved people to Jesus Christ, their only hope.

Moral Determination

*He. . .was glad, and exhorted them all, that with
purpose of heart they would cleave unto the Lord.*
ACTS 11:23

———————

Though we do not have much of it in this age of spineless religion, there is nevertheless much in the Bible about the place of moral determination in the service of the Lord.

The Old Testament tells us that "Jacob vowed a vow" (Genesis 28:20) and Daniel "purposed in his heart" (Daniel 1:8). Paul determined "not to know any thing among you, save Jesus Christ, and Him crucified" (1 Corinthians 2:2). Above all, we have the example of the Lord Jesus "setting His face like a flint" (see Isaiah 50:7) and walking straight toward the cross. These and many others have left us a record of spiritual greatness born out of a will firmly set to do the will of God!

They did not try to float to heaven on a perfumed cloud, but cheerfully accepted the fact that "with purpose of heart they would cleave unto the Lord" (Acts 11:23).

We must surrender—and in that terrible, wonderful moment we may feel that our will has been forever broken, but such is not the case. In His conquest of the soul, God purges the will and brings it into union with His own, but He never breaks it!

*Lord, I may not have the kind of high and lofty calling as did several biblical
personalities, but I surrender myself to Your will and purpose for my life.*

God's Place as Creator

*Thou art worthy, O Lord, to receive glory
and honour and power: for thou hast created all things.*
REVELATION 4:11

We make a mistake if we do not learn to admire God in all things, great and small; for a new rich mine would be opened in our consciousness if we could learn to recognize God in nature as well as in grace!

We do acknowledge that the God of nature is also the God of grace; and it is true that we glorify God's redeeming grace no less when we glorify His creating and sustaining power. When Christ came to redeem us, He stepped into the framework of an already existent nature.

If we will obey and believe, we can go on pushing back the narrow borders of our spiritual world until it takes in the whole creation of God!

At one time, an English merchant and the renowned poet William Blake stood watching the sun come up out of the sea. The bright yellow disk of the sun emerged, gilding the water and painting the sky with a thousand colors. "Ah! I see gold!" the merchant said.

Blake answered, "I see the glory of God! And I hear a multitude of the heavenly host crying, 'The whole earth is full of His glory.'"

Heavenly Father, every time I am captivated by a beautiful nature scene—the pounding waves of the ocean or the rugged peaks of the Rocky Mountains or a crystal clear, star-filled sky—I am reminded of Your awesome creative power. I worship You, Almighty God!

What Really Matters?

For what hath man of all his labour. . .
wherein he hath laboured under the sun?
ECCLESIASTES 2:22

***

It is all but impossible these days to get people to pay any attention to things that really matter. The broad cynic in our modern civilization is likely to ask: "What really matters, after all?"

It is our personal relationship to God that really matters!

That takes priority over everything else, for no man can afford to live or die under the frowning displeasure of God. Yet, name one modern device that can save him from it. Where can a man find security? Can philosophy help him? or psychology? or science? or atoms or wonder drugs or vitamins?

Only Christ can help him, and His aid is as old as man's sin and man's need.

A few other things matter to be sure. We must trust Christ completely. We must carry our cross daily. We must love God and our fellow men. We must fulfill our commission as ambassadors of Christ among men. We must grow in grace and in the knowledge of God and come at last to our end like a ripe shock of corn at harvest time.

These are the things that really matter!

Lord, the world tells me that fitness and finances are the measures
for success and happiness. But I know in my heart that my personal
relationship with You is the one thing in my life that really matters!

....
....
....
....
....
....
....
....
....

Faith Must Be Restored

Take heed, brethren, lest there be
in any of you an evil heart of unbelief.
HEBREWS 3:12

***

The Bible tells about man's being alienated from and an enemy to God. Should this sound harsh or extreme, you have only to imagine your closest friend coming to you and stating in cold seriousness that he no longer has any confidence in you.

"I do not trust you. I have lost confidence in your character. I am forced to suspect every move you make"—such a declaration would instantly alienate friends by destroying the foundation upon which every friendship is built. Until your former friend's opinion of you had been reversed, there could be no further communion.

People do not go boldly to God and profess that they have no confidence in Him, and they usually do not witness publicly to their low view of God. The frightful thing, however, is that people everywhere act out their unbelief with a consistency that is more convincing than words.

Christianity provides a way back from this place of unbelief and alienation: "He that cometh to God must believe that he is, and that he is a rewarder of them that diligently seek him" (Hebrews 11:6). God took the wrong upon Himself in order that the one who committed the wrong might be saved!

Father, You have pursued us passionately and diligently in order that our relationship
with You might be restored. Yet so many have turned a cold shoulder to You. Jesus,
I love You and appreciate all that You have done for me and my family and friends.

Too Much "At Home"

*These all died in faith. . .and confessed that
they were strangers and pilgrims on the earth.*
HEBREWS 11:13

———— ❦ ————

One of the most telling indictments against many of us who comprise our Christian churches is the almost complete acceptance of the contemporary scene as our permanent home!

We have been working and earning, getting and spending, and now we are enjoying the creature comforts known to human beings in this land. You may bristle a bit and ask: "Is there anything wrong with being comfortable?"

Let me answer in this way: if you are a Christian and you are comfortably "at home" in Chicago or Toronto, in Iowa or Alberta or any other address on planet earth, the signs are evident that you are in spiritual trouble.

The spiritual equation reads like this: the greater your contentment with your daily circumstances in this world, the greater your defection from the ranks of God's pilgrims en route to a city whose architect and builder is God Himself!

If we can feel that we have put down our roots in this present world, then our Lord still has much to teach us about faith and attachment to our Savior!

*Lord, although I live at a local address, I pray that You will help me be a
globally minded Christian and that my heart will beat with Yours for this lost world.*

Answering God's Call

The Lord. . .called as at other times, Samuel, Samuel.
Then Samuel answered, Speak; for thy servant heareth.
1 SAMUEL 3:10

When will men and women realize that when God calls us out, He is completely faithful to call us into something better?

In his faith Abraham was against idolatry and idol making, but that was not his crusade. Because of his faith, God led him into a promised land, into possessions and into the lineage that brought forth the Messiah. The call of God is always to something better—keep that in mind!

God calls us into the joys and reality of eternal life. He calls us into purity of life and spirit, so that we may acceptably walk with Him. He calls us into a life of service and usefulness that brings glory to Himself as God. He calls us into the sweetest fellowship possible on this earth—the fellowship of the family of God!

If God takes away from us the old, wrinkled, beat-up dollar bill we clutch so desperately, it is only because He wants to exchange it for the whole federal mint, the entire treasury! He is saying, "I have in store for you all the resources of heaven. Help yourself!"

What a wonderful God we serve! You are looking out for our very best. Lord,
help me to loosen my hold on the things that are blocking the path of Your blessings.

Authority in Preaching

Preach the word; be instant in season, out of season;
reprove, rebuke, exhort with all long suffering and doctrine.
2 TIMOTHY 4:2

Because we are Christians who believe the inspired Word of God and because we believe that the Holy Spirit is the abiding third person of the Trinity, there should be more divine authority in our preaching ministries.

A preacher of this gospel of our Lord Jesus Christ should have the authority of God upon him, so that he makes the people responsible to listen to him. When they will not listen to him, they are accountable to God for turning away from the divine Word.

A preacher under God's unction should reign from his pulpit as a king from his throne. He should not reign by law or by regulation or by man's authority. He ought to reign by moral ascendancy!

The divine authority is missing from many pulpits. We have "tabby cats" with their claws carefully trimmed in the seminary, so they can paw over the congregations and never scratch them at all! The Holy Spirit will sharpen the arrows of the man of God who preaches the whole counsel of God!

Lord, I pray that the pastors in our churches will be freshly filled with Your Spirit,
enabling them to preach Your Word with power and authority from on high.

The Unity of All Things

For it pleased the Father. . .by him to reconcile all things unto himself. . .
whether they be things in earth, or things in heaven.
COLOSSIANS 1:19–20

---

*I*f we are humble and sincere Christians, this should be one of the most welcome thoughts we have ever considered: the work of Christ in redemption will achieve ultimately the expulsion of sin, the only divisive agent in the universe!

When that is accomplished, God's creation will once more realize the unification of all things. We who are men and women, though redeemed and regenerated, are submerged in time; therefore, we properly say that prophecy is history foretold and history is prophecy fulfilled. But in God there is no "was" or "will be" but a continuous and unbroken "is." In Him, history and prophecy are one and the same. God contains past and future in His own Being.

It is sin that has brought diversity, separation, dissimilarity. Sin has introduced divisions into a universe essentially one. We do not understand this, but we must let our faith rest on the character of God.

The concept of the unity of all things is seen in the scriptures. Paul said that God will reconcile all things unto Himself, whether they be things in earth or in heaven!

Lord, sin has spoiled Your creation, and it has ruined the lives of thousands
of people who have died in their sin—with no opportunity to repent. I yearn
for the day when You will reconcile all things to Yourself, but I pray earnestly,
Lord, for the salvation of those who don't know You.

Crossing Over Jordan

O death, where is thy sting? . . . Thanks be to God,
which giveth us the victory through our Lord Jesus Christ.
1 CORINTHIANS 15:55, 57

The prophets and the psalmists of the Old Testament wrestled as we do with the problem of evil in a divine universe, but their approach to God and nature was much more direct than ours. They did not interpose between God and His world that opaque web we moderns call the "laws of nature."

They could see God in a whirlwind and hear Him in a storm, and they did not hesitate to say so! There was about their lives an immediate apprehension of the divine. Everything in heaven and on earth assured them that this is God's world and that He rules over all.

I heard a Methodist bishop tell of being called to the bedside of an elderly dying woman in his early ministry. He said he was frightened; but the old saint was radiantly happy. When he tried to express the sorrow he felt about her illness, she would not hear it.

"Why, God bless you, young man," she said cheerfully, "there is nothing to be scared about. I am just going to cross over Jordan, where my Father owns the land on both sides of the river!" She understood about the unity of all things in God's creation.

Lord, just as Brother Lawrence "practiced the presence of God" in his daily life,
I want my life to be about "apprehending the divine" so that I may have a
steady supply of godly wisdom, spiritual power, and delightful fellowship.

God and the Individual

Blessed is the man to whom the Lord will not impute sin.
ROMANS 4:8

When the eternal Son of God became the Son of Man and walked on this earth, He always called individuals to His side. Jesus did not come into the world to deal with statistics!

He deals with individuals and that is why the Christian message is and always has been: "God loves the world! He loves the masses and throngs only because they are made up of individuals. He loves every individual person in the world!"

In the great humanistic tide of our day, the individual is no longer the concern. We are pressed to think of the human race in a lump. We are schooled to think of the human race in terms of statistics. In many nations, the state is made to be everything and the individual means nothing at all.

Into the very face and strength of this kind of humanism comes the Christian evangel, the good news of salvation, wondrously alight with the assurance for all who will listen:

"You are an individual and you matter to God! His concern is not for genes and species but for the individuals He has created!"

Father God, Your Word says that You knew each one of us before we were born
(see Jeremiah 1:5), You personally knit us together in our mother's womb
(see Psalm 139:13), and You planned each day of our life (see Psalm 139:16).
I praise You, Lord! My only response to this can be to live every day for Your glory.

Saved from Idolatry

Thou shalt not bow down thyself to them, nor serve them:
for I the LORD thy God am a jealous God.
EXODUS 20:5

———❦———

*I*t has been proven often in history that whoever entertains an unworthy conception of God is throwing his or her being wide open to the sin of idolatry, which is in essence a defamation of the divine character.

It is vitally important that we think soundly about God. Because He is the foundation of all our religious belief, it follows that if we err in our ideas of God, we will go astray in everything else.

We would like to believe that there are no longer false gods in the world, but actually we recognize some of them in our own society. What about the glorified "Chairman of the Board" of the modern businessman? Or the storytelling, backslapping god of some of the service clubs? Think of the dreamy-eyed god of the unregenerate poet—cozy, aesthetic, and willing to fellowship with anybody who thinks high thoughts and believes in moral equality. We often encounter the tricky, unscrupulous god of the superstitious; and the list goes on!

Thankfully, we have found that to know and follow Christ is to be saved from all forms of idolatry!

Lord, it is definitely a challenge not to be swept up by the latest media craze or
the hot-selling electronic gadget or the most recent fitness or diet program. I pray, Lord,
that none of these "things" will ever supplant You as the focus and purpose of my life.

Glamour Instead of Glory

Therefore, brethren, stand fast, and hold the traditions
which ye have been taught, whether by word, or our epistle.
2 THESSALONIANS 2:15

———

One ominous sign in the social structure that surrounds us is the false attitude toward anything that can be called "ordinary." There has grown up all around us an idea that the "commonplace" is old-fashioned and strictly for the birds!

This existing mania for glamour and contempt for the ordinary are signs and portents in American society. Even religion has gone glamorous!

In case you do not know what glamour is, I might explain that it is a compound of sex, paint, padding, and artificial lights. It came to America by way of the honky-tonk and the movie lot, got accepted by the world first, and then strutted into the Church—vain, self-admiring, and contemptuous. Instead of the Spirit of God in our midst, we now have the spirit of glamour, as artificial as painted death!

Say what you will, it is a new kind of Christianity, with new concepts that face us brazenly wherever we turn within the confines of evangelical Christianity. The new Christian no longer wants to be good or saintly or virtuous!

Lord, I pray that the pastor and other leaders in my church will so
humble themselves before You that nothing but the sweetness of
the Lord Jesus will attract people to worship You each week.

Getting God in Focus

*But he, being full of the Holy Ghost, looked up
stedfastly into heaven, and saw the glory of God.*
ACTS 7:55

While many are busy trying to set forth satisfactory definitions of the word *faith,* we do well to simply consider that believing is directing the heart's attention to Jesus!

It is lifting the mind to "behold the Lamb of God," and never ceasing that beholding for the rest of our lives. At first this may be difficult, but it becomes easier as we look steadily at His wondrous Person, quietly and without strain.

Distractions may hinder, but once the heart is committed to Him, the attention will return again and rest upon Him like a wandering bird coming back to its window.

I would emphasize this one great volitional act which establishes the heart intention to gaze forever upon Jesus. God takes this intention for our choice and makes what allowances He must for the thousand distractions which beset us in this evil world. So, faith is a redirecting of our sight, getting God in our focus, and when we lift our inward eyes upon God, we are sure to meet friendly eyes gazing back at us!

*Lord, this morning I pray that the inward eyes of
my soul will put You in clear focus throughout this day.*

"A Cheerful Heart"

*Singing and making melody. . .
giving thanks always for all things.*
EPHESIANS 5:19–20

The thankful Christian will turn with true delight to the expression of Joseph Addison in his Thanksgiving hymn, "When All Thy Mercies, O My God," found in many of the better hymnals. Addison gives a mental image that requires music for its expression:

> *Ten thousand thousand precious gifts
> My daily thanks employ;
> Nor is the least a cheerful heart
> That tastes these gifts with joy!*

Here is the spirit of thanksgiving. Here is the understanding of what pleases God in our acceptance and use of His gifts. "A cheerful heart that tastes these gifts with joy" is the only kind of heart that can taste them safely.

While Addison had in mind chiefly the gifts God showers upon us here below, he was too much of a Christian to think that God's gifts would cease at death. So he sang:

> *Through every period of my life
> Thy goodness I'll pursue;
> And after death in distant worlds,
> The glorious theme renew!*

> *Dear Lord, I pray that my life will be characterized by a spirit
> of thankfulness for You and the gifts You have freely given.*

....

....

....

....

....

....

Let Us Be Thankful

Giving thanks always. . .
in the name of our Lord Jesus Christ.
EPHESIANS 5:20

To be grateful to God's servants is to be grateful to God; and it follows that in a very real sense we thank God when we thank His people!

We will always have spiritual leaders, and I think we make two mistakes in our attitudes toward them. One is not being sufficiently grateful to them. The other is in following them too slavishly.

The first is a sin of omission, and because it is something that is not there, it is not likely to be noticed as a sin that is plainly present.

We do make a serious mistake when we become so attached to the preaching or writing of a great Christian leader that we accept his teaching without daring to examine it. We should follow men only as they follow the Lord. We should keep an open mind lest we become blind followers of a man whose breath is in his nostrils.

Learn from every holy man and his ministry. Be grateful to every one of them and thankful for them—and then follow Christ!

Lord, I am thankful for the pastors of small churches who faithfully preach Your Word week in and week out. They do this without much financial support and sometimes without much encouragement. Lord, will You send a special blessing upon them today?

God Gives—and Gives

*Fight the good fight of faith, lay hold on
eternal life, whereunto thou art also called.*
1 TIMOTHY 6:12

We ought to spend more time remembering the blessings and the benefits God is continually giving us while we are alive—before we leave this vale of tears! He gives us forgiveness—so we are to live for Him as forgiven sinners. He gives us eternal life. This is not just a future reality—our life in Him is a present bestowment.

He gives us sonship: "Beloved, now are we the sons of God" (1 John 3:2). In this relationship there are many other gifts we receive from God, and if we do not possess them, it is because we are not God's children in faith!

We ask God to help us, to meet some need, to do something for us—and the Lord mercifully does it. I consider these the little and the trifling things, yet we make a great deal of them. But they are really the passing things compared to the great present benefactions of forgiveness, reinstatement in favor with God, sonship, and eternal life!

*Loving Father, You have given Your created ones so many good gifts! It is baffling,
then, why so many people refuse to put their faith in You. Lord, I pray for
opportunities to share the story of Your goodness with the people within my reach.*

Faithful Stewardship

*Upon the first day of the week let every one of you
lay by him in store, as God hath prospered him.*
1 CORINTHIANS 16:2

God has been pleased to deal with us in a most remarkable way concerning our Christian stewardship and responsibility of honoring Him with the things He has entrusted to us.

The Bible teaching is plain: you have the right to keep what you have all to yourself—but it will then rust and decay, and ultimately ruin you!

This may hurt some of you but I am obliged to tell you that God does not need anything you have!

He does not need a dime of your money!

What you need to understand is that it is your own spiritual welfare at stake in such matters as this.

There is a beautiful and enriching principle involved in our offering to God what we are and what we have, but none of us is giving because there is a depression in heaven!

A long time ago God said: "If I had need of anything, would I tell you?" (see Psalm 50:12).

Brethren, if the living God had need of anything, He would no longer be God!

*Lord, You are a generous God, and I desire to be a faithful
steward of the resources You have given me. Show me how to
best manage my earthly resources for Your eternal glory.*

Live for God's Glory

*That ye may with one mind and one mouth glorify
God, even the Father of our Lord Jesus Christ.*
ROMANS 15:6

It may be difficult for the average Christian to get hold of the idea that his daily labors can be performed as acts of worship acceptable to God by Jesus Christ.

We must practice living to the glory of God actually and determinedly. By one act of consecration of our total selves to God, we can make every subsequent act express that consecration. By meditation upon this truth, by talking it over with God often in our prayers, by recalling it to our minds frequently as we move about among men, a sense of its wondrous meaning will begin to take hold of us.

The New Testament accepts as a matter of course that in His incarnation, our Lord took upon Him a real human body. He lived in that body here among men and never once performed a nonsacred act!

Brethren, we must offer all our acts to God and believe that He accepts them. We should then keep reminding God in our times of private prayer that we mean every act for His glory. We thus meet the temptations and trials by the exercise of an aggressive faith in the sufficiency of Christ!

*Lord, as I face various temptations and trials this week, I pray that Your
Spirit will help me "exercise aggressive faith in the sufficiency of Christ."*

"Why Am I Here?"

Who. . .worshipped and served the creature more than
the Creator. . . God gave them over to a reprobate mind.
ROMANS 1:25, 28

---

*S*ince the first fallen man got still long enough to think, fallen men have been asking these questions: "Whence came I? What am I? Why am I here? and Where am I going?"

The noblest minds of the race have struggled with these questions to no avail. Had the answer lay somewhere hidden like a jewel, it would surely have been uncovered, for the most penetrating minds of the race have searched for it everywhere in the region of human experience. Yet the answers remain as securely hidden as if they did not exist.

Why is man lost philosophically? Because he is lost morally and spiritually. He cannot answer the questions life presents to his intellect because the light of God has gone out in his soul. The fearful indictment the Holy Ghost brings against mankind is summed up count by count in the opening chapters of Romans, and the conduct of every man from earliest recorded history is evidence enough to sustain the indictment.

Apart from the scriptures we have no sure philosophy; apart from Jesus Christ we have no true knowledge of God; apart from the in-living Spirit we have no ability to live lives morally pleasing to God!

Lord, I am grateful for the new life that I have through Jesus Christ.
I pray that Your Spirit living in me will empower me to walk courageously
and morally in this ungodly world. I don't want to be a closet Christian.

Nothing but Sweetness

It was in my mouth sweet as honey: and as
soon as I had eaten it, my belly was bitter.
REVELATION 10:10

Let me caution you about the attitudes of some of the bubbly "happy! happy!" people in our congregations who will insist that the Word of God can never be anything but honey sweet!

Fellow believers, when we digest, absorb, and soak up the Word of the Lord, it becomes part and parcel of our daily lives. It is our delight. It is indeed honey and sweetness. But as we share that same Word in our witness to lost men and women, we will know something of bitterness and hostility, even enmity.

It will follow then in experience that Christian believers who are intent upon being faithful witnesses for Jesus Christ may not always find sweetness and light in their contacts with evil, rebellious people.

We need to pray for men and women in our churches who have determined to set their own agendas—to live their lives as they please! They have determined to manage the influences of the Word of God in their lives.

Dear Lord, I pray for people in other religions and cults who have never read a portion
of the Bible because of indifference or fear. I pray that You will send upon each
of them a spirit of curiosity, prompting them to read from Your living Word!

He Is Our Passover

He took bread. . . And their eyes were opened, and they knew him.
LUKE 24:30–31

❦

What a sweet comfort to us that our Lord Jesus Christ was once known in the breaking of the bread. In earlier Christian times, believers called Communion "the medicine of immortality," and God gave them the desire to pray:

> *Be known to us in breaking bread,*
> *But do not then depart;*
> *Savior, abide with us and spread*
> *Thy table in our heart.*

Some churches have a teaching that you will find God only at their table—and that you leave God there when you leave. I am so glad that God has given us light. We may take the Presence of the table with us.

> *Then sup with us in love divine,*
> *Thy body and Thy blood;*
> *That living bread and heavenly wine*
> *Be our immortal food!*

In approaching the table of our Lord, we dare not forget the cost to our elder Brother, the Man who was from heaven. He is our Savior; He is our Passover!

> *Lord, just as You promised Moses that Your "presence" would*
> *go with him (see Exodus 33:14), I pray that Your presence will*
> *go with me wherever You lead. I will not go without You, dear Lord.*

....

....

....

....

....

The Breath of God

The word that I have spoken. . .
shall judge him in the last day.
JOHN 12:48

Two of the great realities in our midst are surely the promised presence of God and the testimony of His eternal Word!

By the "Word of God" I do not refer only to the book you hold in your hand—paper and letters, pages and ink—sewed together with silk thread. By the Word of God, I do mean the expression of the mind of God: the mighty, world-filling breath of God!

Most of the things men and women talk about cannot be counted among the great realities of life. In October, people talk a great deal about the World Series as a great reality, but by December they have forgotten who pitched and who struck out.

People spend their entire lives in the pursuit of those things that can only perish and fade away. But when it is all over, they are still going to be faced with the reality of the eternal Word of God, the revelation of Truth which God has given us!

Think of the changes that would come if humans would suddenly stop and hear the Word of God!

Lord, I pray that I will not spend my life in the pursuit of
things that won't last. Give me Your eternal perspective, Lord.

....
....
....
....
....
....
....
....
....

Life Flows from God

God saw every thing that he had made,
and, behold, it was very good.
GENESIS 1:31

---

*W*ithout doubt, we have suffered the loss of many spiritual treasures because we have let slip the simple truth that the miracle of the perpetuation of life is in God!

Be assured that God did not create life and toss it from Him like some petulant artist disappointed with his work. All life is in Him and out of Him, flowing from Him and returning to Him again, a moving indivisible sea of which He is the fountainhead.

That eternal life which was with the Father is now the possession of believing men and women, and that life is not God's gift only—but His very Self! The regeneration of a believing soul is but a recapitulation of all His work done from the moment of creation.

So, redemption is not a strange work which God for a moment turned aside to do. Rather, it is His same work performed in a new field, the field of human catastrophe!

Father, that Your gift of eternal life flows through us is a wondrous thought for those
who know You. But for those who haven't received You as Savior, the gift will turn into
an eternal nightmare. Lord, mobilize Your Church to proclaim the gospel as never before.

Let Us Take It Personally

LORD, thou wilt ordain peace for us:
for thou also hast wrought all our works in us.
ISAIAH 26:12

———— ✦ ————

What a difference it makes when we humans cease being general and become pointed and personal in our approach to God! We then come to see that all that God did was for each of us.

It was for me that holy men spoke as they were moved by the Holy Spirit. For me Christ died—and when He arose on the third day, it was for me. When the promised Holy Spirit came, it was to continue in me the work He had been doing for me since the morning of the Creation!

So, I have every right to claim all of the riches of the Godhead in mercy given. What a blessed thought—that an infinite God can give all of Himself to each of His children!

He does not distribute Himself that each may have a part, but to each one He gives all of Himself as fully as if there were no others.

All that He is and all that He has done is for us and for all who share the common salvation.

Thank You, Lord, for all that You have done for me. That You
are a personal, caring God is so unlike other religions. Father,
glorify Yourself among the nations of the world today.

....

....

....

....

....

....

....

....

....

....

Confused about Worship

For ye are the temple of the living God.
2 CORINTHIANS 6:16

───── ✦ ─────

To really know Jesus Christ as Savior and Lord is to love and worship Him!

As God's people, we are so often confused that we could be known as God's poor, stumbling, bumbling people, for we are most prone to think of worship as something we do when we go to church on Sunday!

We call it God's house. We have dedicated it to Him. So, we continue with the confused idea that it must be the only place where we can worship Him.

We come to the Lord's house made of brick and stone and wood. We are used to hearing the call to worship: "The Lord is in His holy temple—let us kneel before Him!" This is on Sunday and in church—very nice!

But on Monday, as we go about our different duties, are we aware of the continuing presence of God? The Lord desires still to be in His holy temple, wherever we are; for each of us is a temple in whom dwells the Holy Spirit of God!

Lord, I want all the rooms in my temple to be clean not only for Your abiding presence but also to be a shining testimony to those I encounter during the week.

Let the Day Dawn

The path of the just. . .shineth more and more unto the perfect day.
PROVERBS 4:18

———— ❦ ————

*T*he Bible tells us that when a person becomes a Christian, it is as though the sun has come up and the day has dawned. Then his experience along the path should be like the glowing light which shineth more and more unto the perfect day!

This brings us to a question: if all Christians are alike in standing and state, why did Jesus point out three distinctions in the Christian life—"some thirty, some sixty, and some a hundredfold" (see Matthew 13:23)?

If we are all alike and have all "arrived" at the same place and state, why did the apostle Paul tell the Philippian Christians—"I have suffered the loss of all things, that I may know Him and if by any means, I might attain unto that superior resurrection" (see 3:7–11)?

I am of the opinion that we cannot experience that which we have not believed. I still think we must instruct and urge men and women, toiling along in average and common Christian ways, to move forward and claim spiritual victory they have not yet known.

Lord, thank You for Your Spirit's ever-present encouragement, teaching, and guidance as I attempt to grow more like You each day of my Christian life.

Everyone May Come

Whosoever will, let him take the water of life freely.
REVELATION 22:17

---

*T*here is a strange beauty in the ways of God with men. He sends salvation to the world in the person of a Man and sends that Man to walk the byways, saying, "If any man will come after Me!" No fanfare; no tramp of marching feet!

A kindly Stranger walks through the earth, and so quiet is His voice that it is sometimes lost in the hurly-burly; but it is the last voice of God, and until we become quiet to hear it, we have no authentic message.

"If any man," He says, and teaches at once the universal inclusiveness of His invitation and the freedom of the human will. Everyone may come; no one need come, and whoever does come, comes because he chooses to.

Every man thus holds his future in his hand. Not the dominant world leader only, but the inarticulate man lost in anonymity is "a man of destiny"! He decides which way his soul shall go. He chooses, and destiny waits on the nod of his head. He decides, and hell enlarges itself, or heaven prepares another mansion!

So much of Himself has God given to man!

Dear Lord, I pray again for my family and close friends. Some of them have not made wise choices and are still on the outside looking in. Lord, I pray that Your Spirit will melt their hearts and that they will come to You at long last.

Where Is the Radiance?

He that believeth on the Son of
God hath the witness in himself.
1 JOHN 5:10

I keep looking, but with little success, for a distinguishing radiance in life and testimony among our evangelical Christians.

Instead of an inner witness, too many professing Christians are depending upon logical conclusions drawn from Bible texts. They have no witness of an encounter with God, no awareness of inner change!

I believe that where there is a divine act within the soul, there will be a corresponding awareness. This act of God is its own evidence: it addresses itself directly to the spiritual consciousness.

Thankfully, there are elements that are always the same among men and women who have had a personal meeting with God.

There is the compelling sense of God Himself—of His person and of His presence. From there on, the permanent results will be evident in the life and walk of the person touched as long as he or she lives!

Heavenly Father, I pray that Your Church will go out into the lost
world exhibiting a "distinguishing radiance in life and testimony."
As a result, may many lost souls be attracted to You, Lord Jesus.

More Than Pardon

*For godly sorrow worketh repentance
to salvation not to be repented of.*
2 CORINTHIANS 7:10

It is a fact that the New Testament message of good news, "Christ died for our sins according to the scriptures" (see 1 Corinthians 15:4) embraces a great deal more than an offer of free pardon.

Surely it is a message of pardon—and for that may God be praised—but it is also a message of repentance!

It is a message of atonement—but it is also a message of temperance and righteousness and godliness in this present world!

It tells us that we must accept a Savior—but it tells us also that we must deny ungodliness and worldly lusts!

The gospel message includes the idea of amendment—of separation from the world, of cross carrying and loyalty to the kingdom of God even unto death!

These are all corollaries of the gospel and not the gospel itself; but they are part and parcel of the total message which we are commissioned to declare. No man has authority to divide the truth and preach only a part of it. To do so is to weaken it and render it without effect!

*Lord, I pray for You to anoint every believer with a "holy boldness"
to proclaim Your gospel and all of its implications. It may not be an
attractive message, but it will be the Truth for those with ears to hear.*

Gifts and Graces

. . .gifts of the Holy Ghost, according to his own will.
HEBREWS 2:4

I go back often to Genesis 24 for the illustration and the figure in the Old Testament reminding us of the adornments of grace and beauty that will mark the believing Body of Christ. Abraham sent his trusted servant to his former homeland to select a bride for Isaac.

The adornment of Rebekah's beauty consisted of jewels and the raiment that came as gifts of love from the bridegroom whom she had not yet seen.

It is a reminder of what God is doing in our midst right now. Abraham typifies God the Father; Isaac, our Lord Jesus Christ, the heavenly Bridegroom. The servant who went with the gifts into the far country to claim a bride for Isaac speaks well of the Holy Spirit, our Teacher and Comforter.

He gives us, one by one, the gifts and the graces of the Holy Spirit that will be our real beauty in His sight. Thus we are being prepared, and when we meet our coming Lord and King, our adornment will be our God-given graces!

Lord, it will be such an exciting day when You come for Your Bride, the Church.
I pray that I will personally be ready to present myself to You, clean in body, mind, and spirit.

"Thus Saith the Lord"

*The LORD giveth wisdom: out of his mouth
cometh knowledge and understanding.*
PROVERBS 2:6

---

*I*n a time when everything in the world seems to be related to vanity, God is depending on His believing children to demonstrate that He is the great Reality; that we are made by God and for Him! The answer to the question, "Where did I come from?" can never be better answered than by the Christian mother who tells her child, "God made you!"

The great store of knowledge in today's world cannot improve on that simple answer! The scientist can tell us the secrets of how matter operates, but the origin of matter lies in deep silence, refusing to give an answer to man's question.

It is important for Christian believers to be able to stand firmly and positively in this declaration: "Thus saith the Lord!" Our chief business is not to argue or to persuade our generation. With our positive declaration of God's Word and revelation, we make God responsible for the outcome. No one can know enough to go beyond this!

*Father, as humans we often try the impossible—we try to explain what in
Your wisdom You have chosen not to include in Your Word! Give us the faith—
and the restraint—to accept and live by the light You have revealed to us in Your Word.*

The Need for Reverence

God is greatly to be feared. . .and to be had in reverence.
PSALM 89:7

———◆———

*M*any persons who have been raised in our churches no longer think in terms of reverence, which seems to indicate that they doubt God's presence is there! Much of the blame must be placed on the growing acceptance of a worldly secularism that seems much more appealing than any real desire for the spiritual life that is pleasing to God.

We secularize God; we secularize the gospel of Christ; and we secularize worship!

No great and spiritually minded men of God are going to come out of such churches, nor any great spiritual movement of believing prayer and revival. If God is to be honored and revered and truly worshipped, He may have to sweep us away and start somewhere else!

Let us confess that there is a necessity for true worship among us. If God is who He says He is and if we are the believing people of God we claim to be, we must worship Him! In my own assessment, for men and women to lose the awareness of God in our midst is a loss too terrible ever to be appraised!

*Dear Lord, forgive me for those times when I rush right in and start
"dumping" my complaints and needs on You without first acknowledging
and honoring You as the Almighty God. I humbly bow before You, Lord.*

More Than a Name

Let every one that nameth the name of Christ depart from iniquity.
2 TIMOTHY 2:19

⸺ ❧ ⸺

There have always been professing Christians who argue and insist: "I am all right—I worship in the name of Jesus." They seem to believe that worship of God is based on a formula. They seem to think there is a kind of magic in saying the name of Jesus!

Study the Bible carefully with the help of the Holy Spirit and you will find that the name and the nature of Jesus are one. It is not enough to know how to spell Jesus' name!

If we have come to be like Him in nature, if we have come to the place of being able to ask in accordance with His will, He will give us the good things we desire and need.

We worship God as the result of a new birth from above in which God has been pleased to give us more than a name.

He has given us a nature transformed, and Peter expresses that truth in this way: "Whereby are given unto us exceeding great and precious promises: that by these ye might be partakers of the divine nature, having escaped the corruption that is in the world through lust" (2 Peter 1:4).

Lord, I pray that the Body of Christ will see itself as the apostle Peter has described believers: "partakers of the divine nature." Perhaps if we see ourselves with that perspective, we will arise to the expectations Jesus has for us as His disciples.

Glory to God

The spirit of glory and of God resteth upon you.
1 PETER 4:14

When the Holy Spirit comes among us with His anointing, we become a worshipping people!

Now, that does not mean that all Christians everywhere must all worship alike—but that under the guidance of the Holy Spirit believers everywhere are united in their praises to God.

When Jesus came into Jerusalem presenting Himself as Messiah, there was a great multitude and there was a great noise. Very often our worship is audible, but I do not believe it is necessarily true that we are worshipping God when we are making a lot of racket. But I think there is a word for those who are cultured, quiet, self-possessed, poised, and sophisticated. If they are embarrassed in church when some happy Christian says, "Amen!" they may actually be in need of some spiritual enlightenment.

If some believer's "Glory to God!" really bothers you, it may be because you do not know the kind of spiritual blessing and delight the Holy Spirit is waiting to provide among God's worshipping saints. I can only speak for myself, but I want to be among those who worship!

Dear Lord, I pray that my worship of You will always be from my heart and without any earthly manipulations or distractions. What a joy it will be to one day stand with all the saints in heaven and worship You as King in spirit and in truth.

Better Farther On

*Then opened he their understanding,
that they might understand the scriptures.*
LUKE 24:45

---

*T*ruth that is not experienced is no better than error and may be fully as dangerous.

Remember that the scribes who sat in Moses' seat were not the victims of error; they were the victims of failure to experience the truth they taught!

We should see that one of the greatest foes of the Christian is religious complacency. The man who believes that he has "arrived" will not go any further; and the present neat habit of quoting a text to prove we have arrived may be a dangerous one if in truth we have no actual inward experience of the text.

The great saints of the past have all had yearning hearts. Their longing after God all but consumed them; it propelled them onward and upward to heights toward which less ardent Christians look with languid eye and entertain no hope of reaching.

May we offer this word of exhortation: pray on, fight on, sing on! Press on into the deep things of God. Keep your feet on the ground, but let your heart soar as high as it will!

*Lord, I pray for people in our churches and for those who work in
Christian organizations. Urge them not to be complacent in their comfortable
situations. Stir their hearts to become more engaged in the battle for men's souls.*

Occupied with Praise

They rest not day and night, saying,
Holy, holy, holy, LORD God Almighty.
REVELATION 4:8

It is surely an erroneous supposition for humans to think or to believe that death will transform our attitude and dispositions.

This is what I mean: If in this life we are not really comfortable talking and singing about heaven and its joy, I doubt that death will transform us into enthusiasts! If the worship and adoration of God are tedious now, they will be tedious also after the hour of death.

I do not know that God is going to force any of us into His heaven. I doubt that He will say to any of us, "You were never very interested in worshipping Me while you were on earth, but in heaven I am going to make that your greatest interest and your ceaseless occupation."

Controversial?

Perhaps, but in the heavenly scene John describes, the living creatures crying "Holy, holy, holy!" rest neither day nor night. My fear is that too many of God's professing people down here are resting far too often between their efforts to praise and glorify the living God!

Lord, may my entire life—including this very day—be a sacrifice of worship
to You so that I am well practiced in worshipping You when I arrive in heaven.

The Secret Working of God

*That being justified by his grace, we should be
made heirs according to the hope of eternal life.*
TITUS 3:7

I do believe in the secret and mysterious working of God in the human breast. I must believe it after finding the forgiving and converting grace of God in the Savior, Jesus Christ.

My father and mother held high human standards, but completely without any thought of God. My parents appeared to be without any spark of desire after God—attitudes that were cold, earthy, profane.

Can you tell me why, then, at the age of seventeen, as a boy surrounded by unbelief—100 percent—I could find my way to my mother's attic, kneel on my knees, and give my heart and life in committal to Jesus Christ?

I cannot tell you why. I can only say that I know there is such a thing as the secret workings of God within the human being who has a sensitivity to hear the call of God. In my own case, I do have the testimony that my conversion to Jesus Christ was as real as any man's conversion has ever been!

My fellow man, if the Spirit of God is still tugging at your heart, thank God—and follow the light!

*Lord, most believers know from personal experience about Your "secret workings" within
the human heart. I pray today that You will do a work in the heretofore hardened hearts of
criminals and terrorists around the world. And may the angels in heaven rejoice at the outcome!*

....

....

....

....

....

....

....

....

Mercy: A Boundless Sea

God, who is rich in mercy. . .
even when we were dead in sins.
EPHESIANS 2:4–5

A human being is never really aware of the great boundless sea of the mercy of God until by faith he comes across the threshold of the kingdom of God and recognizes it and identifies it!

My father was sixty years old when he bowed before Jesus Christ and was born again. That was a near lifetime in which he had sinned and lied and cursed. But to him, the mercy of God that took him to heaven was no greater than the mercy of God that had endured and kept him for sixty years.

I recall the story of an ancient rabbi who consented to take a weary old traveler into his house for a night of rest. In conversation, the rabbi discovered the visitor was almost one hundred years old and a confirmed atheist. Infuriated, the rabbi arose, opened the door, and ordered the man out into the night.

Then, sitting down by his candle and Old Testament, it seemed he heard a voice, God's voice: "I have endured that sinner for almost a century. Could you not endure him for a night?" The rabbi ran out and, overtaking the old man, brought him back to the hospitality of his home for the night.

Father, You are gloriously patient with mankind. I praise You for that, and I pray that You will prod Your believing children to go out and find those who are on the cusp of belief.

Give God the Control

Make me to go in the path of thy
commandments; for therein do I delight.
PSALM 119:35

I know that I am being repetitious—but this needs to be said again and again: our Lord will not save those whom He cannot command!

The lifetime God has given us down here is a lifetime of decisions. Each person makes his own decisions as to the eternal world he is going to inhabit. We must decide to take Jesus for what He is—the anointed Savior and Lord who is King of kings and Lord of all lords! He would not be who He is if He saved us and called us without the understanding that He can also guide us and control our lives.

The root of sin is rebellion against God, and hell is the Alcatraz for the unconstituted rebels who refuse to surrender to the will of God.

There are many arguments about the reality of hell. A man might endure fire and brimstone and worms—but the essence of hell and judgment for a moral creature is to know and be conscious that he is where he is because he is a rebel!

Hell will be the eternal domain of all the disobedient rebels who have said, "I owe God nothing!"

Dear Lord, the grim reality of hell is rarely preached in our churches anymore.
Is it any wonder that the consequences of sin are no longer feared? I pray that
our churches will not shrink from telling the world the whole truth of the Bible.

Revival—and Renewal

Though our outward man perish,
yet the inward man is renewed day by day.
2 CORINTHIANS 4:16

———

I hope some of you will agree with me that it is of far greater importance that we have better Christians than that we have more of them!

If we have any spiritual concerns, our most pressing obligation is to do all in our power to obtain a revival that will result in a reformed, revitalized, purified church.

Each generation of Christians is the seed of the next, and degenerate seed is sure to produce a degenerate harvest—not a little better than but worse than the seed from which it sprang. Thus the direction will be down until vigorous, effective means are taken to improve the seed.

Why is it easier to talk about revival than to experience it? Because followers of Christ must become personally and vitally involved in the death and resurrection of Christ. And this requires repentance, prayer, watchfulness, self-denial, detachment from the world, humility, obedience, and cross carrying!

Father God, I pray for Your Spirit to send "fresh fire" to revitalize the church
in the United States. We have become weakened seed that must be reinvigorated
for the next generation of Christians to be strong and healthy.

Do You Love Beauty?

*There shall in no wise enter into it any thing that defileth,
neither whatsoever worketh abomination.*
REVELATION 21:27

When we look closely at this world system and society, we see the terrible and ugly scars of sin. Sin has obscenely scarred and defaced this world, taking away its harmony and symmetry and beauty.

That is the negative picture. Thank God for the positive promise and prospect that heaven is the place of all loveliness, all harmony and beauty.

These are not idle words. If you love beautiful things, you had better stay out of hell, for hell will be the quintessence of all that is morally ugly and obscene. Hell will be the ugliest place in all of creation!

It is a fact that earth lies between all that is ugly in hell and all that is beautiful in heaven. As long as we are living here, we will have to consider the extreme—much that is good and much that is bad!

As believers, we are held firm in the knowledge that the eternal Son came to save us and deliver us to a beautiful heaven and everlasting fellowship with God!

*Dear Lord, thank You for the glimpses of Your grace and beauty that You show
us in Your creation—a colorful rainbow, a beautiful sunset, a field of wildflowers.
They all remind us of the beauty in store for those who have received eternal life.*

If Jesus Came Today

We will not have this man to reign over us.
LUKE 19:14

---

*P*eople have asked me if our present generation would gladly accept Jesus if He came at this time, instead of two thousand years ago. I have to believe that history does repeat itself!

In our own day, many who want to follow the Christian traditions still balk and reject a thoroughgoing spiritual housecleaning within their own lives.

When Jesus came, many realized that it would mean probable financial loss for them to step out and follow Christ. Also, many of those men and women who considered the claims of Christ in His day knew that following Him would call for abrupt and drastic changes in their patterns of living. The proud and selfish aspects of their lives would have been disturbed.

Beyond that, there was an almost complete disdain for the inward spiritual life which Jesus taught as a necessity for mankind—that it is the pure in heart who will see God!

I am afraid that humanity's choice would still be the same today. People are still more in love with money and pride and pleasure than they are with God and His salvation!

Thank You, Lord, for coming to earth at just the right time according to Your eternal plan. You have revealed God's character to us in a most graphic way. Help us to be faithful to Your Great Commission (see Matthew 28:19–20) until You return as You promised.

The Word Made Flesh

And lo a voice from heaven, saying,
This is my beloved Son, in whom I am well pleased.
MATTHEW 3:17

❦

I have given much thought and contemplation to the sweetest and tenderest of all of the mysteries in God's revelation to man—the Incarnation! Jesus, the Christ, is the Eternal One, for in the fullness of time He humbles Himself. John's description is plain: the Word was made flesh and dwelt among us.

I confess that I would have liked to have seen the baby Jesus. But the glorified Jesus yonder at the right hand of the Majesty on high was the baby Jesus once cradled in the manger straw. Taking a body of humiliation, He was still the Creator who made the wood of that manger, made the straw, and was Creator of all the beasts that were there.

In truth, He made the little town of Bethlehem and all that it was. He also made the star that lingered over the scene that night. He had come into His own world, His Father's world. Everything we touch and handle belongs to Him. So we have come to love Him and adore Him and honor Him!

Lord, You became so vulnerable for us by becoming a helpless baby. Thank You for Your intentional humility. Even in Your birth You showed us how to sacrifice what is rightly ours for the benefit of others. Help me to apply this lesson in my own life so that I will become more like You.

....
....
....
....
....
....
....
....
....
....

Christmas Is Real

Great is the mystery. . .God was manifest in the flesh.
1 TIMOTHY 3:16

---

*T*he birth of Christ was a divine declaration, an eternal statement to a race of fallen men and women.

The advent of Christ clearly established:

First, that God is real. The heavens were opened, and another world than this came into view.

Second, that human life is essentially spiritual. With the emergence into human flesh of the Eternal Word of the Father, the fact of man's divine origin is confirmed.

Third, that God indeed had spoken by the prophets. The coming of the Messiah Savior into the world confirmed the veracity of the Old Testament scripture.

Fourth, that man is lost but not abandoned. Had men not been lost, no Savior would have been required. Had they been abandoned, no Savior would have come.

Finally, that this world is not the end. We are made for two worlds and as surely as we now inhabit the one, we shall also inhabit the other!

Heavenly Father, the historical fact of Your divine visitation gives the world
reason for hope and joy. I pray that the significance of Your birth will
impact the lives of many people who are searching for the meaning of life.

Joy and Wonder

Fear not: for, behold, I bring you good tidings of great joy.
LUKE 2:10

———— ❧ ————

*I*t is tragic that men and women everywhere are losing the sense of wonder, confessing now only one interest in life—and that is utility! Even Christmas Day has been degraded. We ignore the beautiful and the majestic, asking only, "How can I use it? How much profit will it bring?"

The believing children of God once upon a time saw God in everything. They were enraptured with everything before them. There was no common hill—they were all the hills of God! There was no common cloud—they were the chariots of God! They saw God in everything. In our day we never look up in happy surprise!

But let me tell you that it has been a never-failing delight throughout my years to watch little children on Christmas morning. The gifts may be humble, but the child's burst of spontaneous delight and wonder is genuine and rewarding. That incredulous look on the child's face—everything is full of wonder and beauty!

Sad, indeed, for adults to lose the wonder in worship—for worship is wonder and wonder is worship!

*Lord, the announcement of "good tidings of great joy" is every bit as
important today as it was two thousand years ago—for we are still a fallen race,
and the Babe in the manger is still the Savior of the world. Praise God!*

The Happy Morn

For unto you is born this day in the city of David a Saviour.
LUKE 2:11

When we sing "The Light of the world is Jesus," there should be a glow on our faces that would make the world believe indeed that we really mean it!

The Incarnation meant something vast and beautiful for John Milton—and he celebrated the coming of Jesus into the world with one of the most beautiful and moving expressions ever written by a man:

> *This is the month, and this the happy morn,*
> *Wherein the Son of Heaven's eternal King,*
> *Of wedded maid, and Virgin mother born,*
> *Our great redemption from above did bring.*
> *That glorious form, that Light insufferable,*
> *And that far beaming blaze of majesty,*
> *He laid aside, and here with us to be,*
> *Forsook the courts of everlasting Day,*
> *And chose with us a darksome house of mortal clay.*
> *Oh! run; present them with thy humble ode,*
> *And lay it lowly at His blessed feet,*
> *Have thou the honor first thy Lord to greet*
> *And join thy voices with the Angel quire,*
> *From out His secret altar touched with hallowed fire!*

> *Lord Jesus, I worship You today for choosing to put on mortal flesh for*
> *the sole purpose of redeeming mankind. I praise You for Your*
> *single-minded dedication to that most difficult task.*

....

....

....

....

....

December 26

Christ's World of Nature

Then the devil leaveth him, and, behold,
angels came and ministered unto him.
MATTHEW 4:11

Jesus Christ came into our world in the fullness of time, and His own world, the world of nature, received Him, even though His own people received Him not!

It is my own feeling that when Jesus came, all of nature went out to greet Him. The star led the wise men from the East. The cattle in the stable stall in Bethlehem did not bother Him. His own things in created nature received Him.

Dr. G. Campbell Morgan believed that when Jesus went into the wilderness to be tempted of the devil, He was there with the wild beasts for forty days and nights. Dr. Morgan held that there had been a wrong conception, as if Jesus needed angelic protection from the animals.

Jesus was perfectly safe there. He was nature's Creator and Lord. Jesus was in total harmony with nature, and I am of the opinion that the deeper our Christian commitment becomes, the more likely we will find ourselves in tune and in harmony with the natural world around us!

Dear Lord, many people love nature, but they don't yet acknowledge the One
who created it and sustains it. Lord, do something to impress upon those people
that there had to be a Master Designer who set the physical world in motion.

Better Than Gold

That we might know the things
that are freely given to us of God.
1 CORINTHIANS 2:12

---

*E*very Christian believer should be aware that our God has given us definite promises of an amazing inheritance to be realized in the eternal!

The blessings and riches of our divine inheritance are not riches that will come to us for anything that is worthy or superior in ourselves, but will come because of our relationship in faith to the One who is the fount of every blessing.

We must remember that an inheritance has not actually been earned. Such bequests come from One who owns everything and gives to another whom He delights to honor and who can establish his rightful claim.

Inheritance is a right resulting from a relationship. In this case, the right belongs to the children of God by virtue of the fact that their identification as children of God by faith in the eternal Son of God has been established and is in the heavenly records! The apostle said of us: "Men and women cannot imagine or even dream of all the things which God has prepared for those who love Him!" (see 1 Corinthians 2:9).

Lord, I pray that in the coming year my relationship with You will
grow stronger through spending time in prayer and reading Your Word.

Christ's Picture Everywhere

Thou art worthy, O Lord, to receive glory and honour and power.
REVELATION 4:11

We try to sympathize with the writer John as he attempts to describe heavenly creatures in human terms in the book of Revelation. He knew and we know that it was impossible for God to fully reveal Himself and the heavenly glories to a man.

John tries to describe for us the four "living creatures" in Revelation 4. The first was like a lion; the second was like an ox; the third had the face of a man; the fourth was like a soaring eagle. Did you know that for centuries Christians have seen those same "faces" in the four gospels of the New Testament?

God has put Jesus Christ's picture everywhere! Matthew's is the gospel of the King. Mark's, the gospel of the suffering Servant. Luke's, the gospel of the Son of Man. John's, the gospel of the Son of God. Four loving, adoring, worshipping beings, faithfully and forever devoted to praising God!

Make no mistake about it: The imagery is plainly the gospel of Christ. He is what Christianity is all about!

Lord, You are truly what this world is all about: You created it, You hold it together, and You have redeemed it! You are worthy to be praised every moment of every day!

The Lord of All Beauty

They shall see the glory of the LORD,
and the excellency of our God.
ISAIAH 35:2

❦

*T*hink with me about beauty—and about this matchless One who is the Lord of all beauty, our Savior!

God has surely deposited something within our human beings that is capable of understanding and appreciating beauty—the love of harmonious forms, appreciation of colors and beautiful sounds.

Brother, these are only the external counterparts of a deeper and more enduring beauty— that which we call moral beauty. It has been the uniqueness and the perfection of Christ's moral beauty that have charmed even those who claimed to be His enemies throughout the centuries of history.

We do not have any record of Hitler saying anything against the moral perfection of Jesus. One of the great philosophers, Nietzsche, objected to Paul's theology of justification by faith, but he was strangely moved within himself by the perfection of moral beauty found in the life and character of Jesus, the Christ.

We should thank God for the promise of heaven being the place of supreme beauty—and the One who is all-beautiful is there!

Thank You, Lord, for Your beauty that is reflected in the lives of Your servants who
have left the comfort of their own home and culture to serve You in distant lands.
"How beautiful on the mountains are the feet of him that bringeth good tidings" (Isaiah 52:7).

God's Sovereign Plan

Then cometh the end, when he shall have delivered
up the kingdom to God. . . . For he must reign.
1 CORINTHIANS 15:24–25

Many people continue to live in daily fear that the world "is coming to an end."

Only in the scriptures do we have the description and prediction of the age-ending heavenly and earthly events when our Lord and Savior will be universally acknowledged as King of kings and Lord of lords.

God's revelation makes it plain that in "that day" all will acclaim Him "victor"!

Human society, generally, refuses to recognize God's sovereignty or His plan for His redeemed people. But no human being or world government will have any control in that fiery day of judgment yet to come.

John's vision of things to come tells us clearly and openly that at the appropriate time this world will be taken away from men and placed in the hands of the only Man who has the wisdom and authority to rightly govern.

That Man is the eternal Son of God, the worthy Lamb, our Lord Jesus Christ!

Dear Lord, I pray today for the remaining people groups in the world who have not yet heard the gospel message. Without knowing You, Father, many will be lost eternally when the end of the world comes. Lord, raise up specific individuals to take Your Word to those remaining peoples.

....

....

....

....

....

....

....

....

....

The Perfections of God

Give unto the LORD the glory due unto his name;
worship the LORD in the beauty of holiness.
PSALM 29:2

I hope that if I am remembered at all, it will be for this reason: I have spent my efforts and my energies trying to turn the direction of the people away from the external elements of religion to those that are internal and spiritual.

I have tried to take away some of the clouds in the hope that men and women would be able to view God in His glory. I would like to see this sense of glory recaptured throughout the church—too many Christians do not expect to experience any of the glory until they see Him face-to-face!

Within our Christian fellowship and worship, we must recapture the Bible concepts of the perfection of our God Most High! We have lost the sense and the wonder of His awe-fullness, His perfection, His beauty.

Oh, I feel that we should preach it, sing it, write about it, talk about it, and tell it until we have recaptured the concept of the Majesty of God!

Only that can be beautiful ultimately which is holy—and we who belong to Jesus Christ should know the true delight of worshipping God in the beauty of His holiness!

Dear Lord, on the last day of this year, I pray for Your Church in the coming New Year,
that it will be biblically faithful, Christ-centered, and proactive in its fight against the
forces of evil. May the name of the Lord Jesus Christ be praised in every nation!

Scripture Index